TIGER CLI

THE REDHILL SAGA

VOLUME III: 1977-1989

BY

MICHAEL JONES

CIRRUS ASSOCIATES

PUBLISHED BY:
Cirrus Associates (S.W.),
Kington Magna,
Gillingham,
Dorset,
SP8 5EW UK.

ISBN 1 902807 12 X

PRINTED IN ENGLAND BY:
Bookcraft Ltd.,
First Avenue,
Westfield Trading Estate,
Radstock,
BATH,
BA3 4BS.

PHOTO SCANNING BY:
International Graphics Services Ltd.,
24-31 Fourth Avenue,
Westfield Trading Estate,
Radstock,
BATH,
BA3 4XE.

DISTRIBUTORS:
Crecy Publishing Ltd.,
1A Ringway Trading Estate,
Shadowmoss Road,
MANCHESTER,
M22 5LH.

COVER PHOTO: Jim Alderton.
OTHER PHOTOS: credited whenever the photographer is known.

SIGNED COPIES OF TIGER CLUB VOLUME II, *AND A VERY FEW OF* VOLUME I, *BOTH BY LEWIS BENJAMIN, CAN BE OBTAINED FROM HIM: RING 0153 0412382.*

DEDICATION

To the memory of my wife, Norvela

ACKNOWLEDGEMENTS

To Lewis (Benjy) Benjamin for his help and encouragement and for his many contributions to the *Tiger Rag*
reproduced here. Also my grateful thanks to all the other
authors of articles quoted in the book; they are too
numerous to list here. Also to Neil Jensen, David
Hamilton, John Mickleburgh, John Blake, Anne Jones &
Annabel Jones, together with *Flight* and *Pilot* magazines.
To Peter Campbell for producing a good sporting book at
the lowest possible cost. Finally, last but not least, to all
members of the Tiger Club, both past and present.

CONTENTS

FOREWORD

(by Lewis Benjamin)

The Redhill Saga (covering the years 1977-1989) is a fitting finale to the trilogy of books completing the Tiger Club's long love story with that beautiful Surrey airfield.

Written in a contained and very readable manner, Michael Jones again brings to life those last eventful years of flying freedom. Redhill had truly been a pilot's dream world. Cheerful stories crowd the pages, tales that will be read again and again with delight.

But Michael's unique position as the Club's Manager through those memorable years also gave him a prospective denied the hundreds of enthusiastic Tiger Club members, all intent on relishing uncomplicated flying on superb aircraft that were ever available just for the taking, a prospective never before aired. It's explosive stuff.

Against the genuinely bright public face the Tiger Club always presented, a front this influential and vibrant group never failed to show, there dwelt a sinister backdrop of intrigue, virtually unknown to the membership, that threatened our beliefs and existence.

In a revealing and well-considered judgement, the author has delved into the dealings of a bureaucracy nose-led by a Conservative government, seemingly guided by a shameful self-serving expediency. With adroit skill we are taken behind a political façade, peeling away as we go, skin by skin, the trust of a true Conservative – for Michael was ever that – until his once honourably-felt beliefs are compelled to face the ugly truth that a wealthy global entity, as exemplified by our Redhill landlords British & Commonwealth, could, by generous contributions to party funds, cause eyes to close on common justice. And then there was the pain of Wilmington.

Michael fought the good fight for Light Flying and lost, but in his losing he won our esteem.

The Tiger Club has always been blessed with an ever-ready mixture of humour and cheerful determination in the face of adversity – it bubbles over in Michael's book, – so when in 1984 a touch of reassurance was called for, that wise head James Baring found the right rallying words. His prophetic ending still brings on a wry smile.

'. . . Any attempts to write the Club's history leaves those tempted to do so lost for words, or reduced to uncontrollable laughter – or tears. . . .'

We tried, James, we tried.

INTRODUCTION

My father, Norman Jones, began his flying career in the early twenties and was a founder member of the London Aeoplane Club. He also wasted no time in joining 601 (County of London) Squadron of the Royal Auxiliary Air Force, which in 1925 was one of the first to be formed and was apparently known as "the millionaires' mob." Although he forsook flying in the thirties for yachting and ocean racing and served in the RNVR during the war, he rejoined the private flying fraternity in the early fifties, regaining his licence with the Fairoaks Aero Club.

Encouraged by my father, I learnt to fly at Fairoaks on Tigers in 1954/1955. I well remember my first solo, which took place on a winter's day when most of the airfield was marked off as unserviceable due to waterlogging. I obtained my PPL some six months later and then continued my flying on Chipmunks with the Oxford University Air Squadron at Kidlington, which at the time was run more like a flying club than a unit of the Royal Air Force.

In 1957 flying in the RAuxAF came to an end and all the Squadrons were disbanded, including 601, which by this time was proud to have the Duke of Edinburgh as Honorary Air Commodore. However just before this happened, thanks to an introduction from Norman I was able to take up the offer of a ride in a Meteor Mk. 7 from North Weald, a memorable experience and the only flight I have ever had in a military jet.

The founding of the Tiger Club in 1956 by Norman and five other characters does not form part of this volume of its history, but some of the atmosphere of those other organisations which both my father and I had experienced rubbed off on me and contributed to my decision to accept the job of managing the Tiger Club, after its move to Redhill late in 1959 following the closure of Croydon.

The flying club movement during the fifties and early sixties was still relatively strong, encouraged by a government subsidy known as the the petrol rebate. This was administered by the Association of British Aero Clubs (ABAC) and consisted of a sum of money paid – to all *bona fide* flying clubs who were in the scheme – for every hour flown; the sum was varied according to the aircraft used and its officially recognised fuel consumption. Although the subsidy was not large, it was still an indication that the government looked with some favour on flying clubs and, more importantly, unlike the ATC cadet scheme it was spread right across the board. Consequently it was a considerable disappointment when in 1965 the petrol rebate scheme was abolished and perhaps it marked the beginning of the time when governments became finally disenchanted with flying clubs. This was in distinct contrast to what was happening across the Channel in France, where the government was both encouraging flying clubs and a flourishing home manufacturing industry by subsidising directly the down-payment on every new light aircraft ordered by a club. After this the Association of British Aero Clubs for one reason or another changed its name to the British Light Aviation Centre (BLAC) and is now known as the Aircraft Owners' and Pilots' Association (AOPA). Also many flying clubs are now known to the CAA and other authorities as flying training organisations (FTOs).

During this period Norman's interests in the whole private flying movement were of course much wider than the Tiger Club itself. He not only had the necessary vision and direction to make things happen but also he had the personality and resources to put his ideas into practice. He was also assisted by very many loyal and dedicated people, some of whom were paid and others – usually members of the Tiger Club – who were not.

From the time he took over a failing Rollason Aircraft & Engines at Croydon in 1957, the projects and iniatives flowed thick and fast: the manufacture of Turbulents and Condors; the introduction of Jodels and Stampes into Britain; the purchase of Universal Flying Services (which ran Fairoaks and, later, Rochester, and set up flying clubs at Blackbushe and Shoreham; the leasing of Condors to clubs and groups up and down the country; the midget racer design competition and the subsequent building of four Betas in a converted squash court at Redhill; the Dawn-to-Dusk competition; the seaplane; *Pilot* magazine . . . the list seems endless and is by no means exhaustive. Although hardly any of these enterprises were successful in financial terms, most of them benefited sporting and recreational flying generally in the country and the Tiger Club in particular, and after all the Tiger Club was his first idea . . .

However in all this – and it is easy to comment with the benefit of hindsight– there was one major flaw: airfields. Norman, whose background in private flying came at a time when airfields (particularly in south-east England) were a good deal more numerous than they are today, simply did not recognise the problem. To his generation, if one wished to use a light aircraft as a means of transport there was usually a convenient airfield at one's destination – and if not, a farmer's field. The annoying 'prior permission only' (PPO) rule was unheard of and landing fees virtually unknown.

Also during the twenties and thirties there was a flourishing British light aircraft manufacturing industry, a statement of fact which my father was often fond of quoting, but this depended as much on a plentiful supply of available airfields as on encouragement from governments worried by the prospect of another European war. During the sixties the freeholds both of Fairoaks and Redhill became available at prices which at the time seemed grossly inflated but well within my father's means, but again, with the benefit of hindsight, to my eternal regret he never seriously considered the offers made to him. By the time the seventies came round it was too late. Airfield owners started to react to commercial

7

pressures and restrict the use of the few remaining, either through price or regulation, and the anti-aviation environmental lobby was starting to raise its ugly head . . .

The "Redhill Saga" began of course much earlier than 1977, in fact in 1973 when the owners of the aerodrome decided that they could only offer to renew the Club's lease on a very short-term basis. During the Court proceedings which then took place, the judge, in awarding the Club a long-term lease on favourable terms, made an extremely prescient remark, which was that a flying club would have the greatest difficulty in finding another airfield. We were lucky then to have had the right judge.

In a sense also after this we were lucky that the Saga only resumed in earnest some five years later when our landlords finally appeared to decide that the Club was an ill fit – if not a tiresome nuisance – at Redhill and did not suit their long-term plans for the future of the aerodrome. The reason for the timing of this decision is not totally clear but it may have had something to do with the fact that the huge profits being generated by Bristow Helicopters from North Sea oil were beginning to falter and the future of the helicopter training school at Redhill was looking uncertain. Also it is not clear why we were never offered any alternative.

I was already on record on several occasions as urgently requesting hangarage facilities for Rollasons and I had repeatedly advised the aerodrome management that we could afford to pay more rent if we were allowed to carry out *ab initio* flying instruction, if not by the Tiger Club then by an associate organisation; we had the aircraft to do this with the Condor and a pool of qualified flying instructors who were already members of the Tiger Club. Unfortunately these requests were always adamantly refused.

The reason for the Club's survival in a changing world and through the crises of the 1980s lies firmly and squarely with its membership. The very word 'Club' sometimes seems to defy analysis and as far as the Tiger Club was concerned it was always something more than an organisation supplying unique flying facilities for its members with accompanying social attractions. In the hackneyed phrase it seemed always more a question of what the members could do for the Club rather than the other way round and the solidarity in this connection never ceased to amaze me. Whether it was duty pilots, check pilots, attending committee meetings, producing the newsletter, running the Clubroom or organising events of all kinds, nothing was ever too much trouble and many were the sacrifices made. Perhaps it has something to do with the Club Charter which every new member signed and which Norman always liked to repeat on every possible occasion!

This read as follows:

As a member of the TIGER CLUB I undertake:

8

1. Always to go out of my way to assist other members in aeronautical matters.
2. Always to fly with courtesy and with especial attention to the safety and comfort of others.
3. Never to use an aeroplane for any disreputable or unworthy purpose.

But in my view it was more than that and often quite inexplicable. Members came from all walks of life and many went on to reach very senior positions in aviation; as well as airline captains, airline bosses & owners, captains on Concorde, top industrialists and very high-ranking RAF officers, there were masters of the Guild of Air Pilots, a President of the Royal Aeronautical Society and successive Chairmen of the Royal Aero Club.

During the 1980s some people were saying that the Club was 'anachronistic' in the sense of being out-of-date. It was true that by this time there were thriving organisations already in existence representing the Club's three most popular aircraft types: the Tiger, the Stampe and the Jodel. But these clubs were essentially for the owners of these types, not for people who, lacking perhaps the time and the means, simply wished to learn to fly them and to appreciate their qualities. Furthermore the Tiger Club was still unique in providing a variety of single-seat aircraft for its members.

It was also true that by this time there were thriving independent associations running the sporting activities the Club had pioneered during the previous two decades – aerobatics, formula air racing and precision flying. Did these organisations still need the Tiger Club? Perhaps not, but the Tiger Club provided – and still provides – the essential 'means of meeting' for all those people seriously interested in these sports on a weekly if not daily basis. The Committee, which met monthly, was in this respect almost a Club-within-a-Club where all these activities were fully discussed. Also there were other things going on which lacked separate organisations but were still very much valued by members: display flying, the seaplane, foreign touring and even glider-towing. Perhaps in the future there will be others.

Finally during the eighties the Club probably spent more time than previously actually converting new members on to the Tiger Moth so that they could then be checked out all the other tailwheel types including the single-seaters. As explained in the chapters to follow, this sometimes led to difficulties but who can say that the ability, for example, to carry out a perfect sideslip followed by a three-point landing on a Tiger is not 'working to improve the standards of light aeroplane flying'? The fact that there are now more Tigers and other Moths, not to mention Stampes and Jodels, on the British register than ever there were in the sixties and seventies must prove something. There is also a parallel growth in the numbers of classic and vintage cars and motorcycles, boats and sailing craft, not to mention the activity of riding horses for pleasure. Are all these people anachronistic? Other people said that the Club was 'idiosyncratic' in the sense of being eccentric and this charge was made during the mandatory radio controversy. The judge in the case in fact recognised that our objections to mandatory radio were genuine but later referred to the Club as 'this highly individualistic group of flyers' as opposed to more 'orthodox' customers. But is the ability to fly with freedom and responsibility independently of an expensive air traffic control agency 'idiosyncratic'?

The Wilmington episode was very much part of the Redhill Saga and is dealt with at some length. The final outcome probably perfectly illustrates the truth of the old adage that there is no cause like a lost cause! One of our members told me before we started on the planning process that we would need to offer a sum of money to each and every person who might in any way be affected by the opening of Wilmington airfield; but he never mentioned the tariff! I had heard of supermarket chains paying local councils for new roads and playing fields to achieve planning consents, but we were never officially advised that there were any options available in this respect – not that we would have had the necessary resources. The nearest we got to it was to respond to a letter from the appeal for the Alfriston School Swimming Pool fund by a whip-round at a Committee meeting which raised £100! We were not in the same league as supermarkets and stuck to the naïve belief that the issue could be decided on rational objective grounds. In retrospect I remain convinced that the attempt *had* to be made. The Club then needed a home of its own, and in my view still needs one now although the relationship with the owners of Headcorn is good.

This book would not have been written if Lewis 'Benjy' Benjamin had not already produced the first two volumes of the Club's history: *The Tiger Club – A Tribute* and *Tiger Club – The Exuberant Years*. I have followed Benjy's practice of reproducing extracts from the *Tiger Rag* and other sources, including many written by him. Although the events may at times appear repetitive and even commonplace, it still seems a good way of recording the Club's history. Needless to say I have not attempted to imitate Benjy's unique style and presentation. Not only would it have been quite impossible but the years described in this book were difficult years, perhaps less lighthearted and requiring a different approach; they were nevertheless still enjoyable years and infinitely rewarding.

Also I have again followed Benjy in the matter of Appendices and have included a list of the aircraft the Club operated between 1977 and 1989, together with a list of the members who joined the Club during that time.

However I have added two more Appendices: firstly, a list of the Club's major trophies and their recipients, and secondly (most important of all), a list of the members who came to the rescue by buying shares when the Club left Redhill and the Saga came finally to an end.

CHAPTER 1
1977

1977 opened on an optimistic note. The dispute with our landlords at Redhill Aerodrome over the renewal of our lease had been settled. Relations with the then aerodrome manager, Stanley Kerridge, were good and the Club could justifiably look forward to a reasonable period of stability in promoting its declared aims and objects.

We were operating 18 aircraft, comprising some dozen different types and consisting of Tigers, Stampes, various Jodels, Turbulents, a Super Cub, a Fournier RF.4, a Wassmer Europa, various Rollason Condors and a Rollason Beta on a restricted basis. One Tiger could be converted to floats. The aircraft were personally owned by the Chairman, Mr Norman Jones, but were permanently leased to the Club. The Chairman himself had retired to Rye, where he had the use of a disused gravel pit lake on which a seaplane could be moored and a grass landing strip for visitors nearby. Lewis (Benjy) Benjamin, already the Vice-Chairman, had agreed to take over as acting Chairman and continued to produce the Club's newsletter – the *Tiger Rag* – on a monthly basis. I was the official secretary and general manager; Phili Voice and Mavis Harriott ran the office. Rollason Aircraft and Engines, who were an integral and vital part of the Club's operations, had moved from Croydon to Shoreham but continued to overhaul and maintain the Club's aircraft on a day-to-day basis as well as providing a duty engineer at the weekends.

The membership stood at just under 700 and was rising, despite a substantial increase in subscriptions due mainly to inflation. A fifth of the flying members were resident overseas and a further 10% were non-flying – wives, girl friends, supporters and enthusiasts. All were attracted not only by the Club's premises and airfield at Redhill and the highly entertaining *Tiger Rag* but also by the large variety of events and activities, both social and flying, organised by the Club.

The flying rates were also unfortunately on the increase. The Chairman had written in his annual letter to members at the beginning of the year:

"With the constant escalation of fuel prices it is no longer possible to predict the hourly costs of operating the Club's aircraft for more than a few months at a time. . . . The latest fuel price rise, which for some reason is substantially higher on the cost of Avgas than it is for car fuel, has come at a time when we revise the flying rates anyway and for this reason we regret that the enclosed list of flying rates once again shows a substantial rise over the same rates at the beginning of 1976. . . . It is high time that each one of us started to campaign vigorously to obtain some relief or even some return for the taxes we pay on every hour of flying."

The first of the Club's three basic aims was and remains:

"To provide the means of meeting for those who take an active interest in light aeroplane racing, displays, aerobatics and other forms of competition."

There was a Committee to report on and promote all these activities and others, which included overseas touring, seaplane flying and aerotowing as well as social events and the Redhill Clubroom. The Committee met ten times a year and each appointed member volunteered – sometimes after a little arm-twisting – to take on a specific responsibility. Three further and vital Committee functions were to vet applications for membership, to adjudicate on accidents, incidents and complaints, and to review flying standards. The person in the hot seat in this last respect was the Club's senior check pilot and there were around 20 Club members approved by him to carry out both initial acceptance checks on the Tiger Moth and type checks. Brian Smith had taken over this task from Don Henry in 1976 but Don's circular to all the Club's pilots the previous year is worth quoting in full:

During the past few months there have been a number of discussions by the check pilots concerning safety, flying standards, and airmanship generally. Some of the observations/suggestions made by the check pilots are summarized in this memorandum.

One of the functions of the check pilot is to determine, through a flight check in a Tiger Moth, the acceptability of prospective Club members. Check pilots are also responsible, on a continuing basis, for helping to advance the proficiency of all Club pilots. By definition all Tiger Club members have an ongoing responsibility in this effort, for one of the stated aims of the Club is:

"To work for improvement in standards of light aeroplane flying, aerobatics, and private flying generally."

Although the Tiger Club has for years been able to claim, even boast of, high standards of aeroplane handling, there is increasing evidence and concern that this standard is deteriorating. To confirm this observation one needs only to spend an hour on a busy Sunday afternoon watching take-offs, circuit flying, and landings. Many reasons have been advanced as to why standards are deteriorating, ranging from the quality of instruction to the type of aircraft on which new pilots are learning to fly. Nonetheless, conscientious practice and dedication, coupled with true love of flying, should enable anyone who has qualified as a pilot member of the Tiger Club to develop and maintain an acceptable standard of airmanship.

Check pilots may call for a special check of any pilot observed to be flying in an unsafe manner or otherwise demonstrating poor airmanship or inattention to certain fundamental rules. To minimize the need for special checks and to make flying more enjoyable and safer for all, the following suggestions are made:

1. Large circuits, resulting in long straight-in approaches, have recently become a practice with too many pilots at Redhill. One result of long straight-in approaches is that the aircraft glide pattern is very shallow. Since many Tiger Club aeroplanes are biplanes with poor forward visibility, this practice is dangerous. Also similar types flying a normal circuit may not see the 'straight-in' aircraft and a collision could occur. An extended downwind leg will effectively produce a straight-in approach.

2. Circuit safety must rely on a "see and be seen" principle. If all aircraft fly a standard reasonably tight circuit, all aircraft will be clearly visible and every pilot can easily adjust his circuit to give adequate separation.

3. Engines can, and do, fail. There is no sense in flying a downwind leg so extended that a forced landing cannot be made on the aerodrome.

4. The Gatwick control zone, clearly marked in red on the aerodrome chart, is very close to the southern perimeter. Please make sure that your circuit does not infringe on the Gatwick control zone.

5. Low, dragged-in approaches make more noise and complaints will result. There is now an operational motorway on the approach to the west runway, and low-flying aircraft could cause accidents.

6. The runway should be cleared quickly after landing, to the left. There may be other aircraft close behind.

7. A good lookout is essential before taxying onto the runway for take-off.

8. During winter the ground may be very soft in places, with the attendant danger of nosing over. Many pilots take off with the tail too high, and carry out unnecessary wheel landings. The latter are not only indicative of a lack of confidence and skill, but are detrimental to the undercarriage. Except in strong or cross-winds, all landings should be three-pointers.

9. When the north runway is in use, aircraft should taxy out on the eastern side, so as to allow landing aircraft to turn left.

10. The residents of South Nutfield are understandably very noise-sensitive. In the interests of good relations, the village must not be overflown.

11. The new runway directions should be noted, as should the fact that the runway markers are all spaced quite closely and the runways are very narrow.

12. Please take note of the various bulletin boards each time you come to Redhill. Current aerodrome conditions are indicated on the blackboard. The aerodrome chart shows in red the areas which must not be overflown. If you haven't read the aerodrome regulations recently, please do so.

The above pointers are not in any way restrictive. Their observance will result in more efficient and safer flying for all, with less wear, tear and risk to our rare and valuable Club machines. It will also enable the Tiger Club to give the fullest possible effect to another of its aims:

"To provide its members with good sporting flying at the lowest possible cost."

In large part, this is what it is all about. May you have good flying all the way!

Club check pilots were rostered for duty every Saturday and Sunday throughout the year and many of them travelled a long way to do their turn, which was completely unremunerated. One of them wrote to the *Rag*:

"I satisfied one long cherished ambition when I became a member of the Tiger Club. I don't think I ever envisaged becoming a Tiger Club check pilot at that time, but began to think that it might be a possibility a year or two ago. I think it is one of the nicest things that has ever happened to me! One is very conscious of the responsibility entailed in playing some small part in keeping up the standards of what must be the finest amateur flying organisation in the world . . ."

Brian Smith, who had joined the Club in the early sixties as a young enthusiastic supporter and had since, through the self-improver route, become a fully-fledged airline pilot, produced his own circular to the check pilots:

As I write 1977 is two months old; we have had a surprisingly successful year considering the economic climate and it looks as though 1977 may be even better. Sadly both John Burn and Dennis Marshall have decided to step down, and I'm sure we would all join in thanking them for their help and enthusiasm in passing on the tricks of the trade to the newcomers. Replacing them we can welcome Chris Jesson and John Taylor who, as up-and-coming 'younger' members, will fill a necessary role in providing a backbone of experience for the future. Additionally Derek Wright has agreed to help out with type checking, which will take some of the burden away from the Duty Check Pilot during busy weekends.

On the subject of type checks, please make sure you are familiar with all the types on the Club fleet; it looks somewhat stupid if somebody asks you to check him out and <u>you</u> spend half the time searching for the appropriate switch or do not know the various speeds.

Members are now cleared to fly types which they have flown during the previous twelve (not six) months. However, if you are approached by someone who is not sure about some detail to do with one of the aeroplanes he wishes to fly, please take the opportunity to ride round with him for a quick circuit, This is another method by which we can keep an eye on the general standards.

One or two of you have commented that prospective members turn up at Redhill for their initial check without really knowing what is expected of them. To counter this, a general briefing sheet will be sent to each applicant before he undergoes his check ride.

The Club's annual dinner dance, later to be called the Tiger Ball, always took place in February – originally to coincide with St. Valentines Day – and as February was always the worst month for flying it was a good way to chase off winter blues and look forward to the coming season; 1977 was special in that it was the Club's 21st Anniversary year. Benjy described the event perfectly in the *Rag*:

There's no doubt that any Club's 21st is something special, and the Tiger Club's was no exception. There was something in the air weeks before and everyone felt it. It showed itself so early on it shook the organisers, they'd sold every seat within two weeks of the announcement. Fortunately the Arts Club were equal to the challenge and a sort of overflow in the form of a buffet dinner was fixed, which proved first class and was cheaper into the bargain. Then there was the running about arranging the little extras that on the night were to make the evening quite memorable, There was Phili muttering darkly about a cake. 'For 200?' I asked. She nodded bravely. Others were deep in subterfuge getting the odd member to attend (not everyone likes parties, even TC ones) because their presence was imperative for some reason or other, usually to receive an award; thus any reason but the real one was given. Medallions to cast and engrave, awards commissioned. The very secrecy of the whole business lent an air of excitement which visibly built up as the days were counted down.

The Arts Club is, of course, the perfect venue. Too small perhaps to seat everyone, but as an exasperated David Hamilton declared: 'When we *had* the space nobody wanted the tickets!' Nothing induces a want so much as the thought you can't have something . . . ah well! For the 21st Dinner we'd decided to invite all the Founders. There were six. Although I personally wrote to everyone, no one really expected a full house, but with one notable exception we made it. Basil Maile flew over from the States just to be present and even Jimmy Denyer gave being Airport boss in Newcastle a miss to make his first trip south in ages, But although we had high hopes, the man we most wanted to honour couldn't make it. In the letter I read to our Guests that evening:

"You can imagine how disappointed Ann and I are that we will not be able to come to the Founders' Party of the Tiger Club. . . . Do please give my greetings to the Tiger Club on its 21st Anniversary Year.

I am proud that our Aims and Charter are in good hands, and that we have played our part in the last 21 years in keeping sporting flying alive in this country. Also that our Tiger Club ideals have spread to other countries.

Give my special greetings and thanks to Chris Wren who designed our Tiger Club badge (and didn't charge for it). We were as broke then as we are now, but our spirits were as high as they are now, and as they will be in another 21 years.

So here's hoping that you will all enjoy your flying in 1977, and that we shall see you down here at Castle Water during the summer.

Norman (Jones).

PS It is quite remarkable, if one has loyal, capable help, how much one can get done on the telephone, but as Collingwood replied to Nelson: 'Do stop signalling – we all know what to do.'"

Along the top table ranged our many Guests and a more cheerful lot of dinner companions it would be hard to assemble. MC was our very own John Blake, who is the only man I know who can truly think on his feet. His repartee was rapier-sharp and highly entertaining. In our Chairman's absence I welcomed the Guests. Traditionally TC speeches are short, and mine was no exception, probably helped to its end by raspberry-blowing balloons that circled overhead to collapse and drop into someone's wine amid much relieved laughter that it had missed them on its wild flight.

Peter Vanneck replied on the Guests' behalf. If his speech is an indication of some of the hundred he's going to have to deliver during his spell as the next Lord Mayor of London, then I foresee him quickly becoming better known than a certain cat-loving predecessor, and far better value. Not that he's likely to retell the two 601 Squadron stories too often . . .

Chris Wren was in fine form chatting on about his famed (sic) ancestors . . . and finally telling us how he designed our famous flying tiger. It was Basil Maile though who made the first presentation of the evening when he handed over for our Chairman a fine painting of a Tiger Moth presented by the AOPA of America and read the President's letter of goodwill. The significance of this gesture was much appreciated for it was a most charming way to express the rapport that exists between pilots both sides of the Atlantic and in particular it was recognition of Norman's contribution to light aviation.

Perhaps the happiest moment was when the Founders' Medallions were presented. Gold-plated and personally engraved, they were received with a delighted surprise that made it worthwhile keeping this part of the ceremony a closely guarded secret. But there was more to follow. John Blake had been busy gathering everyone's signature onto a vast framed picture which he'd kept covered until the last moment. The unveiling and presentation was no anti-climax, believe me. He had drawn something of a visual history of the Club. It's no good trying to describe it – I must try and get it photographed and reproduced, if Norman will let me, and if I can, in time for the next *Rag*. I accepted the picture and Medallion on Norman's behalf (now, Sir, you know why I tried so hard to get you to come along!).

Somewhere around coffee time and the reading of a telegram from Simon Ames of the AOPA – thank you, Simon – Phili's cake got distributed. I must say it was smashing, even the Catering Manager went around mumbling about its quality. Norma Maile consented to cut it, and promptly did so with the nearest sharp edge to hand – the Hamilton Trophy Sword.

The formal TC Awards were presented by Cordelia Vanneck. To Per-Olof Olsson went the de Salis Trophy; it is awarded to the member who during the first 12-18 months of his membership has done the most for the Club. The Clem Pike Trophy was a most popular presentation and went to W/C Titch Holmes, that most modest and unassuming gentleman who has in a lifetime of real flying done just about everything that can be done in the air, and yet suffers us all with a broadness of mind that belies his senior years. Long may he grace our Committee meetings: his 21 years of Committee service is a record not likely to be equalled.

Steve Thompson walked off with the Air Racing Medallion and Geoff Salt deservedly received the Glider-Towing one. The Aerobatics Medallion went to John Harper and the Hamilton Trophy to Barry Smith. ('Who's he?' whispered my sister. 'Deputy Governor of Pentonville,' I whispered back. 'Cor!' breathed Betty.)

The Dawn-to-Dusk was awarded to Tony Cattle and Mike Wheatley. 'Don't sit down,' someone hissed in a stage whisper; 'there's two more for you.' And so it was that they also received the Best Log Book Trophy and the Long Distance Medallion.

. . . Last award, and certainly not least, was the warmly-applauded presentation of a framed memento to the entire Rollason Team. For 21 years the six members of that team have stood by the Club through thick and thin, always helpful and always friendly. To Dev Deverell, Ted Garman, John and Jim Ellis, Mavis Harriott and Frank Hounslow the thanks of all the Tiger Club pilots. Frank received it to a standing ovation; he couldn't have looked more happy if he'd have tried. Real Cheshire cat he was.

The Dinner was over but the evening was young. If the Arts Club was a bit tight for a seated dinner it certainly came into its own when the diners had dispersed. Downstairs was a discotheque which didn't bend eardrums, plus a comfortable bar, and upstairs the peace and quiet of several elegant rooms with bars in each in which to gossip and toast the evening away. If it is a sign of a successful evening that most of the guests lingered till the very end, then the 1977 Tiger Club Dinner was the best yet. I really think it was!

And in the same issue a letter from Chris Wren was published:

"Two reasons for writing. The first is to make good an omission from my speech at the delightful 21st Anniversary Dinner, so here and now I pay tribute to the chums and ladies who have devoted so much time and effort to the welfare of the Club and the well-being of its members. Never very many but always enough. To coin a phrase: Never before in the field of Club flying did so many owe so much to so few. And few of the few have contributed more than you, Benjy (and I insist that you stifle your editorial modesty and print this!), not only in the way of the *Tiger Rag*, vitally important in keeping our wonderful organization together. Thank you, Benjy! Long may we have the pleasure of your company and the benefit of your hard work. I hereby award you Wren's Commendation, a doubtful honour which entitles you to use the initials 'W.C.' after your name from now on.

Secondly, there seems to be some uncertainty about how the Club began, so I now put the facts on record.

Late in 1956, at the customary end-of-season Racing Championship Dinner at the Royal Aero Club, then at 119 Piccadilly and in its prime, a group of us were sitting round one of the tables. Five of that group were privileged to attend this year's 21st Anniversary Dinner, in alphabetical order: Jimmy Denyer (now Manager, Newcastle Airport); Basil Maile (now a power in AOPA in Washington, DC); Beverley Snook (always a power unto himself); Peter Vanneck (an Honourable power in the City of London and next Lord Mayor – first time in years that I've seen Peter not wearing a sable-trimmed gown); and myself. The sixth and most important member – missing, alas, from the celebratory dinner – was dear Norman.

There may have been one or two more in the group – it was a big table – when Norman looked around and said something like: 'You know, we Tiger Moth people should form a Tiger Club – Chris can design our badge'; and among his other suggestions was that each year's 'Ace' member should be awarded a flying helmet made of tiger skin (not *real* tiger skin, Norman? Still, knowing Norman, it probably *would* have been).

The helmet idea didn't materialize but, as we know, Norman followed through with the main project and I did the badge (incidentally, those wings on the tiger are authentic tiger moth – lepidopterous type, that is). I've sometimes pondered on whether Norman had been contemplating the project for some time or if it was one of his spontaneous combustions.

So three cheers for Norman, two each for Michael and Benjy, and at least one for each of all the other workers who toil to keep us drones happy.

EXTRACT FROM COMMITTEE MINUTES, MAY 1977

New inverted ribbon act discussed. Approved providing great care exercised including the following: always into wind. A minimum of 550 m each side of hoop. It must remain an individual act with named pilot only, i.e. Brian Smith. Trial period '77 season only.

Committee meetings, incidentally, were now held at the Steering Wheel Club because the Kronfeld Club had closed at the end of 1976.

Proposals for new display acts were always discussed and approved in Committee, and needless to say this one was no exception. O.V. 'Titch' Holmes, the Club's long-suffering insurance broker and underwriter, was always present at Committee meetings and decisions such as this needed his agreement. Fortunately he was very experienced and had seen it all before!

Foreign or overseas touring had always been a very important part of the Club's activities, and over the years many close links had been established with Clubs in France, and one in particular in Germany at Osnabrück. Members were specifically approved for foreign touring and there was a significant utilisation of the Club's aircraft, although this had been on the decline, mainly because there was an increasing tendency for members to acquire their own aircraft – so much so that for the Club's organised trips abroad the majority of the machines taking part were privately owned. France was of course the favourite venue, and not just because of the relaxed and friendly atmosphere at most French airfields; as most of our aircraft were either of French design or origin, we felt an instinctive 'French connection.' In 1977 the Club had an organised programme, with visits to Rouen and Osnabrück being run by David Timmis and Wynne Evans, "At-Homes" to Le Treport and Cherbourg run by Tim Corbett at Shobdon and a further "At-Home" to Hilversum, Holland, with the party being hosted by Robin and Phili Voice at their house in Epsom.

An important development that took place in 1977 in connection with foreign touring was the launching of the Club's Hospitality fund, on the initiative of the Vice-Chairman. A fundamental principle of the Club's organised foreign touring was that Clubs on the continent would be invited to Redhill to be entertained by us on a reciprocal basis. The hospitality that members received abroad was so exceptional that from to time we became anxious that we were not returning this hospitality in the appropriate manner. From then on the Hospitality Fund became a popular Club Fund alongside the other two voluntary Club funds – the long-established Legal Fund and the Prize Fund.

The Club's contribution to the art and sport of aerobatics needs no further explanation in this volume of its history. We had introduced and run all the national competitions – and some of the international ones as well – and we had sponsored entries and aircraft for world contests. Two editions of a booklet – *Competition Aerobatics as a Hobby* – had been written by Taff Taylor and published by the Club. But the sport was developing very quickly and the Club's Stampes by now were being superseded by more sophisticated (and noisy) machines. Consequently in 1975 the Club had handed over the organisation of the national competitions, together with most of the trophies, to the newly-formed British Aerobatic Association. This was not to say that our promotion of aerobatics was in any way diminished; Club policy was very much to encourage newcomers by providing an ideal aircraft and training facilities.

Way back in 1968, after much controversy, an agreement had been reached with the then airfield owners and the local Nutfield residents' association that aerobatics could be practised over the aerodrome at certain specific times, which were for two hours on Saturday afternoons and one hour on weekday evenings (in the summer). For years these 'slots,' particularly Saturday afternoons, became extremely popular with the aerobatic enthusiasts, and providing the Stampe or the Tiger was used they were perfectly acceptable to the local residents. The performance of individual pilots could be carefully monitored, taped and criticised from the ground and people felt safe practising precisely because they were flying over an airfield.

Unfortunately in 1975 there had been signs that these long-established slots were under threat. The boundaries of the Gatwick control zone had been extended northward to take in some of the airspace immediately overhead the airfield. Suddenly we received a disconcerting 'order' via Bristow Helicopters that "aerobatics by fixed-wing aircraft will not be allowed over the airfield." Fortunately one of our active flying members, Dick Barnby, was also an ATC supervisor at Gatwick and he immediately arranged a meeting with his colleagues and all concerned at Redhill in order to "formulate procedures to allow performance of aerobatics over Redhill Aerodrome within notified airspace." Eventually a letter of agreement was signed by all parties which allowed aerobatics over the aerodrome to continue at the original times, subject to permission from the Gatwick supervisor and subject to communication by radio between Gatwick and the aircraft concerned using the intriguing callsign 'Tigerbatics.' Again, luckily, primitive portable radios were already being used by the Stampes for the duo formation aerobatic display act; they had the right frequency and their range was just sufficient to raise Gatwick tower. This agreement was renewed annually and appeared initially to work well. However some years later the Club sought a concession and wrote to the National Air Traffic Services:

"Our problem is . . . that attempts to establish satisfactory radio communication have been unsuccessful. Moreover, the pilots who practise over the aerodrome have made it absolutely clear that they are unable to practise aerobatic sequences, very often of a highly complex nature, whilst maintaining a listening watch on 118.6. Consequently aerobatic practice has been taking place in that part of our ATZ which is not in the Gatwick CTZ, which brings the flying much closer to the buildings on the aerodrome and the neighbouring village and at the same time reduces the height available to 500 feet less than that allowed

if radio communication is maintained. We would therefore like to suggest that we might be allowed a concession which would have the effect of realigning the Gatwick CTZ so that, where it passes through Redhill Aerodrome, it does so along the southern perimeter and not through the middle of the aerodrome, a difference of some 500 yards, and that a little more height might be allowed by raising the base of the SRA in the Redhill ATZ to 1,800 feet instead of 1,500 feet."

Needless to say this request was firmly and very politely refused.

As for our two faithful Stampes, G-AWEF and G-ATKC, we were getting worried by the manoeuvres required of them in competitions at advanced level. Consequently, I wrote to Ian Senior, the Club's aerobatic secretary and member of the BAeA committee:

"The manoeuvres required by the advanced known compulsory sequence will have placed an unfair strain on our already overstretched maintenance facilities with regard to the Stampes, and I do not wish to prejudice the future of these fine aircraft. . . it was not until quite recently that I appreciated what was required by this sequence. . . . half vertical rolls are enough for the Stampe, and we are not happy about square or multisided loops. . . . I would be obliged if you would convey to the Board of Management of the BAeA the Club's concern at the lack of consultation when these sequences are devised, particularly if it is expected that Club aircraft will take part. . . . I think that it would be best to assume that the Club Stampes will not be available for competition in 1977 at the advanced level as constituted . . . I have advocated in the past that a formula should be devised primarily on engine power whereby aerobatic aircraft can compete at the advanced level on equal terms. In my opinion this is the only way the enthusiast will be able to obtain satisfaction from the sport at a reasonable price and Clubs can continue to provide aerobatic aircraft, . . . not only for competitions but also for the enjoyment of members generally."

Handicap racing was still popular with Club pilots although the years were long past when a sizeable portion of the entry list consisted of Club machines. The Jodels (the Mascaret and the Excellence) were the favourite mounts. There were frequent grumbles about the handicapping system and the following document was in circulation:

HOW TO HANDICAP AN AIR RACE

First, decide how fast each aeroplane should go. This is impossible, but gets easier with practice. The present handicappers use the results of all the previous air races since 1937, and a mixture of science, intuition, inspiration and sheer imagination; but now that all the entrants have to declare their speed it might be simpler.

Next, measure the course. The pylons are never where the Clerk of the Course says they are, so fly round the course yourself and plot them on a map – preferably at 2½ inches to 1 mile. The distances between the turning points can be measured with a ruler, but it is more accurate to calculate the distances from the grid references. Add on the distances round the scatter points and from the start to the finish lines.

Now allow for the corners. An aircraft turning round a pylon has to fly slightly outside the pylon, so covers an extra distance equal to $(2\pi{-}4\sqrt{2})r$, where r is the radius of turn plus half the wingspan. Assuming a 2g turn seems to work out well in practice. Also, when the aircraft banks, the lift increases, and the drag increases, so the aircraft slows down. (The stalling speed increases too, but that is the pilot's problem.) As it recovers from the bank, it accelerates again, but altogether it loses a certain amount of time on every corner. If you have a taste for mathematics, you can work this out to be roughly

$$\frac{0.8\sqrt{n^2-1}}{\pi\rho g} - \left\{\frac{(w/s)^2}{A(\rho/s)}\right\}$$

per corner, but actually it turns out to be about 2 seconds per lap for everything except Bonanzas and RF.4s. (It is 1½ seconds for a Beta and 2½ for a Cassutt, which is why Michael always beats Tom on the corners. Or it would be if they pulled 2g.)

Then you have to allow for the time taken to accelerate on the take-off run. This is roughly an extra 30 seconds, but it depends how fast the aeroplane is and how strong the wind is. The handicappers have some clever-looking graphs for this, which Colin Britland worked out from the results of the 1948-1964 races, and they allow a bit extra for people who have to crank the undercarriage up by hand.

Now all you have to worry about is the wind. With a Dalton computer you can work out the ground speed on each leg of the course, given the aircraft speed and wind speed and direction, so you can work out how many seconds more or less would be taken on each leg than if the race was run in still air. Add up the corrections for the various legs and you have the answer.

Actually it's much easier if you have an electronic computer in the attic; you make the computer do the sums for all wind speeds and directions beforehand. (If you do not have an electronic computer in the attic, it's probably better not to take up air race handicapping.) Then all you have to do on the day is decide what the average wind is going to be at the time of the race.

If you get it all correct, all the aeroplanes will reach the finish together. This doesn't often happen; but then if it did, somebody would have banned air racing years ago.

By 1977 Formula 1 closed circuit pylon racing with Cassutts, Betas, Cosmic Winds and the like was well established – the first F1 race had taken place in the Isle of Man in 1970. The Formula Air Racing Association (FARA) had been formed in 1972 on the initiative of Fred Marsh, who became its first chairman. I accepted the job of Hon. Secretary and most of the machines were kept in the Redhill hangar. Meetings had been held at many airfields in the UK, usually in conjunction with handicap events and displays, and the previous two years had seen races organised in the south of France and Denmark.

In 1977 a splendid international August holiday meeting took place at St. Valery on the Normandy coast, together with a top-class air show. The airfield, which was on land requisitioned just after D-Day, had reverted to its former owners, Odile Lacuisse and her family, who farmed the surrounding fields and ran the flying club, and whose hospitality was outstanding. The site was perfect for pylon racing, flat and unobstructed and with a clear view of the whole course for all the spectators. The small seaside town and port was (and still is) delightful and Fecamp was not far away. Fred, who had recently swapped his Beta for the rebuilt Cosmic Wind *Ballerina* won the Benedictine Trophy. The French magazine *Aviation* described him as more British than reality and summed up the meeting with the headline *"Les Anglais ont dominé."* After this St. Valery became a popular venue both for F1 racing and a foreign touring weekend.

TO PROVIDE THE MEANS OF MEETING FOR THOSE WHO TAKE AN ACTIVE INTEREST IN . . . DISPLAYS.

As Benjy put it in the *Rag*:

One of the Club's express aims has always been to encourage more members to come forward and participate in this highly specialised branch of the Club's activities. Perhaps it is not widely known but there exists a fund with which to subsidise the very necessary practice needed. If you are interested, contact one of the regular display pilots and get in on the act. I've often been asked how one does begin display flying, and I suppose the simple answer is by ferrying the aircraft to the venues, or turning up by car to lend a hand to the ground-handling teams. After a while one becomes known and trusted – and display flying is all about trust – and then it's a gradual transition to a reserve position and so on into the regular team.

The display practice fund, as it was known, was not in fact an official part of the Club's constitution. The money came from a percentage of the cash received from the display organiser to cover the pilots' flying costs. Originally the Club only staged full displays – perhaps five or six a year – with a Club member as official promoter and risk-taker and who was responsible for all the ground organisation. Gradually over the years the number of full displays dwindled and what were called 'participation' displays became more popular. Bill Chesson, our promoter, had given up the job in 1977 and only one full display was organised – at Kidlington. However the Club participated in 14 other events, some of them abroad. There were many acts on offer and I have counted 20 variations of the basic biplane and Turbulent formations. There were also individual aircraft demonstrations, some of which were performed in machines privately owned by Club members but essentially flying under the Club banner. One such aircraft was the vintage Arrow Active which used to belong to the Club and was operated mainly as a display aircraft on a very restricted basis. In 1975 it was sold to our Vice-Chairman who loaned it to the Club for displays. As Brian Smith, our Senior Check Pilot, explained:

Since the Arrow Active was built in 1932 it hasn't, at least to anybody's knowledge, ventured across the Channel to parts foreign; after reading the tale I'm about to tell, you'll probably understand why.

It started with a phone call to Benjy from some Danish friends who were organising a big rally at Herning, halfway up Jutland. Because it was all done verbally and not booked at least three months in advance Michael was a bit reluctant to let any of the Club aircraft get involved, so it eventually fell to Neil Williams and muggins to fly the Jungmann and Active respectively in order to achieve a degree of British participation.

We met up at Shoreham one glorious Friday morning; they really are the most friendly bunch down there and the chore of clearing Customs didn't seen so bad after all. We set off into a 15 kt headwind bound for Seppe in Dutchland which was a little over two hours away. Neil's Jungmann was the critical aeroplane on range with 2½ hours available compared with 4 hours for the Active, but we both seemed to manage a comfortable 95-100 kt cruise without any trouble. Anyway, we eventually arrived over Seppe and here the fun and games started with a 12 kt crosswind blowing across the only runway, which at least was grass. The Active's landing characteristics are well-known, so suffice to say that crosswind landings are a no-no; with little alternative down we went and after much pedalling and gunning of engine the Active found itself intact on foreign soil for the first time in 45 years.

After a nervous cup of coffee and a spot of lunch we set off for Wilemshaven. Again it was a pleasant run, albeit into that blasted headwind, but we arrived a little over two hours later to find the same situation of crosswind repeated, but this time on a tarmac runway. By this time it began to dawn on me why (a) Benjy hadn't flown the aeroplane himself and (b) why nobody had ever tried to go foreign in the machine. I gingerly touched down on the mainwheels keeping the tail up until it would stay up no longer; so far so good, but then a hint of drift off to the left . . . oh gawd! no response from the back end trying to correct to the right . . . it's going to go . . . quick, pick a gap in the runway lights, point it through the gap and hope for the best. At a terrifying speed (which on reflection was about 10 kt) the aeroplane and I left the runway with neither of us in control and therefore committed to wait until the excursion came to a halt, which it did some several seconds later. Retrieving my heart from my boots I stepped out of the machine and proceeded to taxy whilst strolling beside it in the manner one used to see demonstrated by more senior members of the Club at the races years ago. Needless to say the locals were convinced by this performance that a flying circus had just arrived on their patch.

We were away an hour later bound for Herning. Although flying east we were also heading north so we figured that dusk would fall around eight local. We would have been about right too if it were not for a mass of cloud which appeared on the western horizon and prematurely cut off the daylight like somebody switching off a lamp. By 7.30 you couldn't read a map, 7.35 and you couldn't see the compass, and by 7.40 I was tucked in formating on the flames of the Jungmann's stub exhausts. Herning town was lit up five minutes away and the airfield was marked as being three miles north, although what it consisted of was anybody's guess, We arrived over the town and duly flew north for two minutes; I then made the fatal mistake of glancing at my watch, only to look up to see the Jungmann in the final throws of a wing rock, turn on its side and slide down into the gloom. I followed as hard as I could but my worst fear was confirmed in that Neil was gone and no way was I going to find him. It's difficult to describe the feelings that came on at that moment: fear, panic, apathy, to name but a few. However, the great Smith brain reactivated and came to the conclusion that Neil must have seen something to merit his actions and the chances were he had seen the airfield.

Meanwhile down on *terra firma* a different form of panic was under way. The locals were expecting us, but with the onset of darkness they had convinced themselves that we had diverted to somewhere or other. So there they were, sitting in their Clubhouse knocking back beer and ham when this drone of two unsynchronised aero engines reaches their Danish eardrums. It must have been like a late air raid warning with bodies throwing themselves out of any available exit and making for a vantage point to see what gave. By the time they realised that it was the long-lost British, nothing short of pandemonium had set in with people jumping into anything with wheels and proceeding to construct the most bizarre flarepath you could imagine – with the car headlights pointing up the approach. Neil landed in the middle of this lot, ended up in a sandpit, leapt out of his aeroplane and told them in no uncertain terms to turn the b***** cars around before they blinded me as well.

Whilst all this was going on yours truly was going around in ever-decreasing circles gradually convincing himself that the best thing to do was to spin in and get it over and done with. But all of a sudden I spied a large flock of sheep, which on closer inspection turned out to be 50 or more spamcans parked together and, yes, there was the runway with what looked like some sort of mobile demolition team tearing all over it performing to an invisible audience. The jubilation soon turned to gloom when it became apparent that yet again I was faced with a crosswind landing on tarmac but, just for a change, at night. Anyway, down I went, found the ground and tried again to keep the tail up as long as possible. Down it came and what a sight it was with sheets of flame coming out of the front end, showers of sparks from the skid trailing down the back – a regular firework night attraction. By the grace of someone we stayed on the runway and soon crowds of Danes flocked around to try and discover how we had managed to find the airfield without VORs or some other such gimmick.

The rest of the trip was a bit of an anti-climax after all that. The next day the wind went around 80 degrees and it started to rain, continuing to do so until we crossed the Dutch border on Sunday afternoon. We flew the display in torrential rain and a 400 ft cloudbase, which was a novel experience, looping off the deck to find oneself in cloud going over the top.

During our travels we accumulated a little over 14 hours of flying and looking back I suppose it was fun – but man, was I glad to push the Active back into the Redhill hangar intact on Sunday evening!

Brian also put pen to paper over a display at Bex:

Now the winter has set in would you care to curl up in your favourite armchair and read a tale about flying that's a little out of the ordinary? This yarn revolves around an air show run by an incredibly keen bunch of individuals at a place called Bex, which is ten or so miles from the south-east end of Lake Geneva, down the Rhône valley. During the early spring a delegation visited Redhill in search of ideas for their annual air show to be held in August, and the arrangements soon fell into place with Robin and Phili going out in the Super Tiger, Neil W. taking Adrian Swire's Rapide with Doug and Edna Bianchi and yours truly flying Robin's Cosmic Wind.

We all set off at different times; Robin was first away on the Monday (if my memory serves me correctly). I left early Tuesday morning and Neil cleared through Shoreham that lunchtime – the object being for all of us to arrive by Wednesday in order to cover the Press Day. My routing took me from Shoreham to Troyes in a shade over 2 hours; there I ran into Robin, who had fought his way from Le Touquet in some rather nasty weather, and with the forecast not so good for the Jura mountains he was not that keen in pressing on. Neil was supposedly heading for Beauvais where he had to drop Adrian off and thence proceed in the general direction of Lausanne, which was my next port of call. I set off after a quick turn round at Troyes with Robin hard on my heels but, alas, that was the last I saw of him that day. The weather south-east of Dijon was really rather unpleasant and it turned into quite a fight to get over, or should I say *through,* the mountains that form the natural divide between France and Switzerland.

I landed at Lausanne around teatime and then had to explain to the rather puzzled locals how one could actually fly across Europe in such a small aeroplane without a radio, as well as the difference between a DH.82 and a DH.89, for which they had received separate flight plans. Soon a message came through that Robin was at some obscure airfield on the French side of the hills and obviously intended staying there until the weather picked up. Shortly after this the drone of a couple of Gipsy Queens announced Neil's impending arrival and eventually the *Bamboo Bomber* and its occupants arrived on Swiss soil.

A spot of fuel and a cup of coffee later found us flying together down the Rhône valley; that really was an awe-inspiring sight, the valley about two miles wide with pine-clad 6,000-ft lumps of rock lining the side, with this old biplane and tiny monoplane bumbling along following the river. It made one feel kind of insignificant. Five minutes later we landed at Bex, to be greeted by some rather enthusiastic and excited Swiss gnomes who, after providing certain light refreshments of an alcoholic nature, directed us to our hotel – would you believe a girls' finishing school? At this point the writer came to the conclusion that he was onto a very good thing and later slipped into his pit a somewhat contented pilot, very much at peace with the world.

We awoke next morning to picture postcard scenery, the lake serene and the mountains rising magnificently through the haze; Bleu Leman – that was the name of the school – was perched a couple of hundred feet above the lake just up from Montreux. Our hosts fed us royally on ham and eggs, none of this bread roll nonsense, and by 10 we were on our way to meet the gentlemen of the Press. What a selection of machines they had programmed with Pitts, Jungmann, Blériot, Caudron, Mystère 20 and even a CL-44 among the attractions. We had to fly for the said gentlemen which was a bit worrying because the star attraction – Robin and Phili still hadn't materialised. One of the more memorable moments was later that morning when a group of hang-glider maniacs threw themselves off a nearby mountain which they had been scaling for the past couple of days. All of a sudden the air was full of aspiring birdmen hanging beneath their multi-coloured kites against a backcloth of clear alpine skies and mountains. The peace was shattered by the arrival, true to Club tradition, of Robin in the Tiger, who chose this opportune moment to join the 20 or so hang-gliders flying around in ever decreasing circles, finally flopping down onto the airfield to a great burst of applause from the onlookers who took 'OAA to be some form of advanced kite.

That afternoon we took the opportunity of the incredible weather to venture into the Alps for a bit of sightseeing. Neil, Doug and Edna, Phili and myself piled into the Rapide and set off towards the lake on the slow climb to 10,000 feet. Robin chose the slightly more manoeuvrable seat of his Cosmic although we intended to rendezvous along the route. It took Neil a good 20 minutes to coax that graceful biplane up to our intended height, but when we got there and flew back along our track into the Alps the scenery was more than my literary ability could do justice in describing. Everyone in that aeroplane simply sat mesmerised by the astounding natural beauty around us; even Doug, who usually manages to produce some inane comment, was dumbstruck by the panorama around him. Despite the proximity of the engines one still had this incredible feeling of being at peace with the world; sitting there on the cockpit bulkhead by Neil's shoulder I could sense that he too was moved by what he was seeing, even though we both fly over the area regularly during the course of our respective jobs. Maybe it was viewing it all through the tangle of wings and wires with the song of the engines rather than in the pressurised seclusion of a jet – I doubt that the experience will ever again be repeated,

The rest of the week soon passed, and all too quickly we were flying before the Swiss public on Saturday and Sunday. That was quite an experience in that after flying one was hoisted onto the back of a car and driven along the considerable crowd lines, amid much enthusiastic waving and clapping from the assembled gnomes. Great ego boosting, but more to the point a real pleasure to know that one achieved the object of entertaining the customers.

So homeward with a repeat performance of scratching around the hills to get out of Switzerland. I left immediately after the show ended on Sunday, intent on making Dijon to stop the night with Michel Brandt, the Swiss aerobatic pilot who is also chief designer at Avions Robin. Having only just managed to thread my way through the Juras, we were all somewhat surprised when Robin turned up just before dusk. Anyway, a superb steak plus a bottle of Maçon Rouge soon turned the occasion into a farewell thrash, which probably caused us to view the following morning's weather with slightly optimistic eyes, because in the appalling conditions we both set off for Troyes. Robin soon regained his senses and turned back, but I pressed on, frightening myself silly in the process. Troyes appeared after an hour or so and here I ran into half the French Aerobatic Team who were on their way home from the French Champs. That delayed things a bottle or two, but I found myself at Lydd around teatime being b******* rigid by ATC for not applying the PPO rule – the fact they received my flight plan three hours before I turned up was apparently irrelevant. A bigger bunch of amateur professionals I've yet to meet!

Thence the final hop to Redhill. For all of Switzerland's beauty, the unspoilt expanse of our home aerodrome is still the best site one can wish for, even after such a trip as I have described. Hopefully you have been able to share some of the pleasure I was privileged to be involved in.

The Club's final display of 1977 took place in November and was a unique occasion – the Lord Mayor's Show in the City of London. Our founder member the Hon. Sir Peter Vanneck was the new Lord Mayor. The site was *HMS President* anchored outside the Livery Hall west of Blackfriars Bridge where the new Lord Mayor was taking a 'tot' with the Navy. Neil Williams was in charge and a copy of his meticulous briefing is in the Club's archives. Ron Jacobs described the event:

I was fortunate to be on the Embankment for the Lord Mayor's Show, and a splendid lively show it was, with a City Service theme. For the first time in history and in honour of Peter Vanneck's air and Navy interests, there was to be air participation: a Nimrod, Meteor, air-sea rescue helicopter and a Tiger Club five-biplane formation led by the Arrow Active. The weather was atrocious for biplanes and I feared cancellation, but in true Tiger Club fashion they arrived to the second. Heaving and bucketing about in close formation to the delight and amazement of the thousands lining the route, they swept over Blackfriars Bridge looking more like a Swordfish attack and on past the *President*, where the procession had halted to allow the Lord Mayor to alight and watch the flypast.

Brian Smith and James Black in Tigers were tucked in tight to Neil with the Stampes of Pete Jarvis and Carl Schofield streaming their smoke in the No. 4 and No. 5 spots. Past the ships and up into an immaculate steep turn and down again for the return pass and deafening cheers from the crowd.

This was a day for the professionals and I was relieved to see them climb safely away towards the incoming Nimrod and James Gilbert in the TV Cessna orbiting beyond Tower Bridge. I wondered if John Blake had managed to get a camera to his eye in his heaving open cockpit. As I watched them out of sight, I felt very proud of their performance, and on reflection, Neil could not have given a greater disciplined finale for the Club. Thank you, Neil.

It was Neil's last display. As already recalled by Benjy in the previous volume of this story, Neil died with his crew a couple of weeks later in the treacherous Spanish mountains ferrying a Heinkel 111 to England for film work. A memorial service was given for him at the RAF church in the City – St. Clement Danes. 450 people turned up to pay their respects and to hear John Blake's moving address. Neil's flying achievements and exploits are now legendary and he had recorded many of them in his book *Airborne*. He had joined the Club in 1961 and in his 17 years of membership he flew nearly 700 hours in Club aircraft. His overriding passion was aerobatics and aerobatic competitions and his textbook on the subject, first published in 1975 and reprinted several times, is now a classic on the sport. Although Neil was a professional to his fingertips – he had been trained by the RAF, was a test pilot at Farnborough and, on leaving the service, a much sought-after display and demonstration pilot – he always retained his amateur spirit and his commitment to the Club. Our loss was enormous and very keenly felt by the whole membership.

The inverted ribbon cut, demonstrated to perfection at the 1983 Redhill Air Show. Photo: Author's collection.

AEROBATICS....

"WHAT DO YOU MEAN, IT FELL OFF A LORRY?"

RACING...

"THE CHAIRMAN'S GOING TO BE VERY UPSET— YOU KNOW IT SAID I WAS TO WIN IN THE MINUTES"

GLIDING....

"A NOISE COMPLAINT?"

TOURING...

THE PRIVATE OWNERS,

"ITS 20th BAGLEY, DARLING - ARE YOU IN?"

THE DISPLAYS....

"OF COURSE, WHEN I BOUGHT IT, I DIDN'T KNOW MICHAEL HATED LARGE AEROPLANES."

TO NORMAN —

A 21st BIRTHDAY PRESENT, ON BEHALF OF.....

John Blake's cartoon celebrating the 21st Anniversary of the Club in 1977.

33

TOP: The Sea Tiger G-AIVW – on wheels for a change. Photo: Ken Smith.
BOTTOM: The Super Cub G-AVPT, seen at Scotney Court – on floats for a change. Photo: Brian Hockley.

1978

Early in 1978 a row broke out over the results of the Dawn-to-Dusk competition which took place in 1977. It was customary to declare the results late in the year after a final meeting of the judges' panel at Buckingham Palace chaired by Prince Philip. The trophies and prizes were then presented at the Club's annual dinner dance at the beginning of the following year. The 1977 competition was won by Marylyn Wood and Alan Butcher flying a Rollason Condor but one of the competitors complained that he had been "formally excluded from the results" because of a statement in the judges' report that there were "inaccuracies in his log and his entry form."

By 1978 the competition had grown considerably in status and prestige and had been recognised by the FAI as an international event. The purpose of the competition was to provide a means of encouraging interesting and new ideas for spending a day in an aeroplane and getting as much done as possible. It was not intended to be an endurance competition or even a test of skill. It was judged on the logs submitted, taking into account various criteria such as the type of aircraft flown, its equipment, the pilot's experience etc. and the accuracy of the log. The judges consisted of senior Club members chaired by Prince Philip, who took a very considerable interest in the competition – as did the Prince of Wales, who had accepted honorary membership of the Club in 1971, had visited Redhill and had sent a donation in 1974 towards the event's "administration costs."

All competitors signed on their entry form that they accepted the judges' decision as final and that there was no appeal, but the individual concerned complained via his solicitors that in the interests of natural justice he should be allowed a hearing before the judges. Needless to say this caused the Club considerable embarrassment, particularly since the complainant's solicitors were now sending copies of their letters to Prince Philip's private secretary and threatening legal proceedings.

As a result the Duke's solicitors were consulted and after several phone calls drafted a series of letters for the Club to send in answer to the complaints made. The correspondence dragged on for several months before the matter was finally dropped. The individual concerned later resigned from the Club.

Another row of a different sort broke out early in 1978. In fact as Benjy has recorded in the previous volume it was a continuation of the row which we thought had been settled in 1976 after the CAA had produced their 'discussion paper' on the mandatory carriage of radio in light aircraft. This had produced so many hostile letters and such a widespread storm of protest from all the sporting flying organisations that the idea was hastily dropped. I remember David Faulkner-Bryant – Chairman of the Popular Flying Association at the time – telling me: "We have shot them down in flames."

However in 1978 the matter again raised its ugly head in a different form. Craftily the CAA produced another proposal which actually reached the status of a draft statutory regulation which would empower them, the CAA, to restrict the use of certain aerodromes to aircraft equipped with two-way radio. Our local MP, Sir Geoffrey Howe, then in opposition, was advised of the problem and he wrote on the Club's behalf to the Chairman of the CAA. As a result the proposals were modified "to the extent that the National Air Traffic Services no longer sought powers to preclude aircraft not equipped with radio from landing at certain aerodromes."

But clearly, as we were to learn to our cost five years later, the air traffic control lobby and certain airfield owners were never going to forget "mandatory radio."

The Sea Tiger G-AIVW took to the water again in May after it had been cleverly modified by Rollasons so that it could also be flown on wheels. Tom Freer wrote in the *Rag:*

This does not mean it is now an amphibian, it means that the change from floats to wheels or from wheels to floats can now be accomplished quickly and easily without disturbing the fuselage structure. The benefits are twofold: (i) when not operating on floats it will be operating on wheels instead of doing nothing, so annual utilisation will obviously improve (ii) when required on floats it will be flown to the lakeside, thus avoiding the expense of road transport and re-rigging. G-AIVW is now therefore operating at Redhill as a landplane.

It was a welcome change. Certainly it was not an amphibian, but was it still a seaplane ? The annual circular on flying rates now described it as *"Tiger (floats) £21.00 per hour plus VAT"*!

As for the start of the flying season, Benjy described it in the newsletter in his own inimitable fashion:

"It's the same every year. The moment pilots sniff spring in the air they descend on Redhill. It doesn't matter where they are, it has the same effect. It's like a mating call. Redhill. And in no time at all they're all there, all talking at once, and taking up where they left off last autumn, all as though winter didn't happen. Perhaps it didn't. All that remains to remind us of the snows and rain is the wet patch in the middle of the airfield, and you only remember that when you begin to get stuck in it.

Spring: when the young man's fancy turns to cleaning his aeroplane. Spring: when the locals gleefully reach for their phones and start grumbling. They've missed us. And the practising. It's like show day every day. To see a beautifully spaced five-biplane formation rise up from the N/S runway and thunder over the hangar with a vibrant roar, sunlight gleaming on the bright coloured surfaces, is as heartwarming a sight as any of us who watched could recall.

Outside the hangar all is bustle and polish, like Phillip Wolf's gleaming Staggerwing. Surely there isn't a more concours aircraft in the Kingdom? And mixing it with the busy circuit on that Sunday in mid-April was another beautiful aircraft, as yet in primer, but every inch a thoroughbred, the rebuilt Mew Gull of Tom Storey. G-AEXF is one of the most famous of all light aircraft, for she has won two King's Cups and still holds the 'Cape and back' record. Let's hope she continues to have an illustrious future.

Don Henry, who was now back home in the USA, wrote from Florida that he had now bought his favourite aeroplane – a Stampe fitted with a Lycoming engine – and that with the Club's permission he was going to start a St. Augustine Tiger Club to be affiliated to the parent organisation. The Committee agreed with pleasure, so yet another Tiger Club was formed, in addition to the Tiger Club in Texas run by Frank Price and Tiger Clubs in Australia and New Zealand.

Glider-towing was another long-established and important part of the Club's activities. In the very early days at Redhill members used to tow a glider from Redhill belonging to the Imperial College Gliding Club. All the Club's Tigers were fitted with towing hooks and the Super Tiger was an exceptional tug which – it was rumoured – had actually towed a glider whilst inverted. In 1978 we also had a Super Cub and large-engined Condor available. During an average year 1,500 to 2,000 tows were carried out, making a very useful contribution to Club aircraft utilisation.

In 1978 most of these tows took place at North Weald for the Essex Gliding Club, where a Club tug was based. But members also used to take aircraft away during the summer months to tow at regional and national competitions. Geoff Salt, the headmaster of a large comprehensive school in Surrey and an unfailing enthusiast, was the Committee member in charge. He ran the Tiger Soaring Group (which owned a K.13) and they used to operate most winter weekends at Redhill although soaring was obviously out of the question.

It is impossible in a history such as this to describe in detail all the events and activities of the Club in a single year. It was normal to publish a Club calendar in the spring of each year as part of the *Tiger Rag*. This is the list for 1978; it was typical for these years in the Club's history:

Date	Full Displays
May 1	Beaconsfield
July 2	Bath Racecourse
September 17	Oxford

	Participation Displays
April 30	Old Warden
May 6 & 7	Goodwood
May 21	Brasschat, Belgium
May 27 & 28	Bassingbourn
May 29	Dunkeswell
June 10 & 11	Moorsele, Belgium
June 11	Kenley
June 24 & 25	Leavesden
June 24	Woodford
July 15	Charfield
July 15 & 16	Shobdon
July 22 & 23	Hurn
August 6	Newbury
August 12 & 13	Coventry
August 27 & 28	Halfpenny Green
August 27 & 28	Essex Showground
September 3	Wycombe

	Air Races – Formula One
July 1 & 2	Sywell & PFA Rally
July 15 & 16	Shobdon
August 12 & 13	Redon, France
August 27 & 28	Halfpenny Green
September 2 & 3	Freiburg
September 16 & 17	Thruxton

	Air Races – Handicap
July 15 & 16	Shobdon
July 20	S. Coast Air Rally, Hurn
August 20	Kent Messenger, Rochester
August 28	Round the Island, Sandown
September 9	King's Cup, Thruxton

	Aerobatic Competitions
April 29 & 30	McAully Trophy, Little Snoring
June 3	Air Squadron Trophy, Old Warden
July 1 & 2	Henry Trophy, Sleap
August 5 & 6	Thursford Trophy, Little Snoring
September 23 & 24	Esso Trophy, Rochester

	Gliding Competitions
May 19–30	Nationals, Lasham
June 17–25	Competition Enterprise, Northill
August 5–13	Northern Regionals, Sutton Bank
August 19–28	Euroglide, Nympsfield

	Foreign Touring
May 13 & 14	T.C. Visit, St. Valery
July 7–9	T.C. Visit, Cherbourg
September 1–3	Osnabrück At-Home, Redhill
October 7 & 8	T.C. Visit, Hilversum

Missing, of course, is the Dawn-to-Dusk competition, for which the rules had been modified requiring entrants to fly no more than eight hours –no doubt reflecting worries about the cost of participating – together with a detailed points system to give competitors "maximum information on judging."

Also missing is the Hamilton Trophy, sponsored and organised by Committee member David Hamilton, which took place every year at the end of the season in October. Strictly an "in house" contest and restricted to Club members, it can best be described as a precision flying competition with the added attraction of flour bombing and balloon bursting. It was always popular. Most of these events were written up in the *Rag* or at least reported on in the Committee.

For me personally, the highlight was the Formula Air Race meeting at Redon. Redon is a pleasant small town in Brittany accessible from the sea by the pretty Vilaine river. I discovered on consulting my nautical pilot books that it would be possible to navigate my sailing yacht *Mowgli* right into the centre of the town. So why not go by boat ? Fred Marsh, who had visited the airfield with me earlier in the year to survey the course and make the arrangements with the flying club, agreed to race the Beta *Blue Chip* in my place while I planned a sailing holiday with an all Tiger Club crew.

As it turned out, despite a bit of fog, we made a successful voyage from Falmouth and arrived in time to watch the racing and to collect the prize money cheque from the organisers at the end of the afternoon. Some of the crew abandoned ship for all or part of the return journey but I managed to meet up with Max Druine (son of the Turbulent and Condor designer) who joined the yacht in Audierne for the leg to Cherbourg – all in all a successful land, sea and air exercise! I always used to find that both sailing and sweeping the hangar floor were infallible cures for the occasional bouts of nervous exhaustion I suffered while running the Club daily at Redhill!

Benjy's highlight was the FARA meeting at Freiburg and it was there, by the way, that he met again his future wife, Trudi. He described it in the *Rag*:

I'll say this for the FI boys, they do try to spread the gospel. Not content with recently introducing the tiny racers to France they accepted an invitation to move on down to the Black Forest and put on a Formula I race there.

Tiger Club member Bernd Schillen, from the German Experimental Club of Freiburg, was the instigator. He had come over earlier in the year and then again during the Sywell week to see the races there. He was sold, it just had to be seen in Germany.

Quite how the writer got into this act isn't too clear, but he offered to take over the racing propellers by car and also provide wheels out there/spare pilot/spare seats home. (It's supposed to be reassuring to pilots to know there is always a gash seat home.) In the event I didn't take the props and no one needed a lift home. Never mind.

Freiburg may only look a few inches on a half million map, or just three hours for the racing boys at 150 mph, but I can tell you it was all of eight hours solid driving down the autobahns, to say nothing of the three-hour crawl to Dover and three hours plus on a boat. It was all worth it. Freiburg is a beautiful spot near Baden-Baden, right in the middle of the Black Forest, and the Experimental Club members were warmly hospitable.

But in no way was the idyllic bliss contagious. John Mirley, for instance, didn't immediately catch it. He had towed the immaculate Cosmic Wind *Ballerina* by road, arriving late on the Friday evening burnt up with anger and frustration by some French encounter of the worst kind at Dunkirk. The Customs there had detained him 24 hours on a childish paper technicality. A few beers and a glimpse of some worthy talent eventually did wonders for him, and he was soon back to normal.

Andrew Chadwick and his very professional team arrived by road too and on the *same* documentation had sailed through Customs. The others, Michael Jones & Chris Bellhouse in Betas, Peter Kynsey in Tom Regan's Taylor and Robin Voice in the other Cosmic, flew in. It hadn't been an easy trip for them, for heavy rain and storms had guarded the mountains into Germany. Even David Faulkner-Bryant, representing the PFA in his diminutive Curry Wot, had struggled through, climbing the near-6,000 feet of mountain *en route*. Heaven knows what his rate of climb is, but anything over 2,000 feet must be a valiant effort. His must be the most familiar face in Europe, for he goes just about every weekend somewhere over there. That cheerful smile pushing out from behind all that fungus must do more to cement good relations within the EEC than all the clowns at Brussels.

Bernd tried hard to match the cheerfulness about him but couldn't. It had been a bad week for him. In an endeavour to promote this, the first Formula 1 race in Germany, he had a few days before we'd arrived put on a warm-up event for the Press and TV, matching a Formula 2 racing car with Roland Bousquet's F1 racer from France. They got their story, but in doing so virtually put paid to the race. Roland crashed and the local authorities panicked and cancelled all permission to race. The cancellation was widely published but, since no one explained it wasn't the only event, the crowds that Bernd had catered for simply didn't turn up. I reckon I had the entire 54 Drum Majorettes from Mulhouse playing just for me – and very nice it was too.

Between flying acts the F1 boys did what they could to show the public their paces but all that was permitted was timed runs up and down the runway. They were not even permitted to fly in pairs. But even so their efforts and that of all the flying acts, including a remarkable performance by a Fieseler Storch, were widely applauded. Everyone got clapped. There was a charming Swiss girl called Monika who failed to get her engine started in time for her aerobatic slot and, unable to fly, returned to her starting point and switched off. When she did so she got a great round of applause.

'What did I do?' she asked.

'You switched off beautifully!' someone said gallantly.

I couldn't help thinking what an event it would have been to have put on a full Tiger Club display over there with all the goodies at our command. The Germans haven't seen anything quite like the shows we take for granted. Combine that with the fantastic ground organisation that was on show at Freiburg and it would be an event to remember. They had live music all day, constant supplies of hot food and soups and literally tankers of beer. At night – they don't just turn everybody out at 5 pm when the flying finishes – there was dancing and more food, and each night a huge happy party developed that went on till the early hours. The whole hangar had been converted into a communal restaurant, disco and bar . . . coloured lights, laughter, the lot.

To be honest I can't recall which F1 racer took the speed honours; the best speed, boosted, I suspect, by a bit of a dive, was around 250 mph but without the pylons and a real race it was as nothing. We did go and see Roland in hospital; his battered face was wreathed in smiles when he uncovered a couple of bottles of beer we'd smuggled in.

"I'll be out soon," he said, and we believed him.

Most of us returned to England on the Monday. It had been a long and happy weekend. We'd tried to spread the word and probably succeeded.

"Next year it will really take off," said Bernd undaunted. We believed him too.

John Blake's highlight was a 'Turbulent Sea Story':

I have it on the best authority that this story is impossible. It concerns a flying display that took place at Halfpenny Green near Birmingham during a recent holiday weekend, at which I was privileged to be the commentator.

Now there is a practice, common at such events, whereby the more ferocious or athletic aeroplanes in the programme may get airborne some time ahead of their display slot in order to achieve a more effective entrance – speed, noise or both being of the essence. Thus it happened that the take-off by the Tiger Club's team of Turbulent ultralights (the slowest item on the bill) coincided with that of the Royal Navy's Sea Fury (the fastest). The former cavorted after their fashion before the multitude, while the latter whistled away to hold, lurk or orbit until called upon.

The first day of the display had come and gone; dinner was over, and the conversation over coffee in the bar had become mildly frivolous. The Tiger

Club pilots, gathered around the master of the Sea Fury, were pressing him to accept rides in their diminutive mounts in the wildly improbable hope that he might let them fly his. Nothing came of this naïve ploy, but the adjacency of their take-off times did lead someone to suggest that, on the morrow, perhaps a small formation . . .?

We fell to contemplating the prospect of a 12.500 lb fighter, with 2,500 horsepower and an all-down stall of 80 kt, leading four 600 lb, 40 hp featherweights whose Vne falls short of 110.

'It ruddy well can't be done,' the Turbulent leader stated; but this objection was dismissed and, the joke having been thoroughly explored, the party broke up.

Unlike so many excursions into the brightest heaven of invention, this one stood up to re-examination in the cold light of breakfast. It was mulled over at briefing, and by the time the display was under way everyone was convinced that it *could* be done. So, in due course, Turbulents and Sea Fury got airborne and flew away to sort themselves out. Fortunately the belated arrival of a stick of parachutists from an Islander gave them the necessary time. When finally the formation swept towards the crowd it was a noble sight.

The Sea Fury, whose normal entry resembles an amorous Shire horse keeping an assignation some distance downhill, sailed by nose-high with full flap, the vibrating Turbulents clinging to its flanks *a toute vitesse*, while the drivers crouched low to keep their bonedomes as far out of the wind as possible. Most awe-inspiring of all, I later heard from one of them, was the dominant, all-enveloping thunder of the Fury's eighteen open exhaust stacks.

It was a great victory. Although, once won, I doubt whether anybody will have the temerity to try it again.

LETTERS (an anonymous one on the subject of pre-flight checks):

"So I'm aviating hither and thither in the Stampe the other day (not one of the Redhill Stampes, another one) and I find myself commencing to think that the engine sounds a bit flat. So I amble back to the airfield, throttle back – and sure enough, it stops on me, So I land, which seems to be the judicious move in the circumstances, fire it up again on the ground, and taxy in with the aeroplane sounding like a gate banging in a high wind and me thinking harsh thoughts about the quality of the spark plugs you get nowadays.

Only the trouble isn't spark plugs. The trouble turns out to be the top carburettor bracket fractured clean through and the inlet manifold badly cracked, which leaves carb and manifold wiggling about like a loose tooth with consequent detrimental effects on the fuel/air mixture reaching the engine room. So I do the gentlemanly thing and fly into an hysterical gibbering rage, then I scream for Geoff Masterton, and finally I sit down and think about it a bit.

And what I think is that (a) some of those fractures do not look completely new (b) the flight I have just carried out was relatively gentle – only a few aerobatics – so that I can't see any particular reason why the carburettor should suddenly decide to fall off right then, and (c) a couple of flights back I was out practising Lomcovaks, which might well have put a bit of a strain on things, So the chances are that the cracks and things didn't suddenly develop in the last 10 minutes, but had been brewing up for some time.

Which raises the interesting question of *Why The Hell Didn't I Spot Them* on at least one pre-flight inspection?

Now, understand that I take my flying seriously. When I do a pre-flight inspection I don't just count the wings and climb in, I do an <u>inspection</u>. I pull things and poke things and wiggle things, and in particular I stare suspiciously at things which are known to be prone to breakage.

Or at least, that's what I <u>think</u> I do.

Yet, how sure <u>can</u> one be of one's own pre-flight inspection? If it's your own aeroplane and few other people fly it, you really have no kind of check on your own checking ability – until one day something falls off and you're left sitting there wondering why. You may <u>think</u> you do a thorough pre-flight – but if it's a totally familiar aeroplane and you're not expecting to find anything wrong with it, maybe it's possible to look with the eyes in gear but the brain still in 'Park': maybe it's possible to look but just not bloody well see.

So okay. If the manifold and bracket were cracked before I took off – which isn't proven, of course – then one conclusion is obviously that I'm a BF and I need to sharpen up on the pre-flights before I absentmindedly try to leave the ground in an aircraft which is missing something really important, like maybe the wings.

That's one conclusion – but there's another one too, perhaps, which particularly applies if you're flying an aircraft which nobody else flies very much. And that is to have <u>somebody else</u> pre-flight it for you every now and then: get another pair of eyes on the job, on the grounds that although two people can both make mistakes the odds are mathematically against both of them making the <u>same</u> mistake. Engineers do this with their duplicate inspection system, so why shouldn't we?

Exit one slightly wiser pilot, bellowing for Somebody Else."

And an extract from an exuberant Tom Foxworth:

" . . . Perhaps you've heard by now, but if not let me tell you briefly about my latest non-radio cross-Channel escapade. I flew the London–Paris–London sector in dear old 'CDC about three weeks ago, with Mike Long, a former

US Marine pilot and currently on the editorial staff of the National Geographic magazine, in the other cockpit.

Last summer I wrote to Mike and he answered right away saying he was preparing an article on aviation advances for publication in about a year's time. He'd been invited to fly the advanced transport simulator at Weybridge (all fitted out with TV-tube instruments and other futuristic exotica) which is programmed to fly London–Paris. Since that was the first-ever airline route, Mike suggested we do it in the oldest aeroplane we could find and do it just as it had been done way back in 1919. Then he could do a nice contrast in his article: the way it was compared to the way it will be. Air France came through like gangbusters; they loaned us a Concorde for two hours of photography at Charles de Gaulle, where we landed 'CDC.

Graham Horder flew a C.172 rented from Biggin together with a National Geographic photographer, Jim Sugar, who insisted on the 172 since it is probably the best platform for air-to-air photography. In the three days it took us to do the round trip (we were delayed at first by 65-knot gales, but decided to press on when it abated to 25 knots!) Jim must have shot off 3 or 4 dozen rolls of film, and included in that lot are, I'm sure, some of the greatest-ever photos made of our dear old girl 'CDC. I haven't seen them yet, but am awaiting my chance eagerly. Perhaps a future TC Christmas card or publicity . . . Also, despite what you may have heard about French ATC, they were super to us. In fact, when we pointed out the wind direction at CDG, and the fact that if we were to have to taxy back out to runway 27 again we'd still be taxying next Wednesday, the senior ATC controller, who had come out to poke 'CDC along with other curious and eager hordes, squinted, sized up the situation, then grabbed the mike in the Follow Me car parked alongside.

'This is M'sieu Lemoine . . . The aerodrome is closed for 2 minutes at 1600 Z.'

Then, turning to me with a slight bow, 'M'sieu, be my guest.'

'Fine,' said I, 'we'll fly out to the runway, then turn outbound on runway heading for departure.'

'Non necessaire,' he said with a wave of the hand. 'Beauvais is straight ahead; climb straight out!'

So we took off NW straight from spot S-14 while hundreds of waiting Airbus passengers in the nearby building gaped at the spectacle.

A lovely trip all in all. We followed the 1924 Imperial Airways *Flight Operations Manual and Pilot's Guide*. Highly recommended. . . ."

The dear old girl might have been in for another surprise in 1978. We received a letter from the Captain of the Queen's Flight confirming arrangements for the Prince of Wales to fly in 'CDC. Brian Smith, who agreed to fly with him, took the aircraft to Benson the week before to enable the engineers there to give the plane a look over and the Group Captain also indicated that he would like a trip; the log books were also sent for inspection. The letter went on to specify that the flight was to be contained within a purple zone established over Benson (9 nm radius, ground level to FL50) and was to be along the following lines:

Taxy and Take-off – Demonstration
General handling
Stall
Steep turns
Stall in turn
Practice circuit down to 1,000 ft
Circuits and landings

The Group Captain added:

"We can but hope for a fine day; but clearly the flight will have to be tailored to suit the weather. The following minimum weather conditions have been set:

Cross wind – 10 kt
Cloud – 1,000 agl
Visibility – 3 nm

If the minimum conditions can be met, at least some circuit flying should be practicable. It has not yet been possible to clear the arrangements with His Royal Highness and, I am sure you will appreciate, the pressure of other commitments may necessitate changes to the plan. . . ."

Unfortunately these arrangements were later cancelled but I was assured that it was nothing to do with the fact that 'CDC had flown nearly 14,000 hours in its 45-year life (9,000 of them with the Tiger Club) and had been rebuilt several times!

During 1978 there were changes in the office. Phili Voice left to take up commercial flying. Tessa Lovell returned to look after the membership and Jeanne and Joy Frazer helped out in the office generally. 'Looking after the membership' was no light task; with over 700 members – in that pre-computer age – there had to be a proper system; changes of address and phone numbers (which were frequent), sorting out membership applications for Committee approval, producing the annual membership booklet, working the addressograph for the monthly newsletter and much else besides, and last but not least keeping up the huge membership board in the office on which were displayed cards for every Club member showing exactly on what type or types they were current, which was essential information for duty pilots when giving verbal authorisation for bookings. At least there was one blessing: mobile phones and e-mail addresses had not yet arrived!

The monthly Committee meetings were held at a variety of venues over the years but always in central London – usually a friendly Club; I can remember the RAF Reserves Club, the Kronfeld, the Steering Wheel, the Union Jack Club, the Biggles Wine Bar and the Gates Street Wine Bar. Committee meetings at Redhill were ruled out as likely to be too distracting. In 1978 the Club was honoured to be invited by the Lord Mayor to hold one of its Committee meetings at the Mansion House and there were very few apologies for absence on this occasion.

An important debate took place in Committee in 1978 on a proposal to allow associate flying members to take an intial check on the Condor and to fly it solo before attempting the Tiger check. The main reason was that fewer and fewer new associate members were passing the initial Tiger check without a great deal of familiarisation flying. This not only placed an unfair burden on the check pilots but also on the Tigers. The fact was that whereas the previous generation of new members had mostly learnt to fly on Tigers and other tailwheel types and had probably completed their first solo flight in well under 10 hours, it was now taking newcomers almost the same time to check out on the Tiger because a great many of them had learnt on nosewheel aircraft. Clearly something had to be done if membership of the Club was not to become impossibly restrictive, particularly since new members had to have not only 100 hours as pilot-in-charge but also five hours on tailwheels.

Needless to say the proposal caused controversy but was eventually accepted and later modified into a new category of membership known as 'Provisional Associate' which entitled him or her to take an initial check on the Condor if they could show 75 hours as pilot in charge and without the tailwheel requirement.

A very sad event took place in May that year – the tragic accident to Tony Smith, who was killed flying Bill Colson's Cassutt while practising Formula 1 air racing at Shobdon. It was not an official air race meeting and had nothing to do with the Club as such. FARA ran the meeting to give newcomers a pylon course on which to practise and to obtain some publicity photographs. Tony had become unsighted on the back straight and had struck the top of a tree. It was a grievous loss since Tony was an enthusiastic Club member and an up-and-coming aerobatic pilot. To their infinite credit his parents Geoff and Dorrie immediately joined the Club and presented a handsome trophy in his memory designed by Andrew Chadwick, which was to be awarded annually for aerobatics to the most promising new Club member. Later they were both invaluable in assisting Margaret Burgess in the organisation of weekend teas and lunches in the clubroom.

Another accident occurred later in the year at the aerodrome to the Turbulent G-ARZM, which stalled and crashed in a field on the far side of Kings Mill Lane just after taking off to the north on the north-south runway. Fortunately the pilot was unhurt but the little plane was, as might be expected, virtually a write-off. This provoked a number of lengthy and angry letters from two residents of Kings Cross Lane which was close to the northern boundary of the airfield, one of whom was Admiral of the Fleet Sir Peter Hill Norton, formerly chief of the Defence Staff and later to be elevated to the House of Lords.

Sir Peter used the occurrence of this accident to complain about the actual existence in use of the north-south runway. Copies of the letter were sent to Sir Geoffrey Howe. Sir Geoffrey telephoned me about this correspondence and asked me to send him a draft letter (which he would then amend as necessary) and which would afterwards be sent to him officially from the Club, so that he could send copies to the complainants with his own reply: an interesting technique normally adopted by Sir Geoffrey to diffuse protests about the aerodrome.

To quote from my letter sent to Sir Geoffrey:

"The north-south runway at the aerodrome has been in existence for a very long time, certainly since 1959 when we moved here and to the best of my knowledge since before the last war. A few years ago its northern threshold was moved in some 200 yards from the airfield boundary to give more clearance over Kings Cross Lane for aircraft landing to the south. It is only used when the prevailing wind does not allow the east-west runway to be used with safety and although I have not made any precise calculations, I would estimate from my experience that from the days when we are flying, it is used approximately one or two days out of seven. . . .

Under normal circumstances aircraft would have a minimum of 250–300 ft over Kings Cross Lane. . . . I admit that in the take-off case, when the aircraft is at full power, this may cause annoyance and we are doing our best to reduce this to the minimum. One of the new suggestions under consideration is that we should restrict 'touch-and-go' landings on the north-south runway . . . Some people have adopted the technique of turning left and climbing out before passing over Kings Cross Lane; this course also has its problems in that the aircraft may not have sufficient airspeed to carry out this manoeuvre, nor enough height, and of necessity has to make the turn at rather a low altitude.

This brings me to the accident on 17th September. . . . The pilot concerned . . . resides at Ham Lodge in Kings Mill Lane (when he is not abroad selling cars for British Leyland). Naturally he is more acutely aware than some other members of the need to avoid upsetting his neighbours. I have had a discussion with him since the accident and he has told me that he was turning left between his house and Kings Cross Lane. Unfortunately, due to a bad error of judgement which he honestly admits, he did not have sufficient airspeed on initiating the turn; the aircraft stalled and he did not have the necessary height before hitting the ground. We are distressed . . . about this accident; it is the first of its kind and, I sincerely hope, the last. . . .

I apologise for burdening you with so lengthy a letter and also for the fact that this may not, on the face of it, appear helpful. Whilst we are denied representation on the Consultative Committee it is very difficult for our voice to be heard. Nevertheless I would like to assure you that everything is being done to eliminate unreasonable annoyance to our neighbours and also that we do appreciate in full the anxieties which are always aroused by all types of accidents and incidents in the air."

Incidentally Redhill had been legally designated by the Department of Transport to set up a Consultative Committee on which local residents, local government officials and users of the aerodrome had a statutory right to be represented. The Redhill Committee was run by Bristow Helicopters and the airfield owners. Later, with the help of Sir Geoffrey, we were able to obtain representation. Unfortunately the above letter failed to diffuse Sir Peter Hill Norton, who wrote a further series of angry letters concluding with:

"Unless you are able to give me reasonable assurance that this nuisance will be brought under control I shall regrettably have to resort to litigation which I am prepared to pursue either alone or jointly with others in the highest courts."

We gave what assurances we could and wrote:

"I would like to assure you that we do not use the north-south runway except when conditions make it imperative to do so, and I will take all steps to ensure that this policy is even more rigorously applied than in the past. . . . I can also assure you that every member of the Club, as a condition of his or her membership, undertakes 'always to fly with courtesy and with special attention to the safety and comfort of others,' and if there is clear evidence that any member has behaved in breach of this undertaking the appropriate action is taken under the Club's disciplinary procedures."

These assurances appeared to satisfy Sir Peter and we heard no more on the subject. Later the Senior Check Pilot published a circular in the Newsletter advising pilots that if they were using the northerly runway for 'touch-and-gos' they should always to do so from the threshold of the north-south runway and in all circumstances avoid unsticking near the hangars.

On the whole 1978 had been a highly successful year for the Club. Flying hours were substantially up although they were never again to approach the totals achieved during the decade from the early sixties to the early seventies before the price of fuel went through the roof. Membership was also well up, including the number of members actually flying Club aircraft during the year. Also financially we were breaking even. There were just but two small clouds on the horizon. Our landlords still had not issued us with our new lease, which had been ordered by the County Court over three years previously, and a new aerodrome manager, Mr John Colin Dalrymple, had been appointed at the end of the year to take over from Stanley Kerridge.

CHAPTER 3
1979

Apart from a refusal of permission to hold a flying display at the aerodrome in 1979, the first communication we received from Mr Dalrymple was a few days before Christmas in 1978. He wrote:

"I hereby confirm that with immediate effect night flying by any fixed-wing aircraft from Redhill Aerodrome is to cease forthwith."

The letter then went on:

"It will be appreciated if you will confirm by return whether the Tiger Club meets the minimum requirements for this licensed aerodrome so as to continue to be able to operate at Redhill Aerodrome."

I was astonished by the tone of these communications. The Club had never needed nor had the CAA ever required a statutory licence to operate at the aerodrome because we neither carried out flying instruction nor public transport operations. As for night flying, we had received assurances from the CAA that there was no objection from their point of view; the temporary flarepath we used was not in breach of the regulations in that we were not establishing a 'permanent light.'

In fact the amount of night flying we used to carry out was extremely small – around 20 hours a year on average; it took place only after the short winter weekend days when the clocks had been put back and in ideal weather conditions. We used to lay out a goose-neck flarepath for the Super Cub, Condor and Jodel for members to keep their night ratings current if they had one. To take off and land on a goose-neck flarepath and to be airborne usually on a moonlit night was an activity much enjoyed by members who stayed on in the Clubroom after tea. Mr Dalrymple's next move was to demand *"lists"* – lists of Club members, lists of Club aircraft and lists of aircraft owned by members resident in our hangar. As we later discovered this was to enable him to try and charge Club members for landing fees when they they were flying their own aircraft, despite the fact that our lease was crystal-clear on the matter, which was that the Club paid an annual block landing fee for all its members regardless of the aircraft they were flying.

In the same letter Mr Dalrymple added *"one further point"* which was that *"with immediate effect Redhill Aerodrome has been deleted as a glider-launching area from the UK Air Pilot and that no glider flying activities will be permitted at this aerodrome."* During 1979 Mr Dalrymple made a few 'further points,' which included banning the Club manager or its duty pilots from physically inspecting the airfield and marking out boggy patches, closing the aerodrome over Christmas and the New Year, threats to forfeit our lease and a refusal to accept our rental payments.

Possibly Mr Dalrymple did not wish to be bothered with the clause in our lease which stated that the tenant paying the rents etc. *"shall peaceably hold and enjoy the demised premises . . . without any interruption by the landlords."* Eventually most of these 'points' were resolved but only after endless meetings and correspondence; on the question of gliding this included strong letters of protest from the Chairmen of the Royal Aero Club and the British Gliding Association, and I was also able to circulate a paper about the gliding the Club carried out to a slightly bemused Aerodrome Consultative Committee. The Club's attitude on all these matters was and had always been that we had a lease ordered by a court of law which included the right to use the aerodrome, and a positive covenant to run a flying club for experienced pilots; our landlords had the right to make regulations governing our activities even to the point of strangling them all together but they did not have the right to ban them.

In connection with the 'serviceability' of the aerodrome a disturbing incident took place at the end of 1979 on a bright and sunny Sunday morning. By this time Mr Dalrymple had in his wisdom decided that there was to be an 'Airfield Information Officer' on duty in the ancient RAF Control tower not only during the week but also at the weekends. This person's title and trappings were officially recognised by the CAA, who had invented them to cover the case of people who wished to exercise the powers of an air traffic control officer but without the responsibility.

For the past 20 years during the wet winter months, the Club's duty pilots or myself had the responsibility of checking the airfield surface and designating on the Club's 'Aerodrome Serviceability Board' any areas which were 'no-go' and marking them off as necessary. On this occasion there were the normal 450 metres available at the beginning of the east-west runway for the biplanes and the Super Cub. However a major row broke out after the officer in the tower closed the airfield and banned all flying except helicopters without even bothering to check the surface. The anger in the Club was so intense that it was decided to ignore the ban and continue flying. Eventually the local police were called and after they arrived flying was stopped while the situation was resolved. Everybody calmed down and after a short while flying was resumed for the remainder of the day.

Looking back on these events more than 20 years later I am still astonished. To be faced daily with an aerodrome manager who appeared to perceive that his sole function in life was to make things as difficult as possible for the Club was indeed hard. Needless to say, there was much Clubroom discussion about Mr Dalrymple's role. Some people asserted that he was simply the wrong man in the wrong job, subscribing to the theory that in any hierarchy – and Bristow Helicopters and all the other aviation businesses acquired by British & Commonwealth Shipping PLC, including Redhill Aerodrome (Holdings) Ltd, was certainly a hierarchy –

some individuals were bound to reach such a level of incompetence and to become so incapable of assuming responsibility that their actions inevitably resulted in confusion and discontent. The situation could not continue. Mr Dalrymple would be moved to another position in the hierarchy where he could do less harm.

Other people were not so sure. Mr Dalrymple, formerly employed by Bristows, was rumoured to have 'connections' with the Cayzer family, the ultimate owners of British & Commonwealth Shipping PLC, and was not Sir Nicholas Cayzer himself the actual chairman of Redhill Aerodome (Holdings) Ltd? Mr Dalrymple was simply carrying out policy laid down from above which was, as Benjy was to put it later succinctly in the *Rag:*

My personal thought, and I'm not so charitable as others, is that our landlords want us out. . . .

From instinct, personal observation and my experience of dealing with these same landlords five years earlier I subscribed to the latter view. Mr Dalrymple was a man who was always carefully dressed in collar and tie, well-cut suit and highly polished shoes and he drove an expensive car with personalised number plates. His outlook always appeared to be orientated towards Redhill as an 'airport' with its implications of terminal buildings, aprons and concrete runways. I had the impression that he would prefer to see pilots wearing blazers and flannels, even uniforms, and carrying smart flight bags to which would be attached a radio headset. Pilots wearing overalls, boots and sheepskin jackets were anathema to him as were Tiger Moths, gliders and muddy grass airfields. In a word Mr Dalrymple was interested in aviation, not in flying, and there is a world of difference between the two. My worst fears were confirmed during the following year when he was appointed a director of the aerodrome company.

For most of 1979 solicitors representing both parties were inevitably in the picture. For the Club we were fortunate to have the services of a small inexpensive firm in Ealing who had handled the Court proceedings when our lease was renewed in 1975. They had taken over at very short notice from a large London firm after our barrister, Patrick Ground, abruptly informed me after a conference that it was essential to change solicitors immediately. Both Michael Syson and his father Eric always defended the Club's interests and position not only with admirable patience but also with quiet determination.

Their first task was to put pressure on our landlords at least to provide us with our lease. The first result of this was a series of aggressive and hectoring letters from the solicitor representing the aerodrome, containing not only a number of allegations against the Club – mostly of the "have you stopped beating your wife?" variety – but also a refusal to issue us with our lease unless we agreed to a number of new clauses which would threaten the Club's very survival. Given the general attitude of

Mr Dalrymple, this was hardly surprising. What *was* surprising was that the solicitor who was now engaged against us, Peter Martin, seeking, as he put it, a "final solution," was none other than the very same person who was at that time not only honorary solicitor to AOPA but who had also, several years earlier after handling some problem or other on aerobatics, agreed to become 'honorary solicitor' to the Club if required. To say that I was flabbergasted would be to put it mildly. The only thing I could think of at the time was Dr Johnson's remark:

"Why, Sir, one does not wish to be rude about a man, but they tell me he is a lawyer."

Aside from Clubroom gossip and the Committee meetings, where the problems at Redhill were fully discussed, the vast majority of our members, including 150 overseas, were blissfully unaware of our 'little local difficulties.' During 1979 membership was still on the increase and utilisation of the Club's aircraft was improved, despite further swingeing increases in the price of fuel. As before there was a very full calendar of events including seven aerobatic meetings, two F1 races in France, a handicap air race from Biggin to Ghent (sponsored by Stella Artois, for which I had accepted an invitation to be clerk of the course), a Tiger Moth Rally to Scotland and all the usual foreign touring functions. There were also ambitious plans for the 'seaplane' Tiger including a Scottish lakes tour. Although no full Tiger Club shows were to be organised, the 'participation' calendar was full. The Club was also taking a new initiative:

The Tiger Club are moving into yet another sphere of competition flying for which we are justly proud. Precision Flying, which gives any pilot the opportunity of flying and navigating accurately, is to have its own National Championship. The Hosts and prime movers are, of course, the Tiger Club.

What is the Championship all about? Basically it is divided into four parts: Flight Planning (electronic calculators allowed); a navigation flight; a test of observation of targets and the identification of photographs; together with four different spot landings. The Rules are similar to those which have recently been rewritten (with help from several menbers) for the World Championship.

The British Championship, which is not really a Spectator event, will be held at Redhill on June 2nd/3rd. As this will involve the Club in a day's complex flying, the Committee have agreed to suspend the usual aerobatic slot on June 2nd (thanks to aspiring aerobatic pilots for putting up with another event).

To run the contest is involving a few members in a great deal of hard work but there are one or two areas where assistance would be appreciated. Firstly, anyone who would like to aid the event by offering to be judges, marshallers, observers and the like should get in touch with Michael as soon as possible. We need many hands.

Secondly, and as important, we are promised a number of participating pilots (some overseas members) from Scandinavia, including two from Finland. Would any member(s) prepared to offer the hospitality of their homes (bed and breakfast) for the nights of 1st/2nd June please contact David Timmis.

Finally we intend having a celebratory dinner on the night of 2nd June. Those interested in coming (venue close to Redhill) let Michael know now. The success of this event depends very much on help from all our members and as the Tiger Club is, on behalf of the United Kingdom, to host the 1981 World Championship (regretfully not at Redhill) an immediate success is therefore imperative.

The annual dinner dance to celebrate the past year had been a great success:

This, our 23rd anniversary Dinner and Ball, at least by my reckoning, was a tremendous success. A young lady, shivering somewhat after a visit to the powder room (apparently it was like an ice-box in there), asked with feeling why a Ball in early February. The short answer is, I guess, that originally Bev Snook used to try and make it a Valentine occasion as well, but somehow the 14th doesn't seem to fall right these days – must be the weather. Even so, over 220 turned up and the organisers were soon all too aware that we'd reached the top limit for this venue of the last few years. 130 plus sat down to dinner and nearly 100 others enjoyed a buffet, all finally getting together for the prize-giving and speeches. The menu sported a delightful cartoon by John Blake depicting the waters off Mount Batten, where our Guest of Honour is Commanding Officer of the Southern Air Region, and a launch about to intercept the Sea Tiger just landing with one of the crew saying to the others: 'Before you actually arrest anyone, Nobby, make sure it isn't the Boss.' To see so many familiar faces in unfamiliar garb was part of the fun of the evening. Personally, I found it hard to reconcile some of the provocatively-clad beauties with the airfield image. I tried, of course, but I fear Redhill may never be the same again.

The leisurely dinner over, Benjy arose to review 1978. The ensuing battle to be heard over the raspberry-blowing balloons and the excitement of the tiny aircraft whizzing around wasn't conclusive; put it down to a draw. I thought our principal guest blanched visibly at the reception, but when it was his turn to reply on behalf of our Guests he was probably relieved to find the audience both receptive and appreciative. In an evening such as this it was inevitable that the man who gave us the way of life that is the Tiger Club was much missed. John Severne put it clearly at the end of his speech just how much we owed to Norman Jones. Somehow, but somehow, we must get him to attend next year! Our other two Guests were David and Cherry Cyster. It was in recognition of David's flight by Tiger to Australia just a year ago that the invitation had been extended and glad we were to welcome them.

Katherine Severne kindly presented the many prizes. It fell as ever to John Blake to announce the winners. He was soon into his stride; he couldn't resist remarking on an item in John's speech during which he referred to a flight in an F.104. Boomed John (*all the following to be read in gutteral German/English accent and all*): 'Asked one German of another how could he get a F.104: "You buy a piece of land," replied the other, "and wait."' 36 hours later I still burst out laughing.

A shy Sue Thompson received the de Salis Trophy – awarded to the member who has, in the opinion of the Committee, done the most for the Club within the last 18 months. It was well deserved, if only for her dedication to flying the Tiger in the coldest of weathers! The Club's premier award – the Clem Pike Trophy – went to Bill Chesson for his many many years as Display Promoter. To John Stewart-Wood the Air Racing Medallion for his popular win in the King's Cup, and the Glider-Towing Medallion went again to Peter Ferry, and most deservedly so. To the two Davids, Timmis and Hamilton, the Foreign Touring Medallion for their remarkable trip to Lapland. Andrew Chadwick was again winner of the Hamilton Trophy and the Aerobatic Medallion went to Geoff Masterton amid much wild acclaim. A new award this year, the Tony Smith Trophy, was presented by his parents to his memory; this most handsome engraved silver trophy was given to Alan Dix, the best-placed pilot in the Air Squadron Trophy. It was heartwarming to see Mr and Mrs Smith at dinner and so obviously happy to be with us.

The Dawn-to-Dusk awards turned out to be a near all-female benefit. Pat Holmes not only received the Duke of Edinburgh Trophy but the Bonney Trophy, the Long Distance Medallion and the Icarus Trophy. It was as clean a sweep as ever we'd seen and Pat, who is a most popular person, received a great ovation. Janet Meetoo and Jamilah Nicholl took both second place and the Pilot Trophy.

I think the Arts Club only comes into its own when the diners disperse. For the dancers it was a disco with lights, good music and a place where everyone cheerfully lets their hair down, and the staying power was amazing to see as they danced the night away. Others with stories and gossip to catch up on moved into the bars, and such was the choice that one could choose the huddle and smoky friendliness of the downstairs one or the comfort of the bar upstairs where the barman with a master's touch seemed to know just about every concoction. Tessa and Don Lovell must have realised over £50 for the Hospitality Fund with the Tombola they'd organised and I saw a delighted John Severne leaving hugging a bottle of brandy he'd won; there was no doubt it had gone to a good home. To David and Georgina Hamilton our congratulations on arranging such a fine evening.

I left tired and happy some time after one – I'm told the dancing went on until after two. From the elegant music room came the strains of Chopin movingly played by a member unknown to me. Around her sat entranced friends. It was a little bit of magic that will linger for a long time.

The *Tiger Rag* was as usual the essential vehicle to record Club visits and members' news. Wynn Evans wrote up the trip to Freiburg and Ron Jacobs his in the B-17, and there were letters from Texas and Australia:

Last year the Experimental Flying Club at Freiburg organised a Fly-In which was attended by the Tiger Club Formula I Racers. The meeting was a great success (although they did not get to race, which is another story) and a firm friendship between the Clubs was established. At Benjy's suggestion Freiburg was the first point on this year's foreign touring calendar.

Four aircraft eventually started from Redhill, Ernest Barnes and Dick Thomas in Jodel 'VEF, Eberhard Tramms in a 'vintage' Cessna, Robin Voice in his Cosmic Wind and finally Dennis Sole and me in a Cherokee Arrow.

From here on, I can best give my own version of a most enjoyable weekend. We left Redhill at the gentlemanly hour of 11 o'clock to clear Customs at Lydd. The forecast said there was a cold front with minor waves lying from Frankfurt to Colmar moving erratically slowly south-east and that most of the route would be affected by an unstable south-westerly air stream. Over south-east England it was a beautiful morning, bright, slightly bumpy and with a few light showers. After coping with the incredible bureaucracy which seems to involve one's departure in a light aircraft from the UK we gratefully took off and set course for Abbeville. We crossed the Channel at 3,000 feet, noticing Berck sur Mer still in use as an airfield, the scene of so many past visits. The weather in north-western France was perfect with a cloud base of about 4,000 feet.

We noticed the old town and cathedral at Laon and diverted slightly from our track which was initially to Rheims. Thereafter we proceeded with a short dog-leg to Epinal about two-thirds of the way to Freiburg. Here the sun was obscured by high cloud and the weather started to change as the forecast had predicted. The Vosges mountains which I was seeing for the first time seem a very beautiful part of France and we descended to fly at 500 feet to admire the countryside more closely.

Cloud above us was thickening as we flew east and it was here I noticed a most peculiar phenomenon; over woods we saw innumerable spirals of what appeared to be smoke from small fires, though when we turned to look down no fire could be seen. We assumed it was in fact stratus cloud either forming or dissipating above features in the wood. But what these features were and how they caused it I do not understand; perhaps somebody could explain. Whatever the reason it was very beautiful and rather spectacular, being confined to only over woodlands.

Shortly afterwards the stratus became quite thick and low so that it was impossible to remain below and we climbed just above, flying between layers. The ground in this part of France is a minimum of 1,500 feet above sea level with some peaks about 4,000 feet but we proceeded happily between the layers as we could see perfectly where we were going. However it then began to rain and space between the cloud layers became misty and indistinct so that it was not too plain whether little lumps of cloud were hiding a mountain or not. This necessitated a climb to the safety altitude, which placed us above a solid overcast which remained until we had passed over the Vosges, when one of our passengers discerned the airfield at Colmar beneath us in the mist and rain from an altitude of 5,000 feet. As we were now in the Rhine Valley we made a descent over Colmar to 1,500 feet and proceeded visually in the misty rain across the Rhine Valley. Not having been here before I had no idea how wide the Rhine would be or what it would look like but fortunately our heading was good and again the same passenger obligingly observed the airfield.

The Jodel and the Cessna were not so fortunate, reaching only Metz and Luxemburg and being unable to proceed further as the front disobligingly remained in the same position over the whole weekend. However Robin Voice appeared in the Cosmic Wind at lunchtime the next day so the Club was reasonably well represented.

Our welcome by Ulli Maiss, the Chairman of the Experimental Flying Club at Freiburg, was most warm and cordial. We were given coffee and schnapps in the Clubhouse and later that evening had an excellent meal in the airport hotel as guests of the proprietor, to whom a Tiger Club tie was duly presented as a token of our thanks. Members of the Club very kindly accommodated us in their homes and took us the next morning to see the charming town of Freiburg. Unfortunately it was rather misty so we were unable to appreciate the scenery to its full extent, but the town nestles at the foot of steeply-wooded mountains with vineyards on some of the steeper south slopes. It is a medieval university town with tremendous atmosphere. There are many street musicians: we saw a one-man band, a bagpiper, a flautist playing Bach's musical offerings, a violinist, a peasant band and two string quartets.

That afternoon we were taken by car to Ulli Maiss' house in your actual Black Mountains. This was about 3,000 feet above sea level and we came above the mist, which still persisted in the Rhine Valley, into bright sun. The atmosphere and fragrance of the country is unusually pleasant. The fir trees grow to an extraordinary size and extremely straight. The vegetation at 3,000 feet is quite different from what we would find at this altitude in the UK;

grass, hardwood trees and arable crops all seem to be grown with fair success in spite of the altitude. The farmhouses are part of a huge barn with the fodder on the top floor and the house and cow sheds on the ground floor. Some of these seem to be of a considerable age.

That evening we were given an excellent barbecue in the Clubhouse and imbibed quite freely of the excellent local wine. It really was a very enjoyable evening and we were made to feel most welcome. Two of the members played a pianola and a piano accordion and, starting with *God Save the Queen*, the dancing and revelry continued (so I am informed) until 4 o'clock in the morning.

Sunday dawned a really foggy day but fortunately it cleared sufficiently for us to take off at about 10 o'clock, and by 2,000 feet we were in the sun admiring the Black Forest and the lower slopes of the Vosges, which were quite clear. On the return we were able to see those parts of the Vosges we had missed, which were indeed spectacular with steeply wooded slopes of mixed trees coming to steep ridges. We flew low over several of these to experience the sensation of crossing the ridge at 100 feet above the ground and seconds later being 1,000 feet above the ground in the bottom of the valley. The weather in central France was a little hazy and on reaching the Channel coast we found the weather in England was very bad. However Lydd was reasonable and we landed here to find Eberhard Tramms had also just returned. By the afternoon it had cleared sufficiently for us to follow the railway line back to Redhill. Ernest Barnes had wisely returned the previous day, while Robin Voice left Freiburg on the Sunday afternoon and, after transacting various business he had on the Continent, returned to Redhill on Monday.

All in all this was a most successful and enjoyable visit and it is only a great pity that the weather was so unfavourable for us. We have some marvellous memories of our welcome there, of the town and the Black Forest, sitting in the sun sipping the German wine and listening to the bells of the Churches echoing across the mountains. We have invited the Freiburg Club to Redhill on the second weekend in August and hope to be able to return some of their hospitality.

AN EX-LANC PILOT REFLECTS ON A B-17

Being a member of the Tiger Club can provide the occasional rare moment and sometimes a real highlight. I certainly experienced mine whilst gazing rapturously at the Flying Fortress at a recent air show. My reverie was interrupted by Keith Sissons saying: 'Would you like to come up in the Fortress?' After a respectable pause, I accepted.

58

As you approach the aircraft you can sense the atmosphere emanating from her and all the Army Air Corps' planes she represents. I half expected the door to open and the old crews to emerge.

Sally B arrived over here in 1944 and has been flying ever since, a tribute to the band of enthusiasts who have kept her in such remarkably good condition. The all-volunteer crew consists of two pilots and two Flight Engineers; Keith and Don Bullock as Captains alternate the shows.

The feeling of nostalgia increases as you climb into the aircraft, past the waistgunners – five positions, – no Lanc main spar to scramble over but a narrow catwalk over the bomb bay and up into the cockpit.

It was a wonderful feeling to settle in the right-hand seat as Keith explained a few things and I tried to absorb., There was a clever-sounding automatic electrical control for the turbochargers. The throttles had a central control bar that seemed more restricting than RAF types. We would be using about 2,300 revs and over 20 ins boost and 130 mph on the climb-out.

Getting close to slot time I reluctantly vacated the seat and moved back to the port waist position. Taxying through the vast crowd on outers was safely accomplished with *Sally B's* helpers parading the wing tips.

Waiting at the holding point, my excitement mounted as the Navy finished their show, the Fury passing over my gunsight looking much like a FW.190 (I'm no Chris Wren!). Engines at full blast, brakes off and we leap forward flapless into a 20 kt wind from starboard. . . . The aircraft is soon clear and climbing away. Any previous ideas I nurtured of the Fortress as a stately straight and level old bird were quickly dispelled as Keith stood her vertically on the starboard wingtip and down for our first low pass.

The next few minutes were sheer delight; the cabin is quiet, pulling smoothly positive, there's not the discomfort of a Lanc corkscrew. The very spirited show concludes with the inevitable run down the valley, for the householders to view us from above! Up from nowhere for the final low pass, a steep climbing turn continued round to the threshold (Spit fashion), everything down, 100 mph over the hedge and we're neatly down.

Backtracking down the active we clear past the waiting Me.108. I can't resist one little squint as it traverses the point 5. When the Cyclones are shut down, old *Sally* wheezes and settles. In the ensuing silence I ponder. How can I ever complain next time I'm down for duty pilot on a wet day after a perk like this?

LETTERS

6 January 1979   Box 672, Hillsboro, Texas 76645

"Dear Benjy: The grass is always greener on the other side of the Atlantic – and at Redhill Aerodrome it was as green as ever during our family's visit in August 1978. It had been eight years since I last flew a Tiger Moth, but check-pilot Tony Baptiste kindly helped me polish some of the rust from my airmanship in 'CDC. Later I was able to take Stephen (14 years old) for his first ride in a Tiger.

I was surprised by the apparent lack of available Tigers at the Tiger Club. Rather sad. Of course one was on floats at the time and in spite of Tom Freer's offer to let us sample the delights of this combination, we just did not have enough time and weather available to get down to fly it. The Stampe was as lively and responsive as ever and I enjoyed a few minutes cavorting over the Surrey countryside – just like old times.

The Club is just as wonderful as ever with friendly, helpful people. We met some new and some of the remaining old faces – I just wish our visit could have been longer so that we could have met more and spoken longer. Perhaps we'll be able to make another visit one of these days. In the meantime we would always welcome a visit from any members passing through Texas in their travels. To help make up for the lack of Tigers, I noticed a considerable increase in the numbers of private owners, home builders and 'do-it-yourselfers' in the hangar. This is more like sport aviation in the US, where there are few Clubs as we know them in England.

Happy New Year!
NICK POCOCK"

Letter from "down under" (by Bill Goldstraw)

Croydon, Victoria, June 1979

"Winter is with us again and with it more civilised temperatures and short take-off runs in the Tiger. The latter continues to go well but the aviation scene is changing dramatically owing to a doubling in the price of Avgas (to £0.92 a gallon) and a total drying up of 80 octane. We hope the latter is temporary but anything could happen. There is even a shortage of 100 for reasons which are not spelled out but which I suspect depend on the low political 'pull' of general aviation.

In March I was able to resurrect the Tiger Moth formation team for an air display at Berwick. Later in the year we did our annual "dawn patrol" flypast for the Anzac Day dawn parade at the coastal town of Torquay. David Allan was prised away from his legal studies and house improvement duties to perform very ably at No. 3. At RAAF Point Cook changes have been made for the better and a nucleus of keen flying types has suddenly appeared who actually like flying, especially in Tiger Moths.

Tiger Club member and occasional correspondent Roger Meadmore coaxed his Tiger Moth 'TSG round the "Tiger Moth Air Race" course successfully (though a Pt. Cook type won – for the second year running), but spends more of his flying time flying his hot-air balloon and generating many 'hairy' stories in the process. One of the latter appeared in a feature article in the local edition of *Playboy*!

You will of course remember our antipodean motorcycling fiend Arthur H. I haven't seen Arthur for some time but I was sad to hear that his Tiger Moth 'FAH was blown over at its moorings at Berwick earlier this year and written off. Poor Arthur was miles away at the time but immediately bought back the wreck when he heard of the mishap. I believe he intends to rebuild. A very sad affair, for A. has had that aircraft for many years – 15 at least – and was always most helpful in lending it to us for display.

I paid a quick visit to the HQ of the Tiger Club of Australia at their airfield near Maitland (NSW) last September. Enthusiast and prime mover Bill Hitchcock was an excellent host and a formidable salesman for the Club and its activities. There are some immaculate Tigers (privately owned) at Maitland. The restoration work carried out there is of a thoroughly magnificent standard and such as to make Rollasons sit up and take notice. Their engineer is a perfectionist (judging by the work I saw) and in his hands DH.82s in that part of the world will drone the skies for many years yet. I suppose he is lucky to have owners who can afford to pay for the best but it is nice to see genuine craftsmanship still in evidence.

I was at Maitland at a quiet time and saw little of their flying activities. The Club involves itself with a number of air displays each year and is very active in promoting sport flying. The annual (by now) Tiger Moth Air Race is a much publicised and tidily organised event which draws participants from all of the nation (last year one aircraft was flown nearly 2,000 miles from Western Australia for the event). . . ."

QUOTES OF THE YEAR

"Would you accept another 50p per gallon price rise to secure the supply of Avgas?" (Shell spokesman)

'There is still room for sporting aviation here. . . ." (Norman Tebbitt MP, Minister of State)

During 1979 the Club came into possession of two new trophies known as the Sportair Trophy and the Sportair Lady Trophy. Through the good offices of Gordon Franks these were donated to the Club by their owners Mr and Mrs Haley. Sportair was at one time an enterprising flying club based at Biggin Hill using Fournier RF.4s and RF.5s for *ab initio* training. It had been run by two Tiger Club members, Brian Stevens and Neil Jensen. As its name suggests, its philosophy and ideals were very similar to those of the Tiger Club; its members were regular participants in handicap air racing and performed an excellent solo and duo RF.4 display act. Many people who trained at Sportair subsequently became welcome and prominent members of the Tiger Club. In 1972 we had done a deal with Sportair whereby we bought an RF.4 and they bought a Rollason-rebuilt Stampe. The RF.4 immediately became highly popular with Club members and in 1979, despite the room it took up in the hangar and occcasional undercarriage problems, it was more then justifying its keep. It was eventually agreed that the Sportair Lady Trophy would be awarded to the Club member highest placed in the standard class aerobatic points championship and that the Sportair Trophy would be similarly awarded to the Club member best placed in F1 racing.

In December 1979, in connection with Formula 1 Air Racing, I was very busy with others in FARA organising an International 'Rules' Conference. This was to take place in London at the In and Out Club – courtesy Fred Marsh. The reason for this rather ambitious exercise, which strictly speaking had nothing to do with the Club, was that a row had broken out in America between two groups of F1 racer owners and pilots over the class rules and alleged 'cheating.' The rules governing the specifications of F1 airframes and engines are of necessity fairly complex and, without very tight inspections, open to different interpretations; a splinter group had been formed in the US breaking away from the official United States Air Racing Association and running its own meetings to different rules. The idea was to invite representatives from both sides to come to London and, to put it bluntly, knock heads together to agree one International rule which would be acceptable on both sides of the Atlantic. A surprising number of people turned up all the way from California and from France.

On the face of it, with the help of some skilful chairmanship from Anne Welch and plenty of socialising, the conference appeared to have been a success. However we learnt later than in America the rift had not been healed and that consequently there could be no International rule. I instinctively feared that, without an International rule properly enforced, the sport, which had huge potential for sponsorship, would never really 'take off.'

The country's political scene was not generally a Club topic for discussion but we could not help noticing that 1979 was the year that Margaret Thatcher and the Conservative Party swept to power in the General Election on a programme to encourage "wealth-creating private business, free markets and limited government." Sir Geoffrey Howe, our local MP, who was now the Chancellor of the Exchequer, might not have too much time for our problems. Was the Tiger Club a "wealth-creating private business" and would there be "limited government"? We hoped so.

CHAPTER 4

1980

The Chairman's letter to members at the beginning of 1980 was concerned not only with the crisis in the cost of aviation fuel but also for the first time touched upon the problems at Redhill. In fact from now on through the *Rag* and elsewhere members were kept fully in the picture:

As everybody knows, there has been a continued surge in the price of fuel during the past year and, for reasons which are not altogether clear, this has affected aviation fuel a very great deal more than motor fuel. In fact we have had to suffer seven separate price rises which in total has increased the cost of fuel by 75%. As a result we have had to make increases and surcharges during 1979 to try and keep up with this and we will have to continue to do this during 1980 if the present trend continues. At the same time other operating costs have also increased in line with inflation and this means that the flying rates on the enclosed list show a really large increase on those prevailing a year ago; it is clear that the cost of fuel is now a quite unacceptable proportion of the cost of running a light aircraft and, although we can be thankful that the threat of a further increase caused by the abolition of the road fund tax appears to have receded, it does seem that it is again high time that the fuel companies and the responsible authorities put their heads together to see if an acceptable formula can be found to use the lower-priced motor fuel in unsophisticated light aircraft. In the meantime, it is essential that all members using Club aircraft exercise the maximum possible economy with power settings.

We regret that we also have had to raise subscriptions yet again; this is to take account of the increased VAT introduced last year and also to budget to some extent for the likelihood of increased airfield charges which are paid by the Club on behalf of all members.

Finally, as some members will know, during the past year we have experienced certain difficulties in our relationships with our landlords at Redhill aerodrome. We believe that the difficulties have arisen mainly as a result of misunderstandings on both sides: we are now in the process of finding a solution acceptable to all concerned. Meanwhile, although the standard of airmanship is as high now as it has ever been in the history of the Club, it is particularly important that we maintain this reputation, not only by showing extra special consideration for the safety and comfort of others but also by taking extra care to comply with all aerodrome regulations; these are currently being revised and agreed with the aerodrome owners and they will shortly be circulated to all members with an up-to-date copy of the Club Rules.

On the thorny question of the Club's relations with its landlords, a round table 'without prejudice' meeting took place in January at the Chequers Hotel in Horley. In addition to the presence of solicitors on both sides I had invited two members to attend, Ken Smith and Roger Graham.

Both were regular users of the aerodrome. Ken was a very senior member and had wide business experience. Considerably concerned at the deteriorating relations, he already had had a private meeting with Mr Dalrymple. Roger was a young barrister well versed in the intricacies of the Air Navigation Order and a very keen aerobatic pilot. Mr Dalrymple was joined by his immediate boss and director of the aerodrome company, George Russel Fry DFC. George Fry was also in fact a long-standing – although not very active – member of the Club. He had joined in 1960 when Bristow Helicopters had arrived on the aerodrome to occupy the hangar next door to ours, and he used to enjoy keeping his hand in on the Tiger. Bristows was then a comparatively small company and George Fry was its chief acccountant. He was completely aware of what the Club stood for and its aims and achievements.

But Bristows, with the expansion of North Sea oil, was now a very large operation indeed and George Fry, now driving a very expensive car – also with personalised number plates – not only was its managing director but was also directly responsible to the bosses of British & Commonwealth PLC. In view of his membership of the Club, I entertained fond hopes that he would have the Club's charter in mind and *"always go out of his way to help other members in aeronautical matters."* But for him the conflict of interests was just too great; yet he continued to renew his membership each year and the Club never put any pressure on him to resign.

The 'round table' meeting appeared to be successful in that the other side seemingly accepted that they could not alter the terms of our lease without our agreement. They also accepted that they could not ban both night flying and gliding outright. They also protested vigorously that it was not their intention to get the Club off the aerodrome. On the other hand, despite the fact that we had a lease ordered by a court with provision both for rent and rent reviews, they persisted in repeating that our presence on the aerodrome was 'uneconomic' and also they insisted on maintaining their forfeiture proceedings for alleged and unspecified breaches of aerodrome regulations. There was also an ominous silence on the subject of members' landing fees. However we remained optimistic and a few days later a further smaller meeting was held in London, at which we were able to agree a final version of the aerodrome regulations which permitted both gliding and night flying, and the important point that the aerodrome would only be closed 'after consultation with the lessees.' It was also agreed that a new and important rule would be incorporated into the Club's own constitution:

XVIII AERODROME REGULATIONS

The TIGER CLUB does not have exclusive flying rights on Redhill aerodrome. Membership of the Club does not excuse anyone from failure to understand or comply with regulations made by the owners – Redhill Aerodrome Holdings Ltd. All Aerodrome Regulations are agreed with the Owners. They are displayed on the Club Notice Board and copies are available from the Club Secretary on request. They are subject to changes without prior notice. All pilots are responsible for making themselves aware of any changes, which will either be published on the Club Notice Board or communicated verbally by the Duty Pilot.

To my disgust and annoyance, on a perfect spring Sunday in March, the 'man in the tower' suddenly and without giving a reason refused permission for gliding to take place, and inevitably a confrontation took place with Mr Dalrymple over the telephone. His solicitors later wrote weakly: "Did we not realise that at both these meetings agreements had been made 'without prejudice'"? We were again back in a cold war situation as far as the aerodrome was concerned. Some weeks later George Fry wrote to Norman Jones, our Chairman and still the actual leaseholder, but now aged 75 and in retirement with a young family down at Rye; my father sent me a copy of his reply:

"Dear George,

How nice to hear from you and thank you for sending me copies of the latest correspondence which I will study with a lot of interest and talk over with Michael.

We have a landing strip down here and if any of your chopper pilots feel like a seaside cross-country this summer, please drop in. The only thing to look out for is sheep and they are well-trained.

I would like to have a talk with you sometime about the future of Redhill. As you know we have been there a long time and all the Tiger Club members are very fond of it. But I am told that West Malling is going to be activated for business and recreational flying. It would cost quite a lot to move in there and might not please all our members.

It is nice to feel that we can work together and help each other solve our own particular problems.

All the best.

Yours sincerely,

Norman Jones MBE"

George Fry's reply to this letter has not been recorded for posterity.

Aside from the aerodrome situation, life at the Club continued as before. The annual Dinner Dance had again taken place at the Arts Club, with a somewhat reduced attendance and perhaps with less than the usual bonhomie. Cliff Robertson, a member since 1965, and through whose good offices the Clubroom at Redhill had received the old Brevet Club bar, missed a flight from the USA and his slot as guest of honour; Peter Vanneck stood in in his place.

Check and familiarisation flying was again in full swing and Brian Smith put out another circular to check pilots:

I last put in a circular towards the end of 1978; happily there has been little need to raise any matters since then and I think that you will agree it says something for the 'system,' all things considered. The idea of putting ab initio *tailwheel pilots onto the Condor before attempting the Tiger has been going for a year or so and seems to be producing the desired results. Familiarisation hours appear to be steady, and to date I can only recall one case in which it proved impossible to let a pilot loose on his own; again indications are that our standards are remaining at an acceptable level and the system of cross-checking each other is paying dividends. Keep up the good work.*

As most of you know, there have been some recent comings and goings. Chris Jesson has finally become an airline pilot and has been pushed up to Aberdeen so as to bolster the numbers, Jim Alderton, Tim Barnby and Alan Dix have joined the fold; may they spend many happy hours being bounced all over the aerodrome. . . .

Thanks to Barry Smith (and Sue Thompson) we now have an electric hat available for familiarisation and check flying. Enclosed is a key – if I haven't already given you one – to locker No. 17/18, which is situated to the left of Michael's office door and is marked 'Norman Jones.' The theory is that no self-respecting thief is going to break into the Chairman's locker.

With the cost of flying going through the roof I cannot stress enough the need for thorough briefing/debriefing sessions. It saves a lot of time and a vast amount of money, so please ensure you cover this aspect properly.

During the spring I will try and arrange to fly with all of you, just to make sure that we are all talking the same language. In the meantime keep in touch. Thank you for your continued efforts and have a pleasant year's aviating in 1980.

The highlight of the Club's very full calendar for 1980 was the Croydon Airport Air Show. Although there had been virtually a full display at Sanicole in Belgium in 1979, this was to be the first full Tiger Club air show as such since the Oxford event the previous year. Benjy found himself wearing two hats and of course described the action perfectly in the *Rag* both before and after:

The flying display season begins this year with the first full display we've put on for quite a while and at, of all places, Croydon. I'm so closely involved with this exciting project that I reckon the best way to tell this most extraordinary tale of how it all began is to leave it all till afterwards and then, with the story complete, tell all. The event is promoted by the London Borough of Sutton to commemorate Amy Johnson's 50th Anniversary of her Australian flight – for the purist it's 50 years to the day. The event is getting so much publicity it should be a sell-out. Highlight will certainly be the re-enactment of her take-off in a most original Gipsy Moth currently being rebuilt and resplendent in Amy's original colours. I'm sufficiently superstitious not to name names or even commit myself to other than generalities, but enough to say that conversation at Redhill seems to be of little else with everyone wanting to go. It was enough to drive Michael to yet another of his *bon mots* when he suddenly cried: 'I wish Amy Johnson had never been invented!' It's on the Bank Holiday Monday, 5th May. Details of aircraft and programme and so on are in the capable hands of Robin Voice. That considerable practice is taking place every weekend goes without saying. I can reveal just one item for that day. Keith Sissons will be overflying Croydon in the Sea Tiger – having made the not inconsiderable pilgrimage to the celebrations up at Amy's birthplace in Hull on the previous day. That and the variety of aircraft offered for the occasion has been nearly as remarkable as the prospects of a day's flying at Croydon 23 years after it was closed. Unfortunately most offers have had to be refused but they included a DC-3 and a Ju.52/3M.

Of the claim to have been the last pilot out of Croydon – and there have been many – that of our Chairman, Norman Jones in a Turbulent, is a strong contender. The Tiger Club has had a long association with the airfield and all the Turbs and Condors were built and originally flown there. . . .

Just before the turn of the year Ron Jacobs who, when he isn't being Ron and flying Tigers, is the publisher of the *Evening News* asked whether the Tiger Club could provide a Tiger to overfly Croydon on May 5th 1980, to help both commemorate Amy Johnson's famous solo flight to Australia 50 years earlier, and launch a book. Someone had obviously bent his ear. One of the Croydon Airport Society's members, Doug Cleuett, in conjunction with a couple of collaborators, was aiming to publish Vol. 2 of the history of that airport, and what better way to do it etc. . . . Now as it happened Doug was, and still is, a senior member of the Sutton Central Library, the Chief Librarian of which had offered to help launch the publication with a small civic reception. The sight of a lone Tiger above might help.

Ron and I went to meet the library chiefs. Incidentally the library warrants a story to itself for it's probably the biggest, busiest and best library in all of Europe. Present was its head, Roy Smith, a true entrepreneur if ever I met one, Martyn Kempson and Peter Smithson, his assistants, and Doug and Peter Elliott, the PROs. Before an hour was out the overfly had progressed to a wild but enthusiastically supported idea to re-open Croydon with a full display and mini county show in one. If it's one thing having an idea, it's another to get it through a County Council Committee, yet in early February

67

the concept got unanimous backing, a lot of raised eyebrows and £15,000 to set it all up. I represented the Tiger Club and was asked formally if we could do it. I said yes. Would you also organise the day for us? I put on another hat and cheerfully agreed. 12 weeks remained. 'Short notice' was putting it mildly!

By mid-February I'd moved into an office in the library and if I had any ideas that the project would require a day or two a week, I was quickly disillusioned. From day one the phone didn't stop ringing. Was it true? I even had one call from the CAA Airports Division but he was only yet another disbelieving enthusiast who wanted to believe but couldn't accept it yet. Peter Elliott, the PRO, got off to a quick start with a Press Release that put me in at the deep end. An air show? Joy-riding? From Croydon? Disbelief became universal. Not that anyone objected, on the contrary, everyone was for it, but had I seen what was left of the old place? There wasn't room to swing a cat. Had I seen it indeed! Privately I'd paced and re-paced the hallowed ground. Mentally I flew sortie after sortie assessing the problems. It could be done but only by the right pilots in the right aircraft. I asked Brian Smith, our chief pilot, and Robin Voice, whom I'd invited to be the Display Director, to walk the strip too. Both came down firmly: can do. I reckoned 25 or so aircraft was top whack and everyone had to be hand-picked. And I didn't deviate from that concept albeit I was sorely tempted as the weeks went by. I estimate I received well over 100 requests to land at Croydon; heaven knows what the final total was, for once the others knew I was unbending they also said no.

I did say yes to one. I got back to my office one evening and on my desk was a little note: 'Please can I come to the party? I've a Gipsy Moth. Ring Ron Souch,' and there was a telephone number. I had already asked Sue Thompson to take on the task of representing Amy Johnson for the big day. I knew she flew Tigers often and well, and who was to be churlish whether or not she flew a DH.60 or DH.82 except the purist? Gipsy Moths were few and far between, in fact I only knew of two in private hands and neither were likely to let an unknown fly such a rare bird . . . and yet, Ron not only had an original Gipsy Moth which he had totally rebuilt, but in some fateful way Ron had always planned the aircraft to be an exact copy of Amy's *Jason* right down to the tiniest detail. The only visible variation was in its name; he called it *Joan*, after his wife. Even the lettering was painstakingly to the original. He said modestly when he brought the aircraft to Redhill for a Press call: 'I've tried to rebuild it to a factory-fresh finish.' To see it in all its original glory was a stunning experience. It *was* new, it was exactly as it must have been 50 years ago. The big question for me was not whether or not he came to Croydon but would he let Sue fly it? It had taken four long years to rebuild and it wasn't finished until a short three weeks before the day.

At 3.15 pm May 5th Sue flew Ron's superlative DH.60 out of Croydon before a wildly enthusiastic Press, sent on her way by Amy's sister, Molly Jones, and the good wishes and encouragement of that vast crowd. She flew to Gatwick and another big reception as a commemorative plaque was ceremoniously handed over to BA in its first leg to LAP and on to Quantas *en route* to Port Darwin, Australia.

All this was just one highlight. Back in February and March there were many other items to consider. The flying side was relatively easy to arrange. I invited some dozen visitors, all representative of Croydon in the '30s, among them beautiful examples of de Havilland's art: Puss Moth, Hornets, Leopard and another Gipsy Moth. A Comper Swift, the Active and immaculate Mew Gull, a Redwing and Proctor. I even wanted to joyride so I stuck my neck out and asked the CAA to license Croydon for me. They would have done it but I had second thoughts. Joy-riding, even with Islanders, off 410 metres hard by 8,000 occupants of a housing estate was possible but not really on. I dropped the idea with some relief.

I discovered something else. We've many friends, often long-suffering, but friends nevertheless, within the CAA. They supported the whole project from square one and I discovered too that most of them were flying men. It made me realise how few real difficulties would exist in our world of flying if we really communicated, and I just don't mean letter-writing. Another example of communication comes to mind. 8,000 folk now live where once we finished our landing run, an industrial estate now straddles the threshold, yet not one complaint was recorded at the prospect of flying returning to Croydon Airport. Before a tractor began to cut the grass, moves were afoot to keep the local community fully in the picture. Everywhere pride was engendered. It was *our* heritage, *our* airfield. Exhibitions in local libraries and talks in local schools prepared the ground. One Tiger Club member, a school inspector by profession, personally circulated an illustrated set of data to 1,000 schools in the area. The PR for this event is also a story in itself.

Of the actual airfield little enough remained. The long north-south run was no longer viable for it was marred by a continuous diagonal ridge which must have been thrown up by the building development; besides, at each end the once pristine turf had been churned up and allowed to return to scrubland where reposed the refuse of years. During that bleak February the Sutton Parks Department began a programme of reclamation, taking on a job that local contractors considered beyond them. They patiently worked on through into the spring and restored some hundred acres or so. If nothing else the big day had given back some good land for the locals to enjoy. Even a litter collection was organised by the local Scout groups and several skips were filled. Everyone was getting in on the act.

The space finally chosen for the landing area was roughly east-west. It measured 450 metres overall, fronted in the east by factories and in the west by a building site. From the air it looked ridiculously small, so every pilot was invited not only to practise short landings but to come along and walk the strip for himself. On the day every landing was safely completed within half of the available distance; praise indeed for the quality of piloting, and some of the mounts were hot indeed. To see the Proctor, Mew Gull, Active and Swift put down so sweetly did my heart good. I said earlier that arranging the flying side was relatively easy, but providing the ground facilities for an estimated 50,000 people was nothing if not challenging. One passes lightly over the seemingly impossible. Inter civil service procedures were a continuing mystery to me and here the brilliant diplomatic ability of Roy Smith persevered when I would have blown my top with exasperation . . . and he always won, but at what cost I will never know. Forget at once the image of civil servants sitting around drinking tea and knocking off at four. Roy and his team lived on black coffee and were invariably still at work at eight of an evening and often later. Whatever civil servants do elsewhere, it's not like that in Sutton. Nor were they alone. My small team of rough, cheerful parks men were invariably on site by 6.30 am and would only leave when they had seen me off, content only when I was satisfied, and never before six of an evening. I pay humble tribute to as fine a bunch of men as any I have met.

We didn't miss the odd strike either. The first to clobber us was NALGO, who not only stopped the rate demands being sent out, but instructed their members not to co-operate with consultants. At a branch meeting they reluctantly concluded I was one, but with kindly initiative not once did they allow me to feel in Coventry. But worse was to come. A big and very costly supplement was planned for free distribution to 100,000 homes by the local paper. Then the printers went on strike and only 22,000 escaped the net, and these were to be hastily snapped up as collectors' items. A hurried replacement was arranged. 50,000 smaller illustrated programmes were printed in just two days, two days before the show, by non-union labour. To have all the Press there and to have all the TV teams as well, and then to have the lot wiped off the screens and nationals by an ill-timed invasion of the Iranian Embassy was hard to bear – but it happened. And the weather? The plusses were a steady 15 mph right down the runway, no rain, high cloud, good vis and the occasional glimpse of the sun. The minus was the chill edge to that north-easter.

The nitty-gritty was the show the Tiger Club put on. It was magnificent. The rehearsals and careful preparation that had gone on backstage had paid off. From the opening Balbo of nine aircraft through every following act the public saw a display that had no equal. The memory of that once great airport could not have been served better. Everyone was filled with delight and not a little nostalgia that their Croydon had briefly come to life again.

When all had gone and at long last Croydon lay deserted, the threat of the 80s, vandalism, over our heads – for the site had been a nasty battlefield the previous night – yours truly drove slowly over the ground to check that all was as secure as we could make it and could only chuckle at what was to be my last act on the day as organiser: I locked the doors to the loos. Time: 8.30 pm. It had been a long and happy day.

The London Borough of Sutton was also happy. The following letter was received by the Club the next day:

"Can I through you pass our thanks on to all your members who turned up and did their stuff so well on Monday? Notwithstanding a few problems there is little doubt that the day was an outstanding success and that was in no small part due to the brilliant skills of the Club. . . .

It was so very clearly seen as quite an aviation coup to get the aerodrome back in use in such a dramatic fashion and the day had enormous historical importance. . . ."

One newcomer to the Club in 1980 was Charlie Shea-Simonds, soon to take over as editor of the *Tiger Rag* and later to become Chairman of the Royal Aero Club and the founding father of the Tiger Diamond Nine formation team. He was also, incidentally, one of the inspirations behind the Club's Garden Party idea which was to be a great success in the years to follow. Charlie was soon demonstrating his journalistic skills in the *Rag*:

We'd been talking at the Royal Aero Club Council Meeting about co-operation between aviation sports and the discussion continued in the wine bar afterwards. David Faulkner-Bryant took the plunge.

'How about my doing a parachute jump?' he asked.

'No problem,' says I, and then, rather tongue-in-cheek, I suggested: 'Swap you for a ride in your aeroplane.'

'Done,' he says, and I can hardly believe my ears – will he really let me loose in his Currie Wot?

Exactly a month later it actually happened. The Saturday had been devoted to David's undergoing the necessary and undignified physical exertions of his sport parachute training – and that's another story! On Sunday we drove to the Tiger Club's base at Redhill where the hangar full of beautiful aeroplanes set my mouth watering. My first encounter with a Currie Wot had been 11 years ago when I was Chief Instructor with the Northumbria Parachute Club at Sunderland, where I had lusted after the one belonging to Les Richardson. But it was even more of a daydream then as I didn't even have a PPL. But now, having flown a few interesting aeroplanes

(Rapide, Tiger Moth, Auster, Maule, Zlin, Emeraude and Piper Cub being a few of the taildragger types recorded in my log book), I was hoping I had the necessary combination of ability and humility to conduct the gorgeous little aeroplane that now confronted me.

David's 65 hp Mikron-powered Wot was to be the smallest aeroplane I had flown to date, but in spite of her size she gave the reassuring impression of being a rugged, sturdy little bird. David's briefing was brief and concise, pointing out the neatly-arranged knobs and dials, warning me of a flat spot at around 1,500 rpm, giving me the necessary power settings, stall and approach speeds and reminding me that, in spite of wot I may have heard, it was still pull for 'up' and push for 'down.'

After a couple of warm-up circuits from David and his final encouraging words about a not-to-worry-about noise from the undercarriage just after take-off, I found myself firmly strapped into the tiny compact little cockpit and taxying 'Zulu Whisky' out across the grass. I was as excited as I had been on my first solo. A little burst of throttle and a dab of rudder and she responded quickly to my request for change of direction. . . . I tested the back pressure and we were airborne. 'Zulu Whisky' was alive and throbbing with the thrill of being in her natural element and I became intoxicated with sharing the experience. The controls were light and responsive, the tiny engine throbbed away contentedly and the needle of the ASI flickered on the dial recording our speed of progress across the Surrey countryside. The total experience is impossible to describe adequately, suffice to say the flight was utter magic and the Wot was a complete delight.

All too soon it was time to return to Redhill and to persuade 'Zulu Whisky' to abandon her enjoyment of the sky. Downwind checks, turn base leg, ease back on the throttle and trim to 60. With Mikron popping gently away in front we slid towards the green turf. A touch of back pressure and even that's too much – she wants to fly again, she's so responsive on the elevator. I let her sink to the ground. It's not a tidy arrival: a gentle bounce first to show me that she's the boss – 'Sorry old girl, you've simply got to stay on the ground' – and the second time it's three points permanently on. I taxy back with great reluctance and with the regret that I haven't got David's 400-plus hours of experience on this gorgeous flying machine. He's there waiting for me. I switch off and sit there savouring the experience. I know from his grinning bearded face that he doesn't have to ask wot I think of her. My words of thanks are inadequate. Wot an aeroplane!

"27.6.80   *14834 Kaler Road, Houston, Texas, 77060*
Dear Michael,
For 18 years I've looked forward to coming to Redhill and flying·those beautiful airplanes in the Tiger Club hangar. I couldn't have been any more pleased unless I personally owned them. Starting with Joy Frazer, who makes any room nicer to walk into, Benjy's bouncing personality, Jim Alderton's patience and expertise checking me out in G-ACDC, which is a joy to fly, Margaret Burgess whose gracious hospitality made my stay in England so pleasant, Gregory Burgess for inviting me to share some of the "Pub" night life, Roger Graham for his knowledge and wit about flying, the law, history and aerobatics, and everyone associated with the Tiger Club. Thanks for everything – the 18 years was worth waiting for and I hope to return in the near future.
    Sincerely,
    CHARLES 'BUCK' METZ"

The Club hangar normally housed around 30 aircraft, half of which were privately owned by Club members, including many single-seaters. Every Sunday evening at the end of the weekend's flying it was a major undertaking to 'pack' the hangar, requiring skill, practice and patience. Also there was a long list of Club members anxious to snap up a slot if one became available.

Then during 1980 our neighbours Tiltman and Langley decided to make their hangar available, and also some time later acquired the lease of part of the former Home Office hangars (the other part had been taken over by a frozen food company, much to the anger of the local Nutfield villagers, who were in constant dread of industrial development at the aerodrome). Consequently Club members rushed in to take up the newly created space.

Also many more members now owned their own aircraft than previously, usually tailwheel types and very definitely of the sporting variety. The fact that the great majority of these new arrivals on the airfield not only belonged to Club members but also in most cases were precisely the same types as operated by the Club (Tigers, Stampes, Jodels and the like, in fact the very type of tailwheel aircraft which would normally be attracted to a grass airfield), seemed to cause Mr Dalrymple extreme irritation. The policy of the aerodrome management was now, with an 'airfield information officer' in residence in the tower at the weekends, to collect as many landing fees as possible, and most of these newcomers were exempt from paying landing fees by virtue of their Club membership. Individual landing 'fees' – or, as the French more appropriately call them, *'taxes d'atterrissage,'* and which also in France were unheard of on a grass airfield – were at this time very serious money and totally unjustified by the facilities available at Redhill.

Mr Dalrymple now chose to ignore the legal agreement in existence and harass and intimidate members into paying separate fees, particularly those parking their aircraft in the adjacent hangars and, of course, members arriving in their own aircraft to meet their friends, be seen and quite often to fly a Club machine. One member was informed that "the Tiger Club's days at the aerodrome were numbered" and that "should you refuse to accept these (landing) charges I shall be forced to withdraw my permission for you to use the aerodrome."

Another member sent me a signed and legally witnessed statement:

"When I landed at Redhill earlier today in the Cub, I went up to the tower as they had told me to report after landing when I called to PPO. They informed me, politely but firmly, that I owed £3.00 landing fee and went on to say that:

1) The Tiger Club lease expires in 'a few months.'

2) We as a Club would then be kicked off the field.

3) Another pilot who had refused to pay his landing fee had had his licence revoked by the CAA when the case was drawn to their attention.

4) All those who refused to pay individual landing fees were being taken to court over this refusal.

Naturally, having been a member here for the past eight years, I was quite upset by all this. I'm not sure just what the facts are, but I feel that my freedom to fly in and avail myself of the Club facilities is in jeopardy.

They went on to tell me that if I didn't pay the aforementioned landing fee that they were 'sorry, but we cannot give you permission to take off.'"

The complaints from members were fast and furious and, if 'extortion' means obtaining money by intimidation, this was extortion. The Club's view was that we had a duty to protect the interests of all our members equally, whether they were flying Club aircraft or their own. As a result of the changed situation on the aerodome, it might be necessary in due course to propose a compromise and institute a system involving payment of an acceptable block fee for resident aircraft, but never would we agree to waive our members' rights to exemption in the matter of landing fees. I sought to explain the whole imbroglio to members in a long article in the *Rag* in the summer of that year – all the interconnected and intertwisted aggravations, landing fees, aerodrome regulations, AFIS, permission to land and take off, the Air Navigation Order and the rest. I think most members understood, but now their enjoyment of their flying and their Club was beginning to be quite seriously affected.

Two members thought that Gatwick was the problem and wrote to the *Rag*:

74

Apropos Michael Jones' article in the *Tiger Rag*. Something has been nagging at the back of my mind now for some time and I think it deserves an airing.

Michael wrote: '. . . with their suspected aim of removing the Club from the aerodrome.' Does all this tie up with the rapid growth of Gatwick? Now that more and more airlines are being directed there it becomes obvious that the heavy end of General Aviation can't be welcome there, so what better than to move it all out lock, stock and barrel to a satellite field, i.e. Redhill?

Unfortunately it isn't as crazy as it sounds, and we would be unwise to dismiss the scheme as impractical – it isn't. We may not just have a landlord problem, but a political one as well.

But it would ruin the peace and beauty of Redhill. A runway (applied for), jets, noise and even light scheduled movements would do to the locality what the steamroller growth of Gatwick did to that once beautiful part of Surrey.

Can any member of the Tiger Club give a satisfactory explanation as to why it is now considered necessary to have an Aerodrome Flight Information Officer – what a magnificent title – on duty throughout the weekend?

During the week when Club flying is minimal, if the helicopters need the service then, of course, it should be provided and rightly so, but why at the weekend?

In these days when aspiring pilots seem to be taught to rely upon what they hear rather than what they might see, there are some people who claim that an aerodrome Flight Information Service Unit is essential; however I, for one, would not agree with this view. Despite what some aerodrome operators might feel, the original concept of the AFIS both in status and description has never changed. The AFIS is an Information Service for pilots, nothing more. It is necessary for a pilot to take what action he feels to be necessary for the safe and efficient conduct of his flight in the light of the information given by the AFIS.

The final responsibility continues to rest where it should do, in the cockpit and not in the "Control Tower."

This takes me back to the question, why then an AFIS seven days a week? Could the answer be that we are seeing the thin end of the wedge, not to get rid of the Tiger Club but for the ultimate development of Redhill into a GA satellite for Gatwick? This is not as far-fetched as might be thought; consider for a moment the fact that the BAA would be glad to see the back of General Aviation at Gatwick. Furthermore there is talk of extending the Gatwick Zone northward to include Redhill; already half the aerodrome lies within the Gatwick Zone. Such a move would enable Gatwick to control the flow of traffic in and out of Redhill. . . .

Another tactic freqently adopted by our landlords at this time was to complain not only about breaches of aerodrome regulations but also 'poor flying discipline.' In fact I sometimes had the distinct impression that it was not 'poor flying discipline' that was at the root of the landlords' problem but the sort of flying we carried out and the type of aircraft we flew. For example: a glide approach in a Tiger with a steep sideslip landing, a practice formation with two or three Turbulents, a spot landing competition, a low-level circuit in bad weather, were these examples of poor flying discipline? We did not know but the effect of this generalised sort of complaint made to anyone who cared to listen had a bad effect on morale in the Club. Furthermore, although I knew that George Fry had instructed the previous aerodrome manager, Stanley Kerridge, to keep a record of what he described as our 'misdemeanours' the complaints were never actually proceeded with.

The Club rules were very clear on the subject of complaints:

XXIV COMPLAINTS
Any member reported for or seen carrying out bad or dangerous flying or flying which on the face of it is a breach of either the Aerodrome Regulations or these Rules or the Club Charter may be grounded forthwith by the Senior Check Pilot, a Club Check Pilot, a member of the Committee or the Duty Pilot. After examination of all the relevant facts, the matter will be brought before the Committee and a decision for or against the grounding and, if required, the period of grounding, will be recorded and the member informed. The Committee may issue any such reprimand as it thinks fit.

The 'relevant facts' as far as the landlords were concerned were rarely if ever produced. The Committee's response to this worsening situation was to form an Aerodrome Sub-Committee to be chaired by Barry Smith, who in real life was one of Her Majesty's prison governors. He wrote in the *Rag*:

The Committee, in the time-honoured fashion of organisations faced with a problem, has acted decisively and formed a Sub-Committee! To be fair though, we who now form the aerodrome Sub-Committee are determined either to provide effective asistance or to disband ourselves.

The members are Barry Smith, who will liaise between the Sub-Committee and the main Committee, Neil Jensen, Roger Graham, Anthony Preston and Mike Dentith. It is possible that we may ask others to help us from time to time to deal with specific issues.

Our aims might be summarised as performing as a sort of think-tank to advise the Committee on aerodrome policy, making suggestions to help with immediate problems as they arise and, we hope, supporting Michael in the very difficult job he has in the day-to-day situation and providing a source of guidance to all members, particularly Duty Pilots.

To this end we would stress that if, on a weekend day, Michael or Brian Smith are not immediately available to advise on a problem any one of the

Sub-Committee could be contacted, by telephone if necessary, if a Duty Pilot is presented with a situation to which he or she does not know the answer. We may not know the answer either, but at least we ought to be able to provide some consistency of response!

We shall obviously be dependent on feedback. It is important that individual members who have difficulties with the aerodrome owners, particularly over matters of flying discipline and the observation of regulations, let us know. A note to me at my home address or left with Michael at Redhill will suffice.

It would be easy to-fall into the use of combative terms like 'fight' and 'struggle' to describe the present situation of the Club vis-à-vis its landlords. Certainly some of the behaviour of some of the landlords' employees suggests that they are seeking a confrontation, with what end in view one can only guess.

Some members are, I know, attracted by the theory that the aerodrome owners are encouraging deliberately provocative attitudes in their employees, presumably in pursuit of a policy of making life so uncomfortable for the Tiger Club that we shall be persuaded to seek a home elsewhere. . . .

If the AFIS officers at Redhill are confused about their own role, which they illustrate by behaving from time to time like the Air Traffic Controllers they are not, and are predisposed to see Tiger Club members as arrogant and unwilling to conform, then it is hardly to be wondered at if misunderstandings arise. . . .

The Club believes that its rules and regulations impose adequate discipline on the activities of its members, and that our safety record bears this out. This can only be so if members punctiliously observe those rules and regulations. If we are to argue that booking out for cross-country flying in the Club movements book, or for aerobatics or formation practice in the Club intentions book, meets all reasonable requirements, then such booking-out must be done conscientiously.

If we argue that our standard of airmanship and competence is sufficient to allow display practice over the field with perfect safety it does not follow that a few Tiger Club members can ignore normal circuit discipline in the apparent belief that their Tiger Club membership makes them some kind of aces.

We want Tiger Club members to be able to continue to enjoy their flying at Redhill, and to do so in safety. It is necessary to realise that the environment is now dominated by elements who do not see aviation as a pastime to enjoy but as a field for commercial enterprise. Co-existence is not impossible.

Barry, who would not have described himself as a 'hawk,' – and on the aerodrome issue the Committee was inevitably divided into 'hawks' and 'doves' – was rather more specific in his circular to Duty Pilots:

Although there is some recent evidence that things are improving a little you will be aware that the Club has had a difficult situation on its hands for some months at Redhill.

In the current situation it is even more important than ever before that the Tiger Club Duty Pilot is on the ball.

To put it at its most basic, efforts are being made to insist that a number of the Duty Pilot's traditional responsibilities are transferred to the Aerodrome Flight Information Service Officers in the tower. This the Club is resisting.

In these circumstances it is absolutely vital that people scheduled for duty turn up to perform it, or find a replacement, or at the very least let the Club know that they won't be there. Please remember to book yourself on and off duty.

A new set of Notices and Guidance for Duty Pilots is displayed in the briefing room. Please study it.

Turning to more specific issues on which it might be helpful to outline the Club's position, I will concentrate on those that have already given rise to difficulties.

a) Landing fees
The Club's lease clearly allows members to land at Redhill whether visiting or resident without payment of a landing fee. Although a new lease should have been given us by the aerodrome owners some time ago there has so far been no question of altering that situation when the new lease is in force. We are, of course, aware that the aerodrome owners' employees are under instructions from the Aerodrome Director to charge landing fees, and that this has already given rise to a number of arguments.

The only advice the Club can give Duty Pilots at this stage is that there is no requirement for members to pay this money.

b) Booking out for cross-countries ending in landings away
(Notes and Guidance para 18)
The Club's movements book meets all reasonable requirements for booking out. It is important that Tiger Club pilots make the appropriate entries in the Club book. The Club does not, however, insist on its members booking out in the tower as well, nor does it recognise anyone else's right to do so.

The Customs & Excise have expressed no dissatisfaction with this procedure, though the argument that it is necessary to book out in the tower to meet their requirements has been advanced from time to time.

Enquiries from the tower about the destinations of departing Club aircraft should naturally be dealt with courteously, and there is absolutely no reason why the Duty Pilot should not give the requested information. The important point is that the pilot has booked out <u>at the Tiger Club.</u>

(The foregoing applies at weekends when a Tiger Club Duty Pilot is on duty and an AFIS <u>which we do not need</u> is in being. Obviously during the week when helicopters are flying the AFIS has a role to play and it would be sensible to continue as we have in the past to inform the tower of <u>all</u> Tiger Club movements.)

c) <u>Special flying</u>

(Notes and guidance para 20)

It is important to remember that AFISOs do not control, only give information. Their <u>permission</u> is not therefore necessary before any particular type of flying takes place at weekends, but obviously it is both sensible and courteous to inform them beforehand what one proposes to do.

d) <u>Gliding</u>

It is unlikely that a Duty Pilot will find himself having to make decisions in this area since Geoff Salt is fully in the picture and will undoubtedly have discussed with Michael any proposed gliding activities.

It is greatly to be hoped that this and other matters will be clarified when our new lease is in existence and when revised aerodrome Regulations for Redhill are finally agreed.

Suffice it to say at the moment that gliding <u>may</u> continue when runway 10/28 is in use, one glider only operating and the normal BGA operational regulations applying.

A word of advice if a Duty Pilot is told that the airfield is unserviceable at a weekend by one of the owners' employees and finds himself in disagreement with this opinion. Ask for and record the reason given for the unserviceability and then, if satisfied that there is no threat to safety in doing so, permit flying to proceed. . . .

We have every reason to hope that, given common sense on all sides, the situation will improve. Indeed there are already signs that it is at least not deteriorating any further. It seems important that we all know as far as possible where the Club stands and that is why I am writing to all on the Duty Pilots' list. I shall try to keep you in the picture as developments occur. Our posture should be polite firmness in our dealings with the landlords.

Barry may have written that there was evidence that the position was improving. I was thinking that he was whistling to keep up his spirits. The fact that we still had not been issued with our lease ordered by the county court over five years ago was both humiliating and very worrying, not only to me but also to Graham Plumbe, our surveyor, because the date for our first rent review had already passed and all our rental payments were still being refused.

I asked our lawyers what we should now do to have our lease restored to us. Their advice was clear and categoric: the Reigate County court would, if formally requested by our solicitors, issue a notice to the "Directors and Officers of Redhill Aerodrome Holdings Ltd that unless they obeyed the directions contained in the (court) order they would be guilty of contempt of court and liable to be committed to prison." The request was made and what effect the notice subsequently had on Sir Nicholas Cayzer Bt., Lord Rotherwick, George Fry *et alia* I was not told but at least I felt that we were taking some positive action.

Accidents and damage to Club aircraft came up from time to time on the monthly Committee agenda. The Club rule on the subject was also very clear:

XXV DAMAGE TO CLUB AIRCRAFT
If damage is caused to any Club aircraft for whatever reason – the member in charge must submit a written accident report to the Club Secretary immediately. This report will be considered by the Committee and if the accident is decided to be due to bad airmanship the member concerned may be fined a sum not exceeding £250. The member concerned may also be grounded in accordance with the provisions of XXIV (above).

There were four such reports in 1980. A Turbulent suffered an engine failure on take-off at an airfield in the north of the country for a reason that the pilot was unable to explain. The Stampe G-AWEF suffered serious damage after nosing over on landing at Redhill, also for a reason that the pilot was unable to explain, although there was strong circumstantial evidence that the handbrake had been left on. Fortunately in neither case were the occupants hurt. There were two other minor accidents both occurring to touring aircraft whilst abroad.

All accident reports to the Committee were kept strictly confidential but a few made both entertaining and instructive reading and I am sure that the authors of the following – who remain anonymous – will not object to their publication after the passage of time. The first occurred to the Wassmer:

"On 5 September 1980 I took charge of the Tiger Club's Wassmer WA.52, G-BDSN, for the purpose of attending the air meeting at St. Valery. I piloted the aircraft from Redhill to St. Valery, stopping at Biggin Hill and Le Touquet on the way. With me in the aircraft was another Club member, Miss P., who was to share equally with me the costs of the expedition. Miss P. is an experienced pilot and a flying instructor, but she did not on the flight to St. Valery act as a member of the crew.

It was Miss P.'s and my intention to return to England during the afternoon of Sunday, September 7. In the morning I filed a flight plan by telephone to Deauville and later told Miss P. that I had done so. We agreed that we would try to depart from St. Valery at about 15.00 local time, but we both recognised that this might not be achieved because of the air display.

Miss P. then said to me that since she was paying half the cost of the expedition she would pilot the aircraft on the return flight, although I could sit in the left-hand seat. I agreed to this and we arranged to meet after lunch to have the aircraft fuelled.

At about 14.10 local time I taxied the aircraft from where it was parked on the grass on the north side of the runway to the fuel pumps. Miss P. was with me. When we reached the pumps I suggested that Miss P. should carry out the pre-flight inspection while I sought the fuel pump attendant. After a short time I found him. He filled both tanks and put in a litre of oil. After carrying out the pre-flight check Miss P. left the aircraft for a short time.

When she returned it was necessary to move the aircraft from the fuel pumps so as to allow other aircraft access to the pumps. I suggested that Miss P. sit in the aircraft and steer the nosewheel while I pulled the aircraft by the propeller. As Miss P. was about to enter the aircraft I said to her that, since she was going to be the pilot, she had better sit in the left-hand seat, because it is easier to pilot the aircraft from that position. She got into the left-hand seat and I pulled the aircraft towards the intersection of the taxiway and the runway.

I stopped the aircraft about 30 yards from the caravan from which the meeting and air traffic were being controlled, and told Miss P. that I was going to the caravan to see when we could get away. She remained in the aircraft.

I went to the caravan and spoke to the man in charge, an officer in the French Air Force. I asked him when he could let us go. After some thought he said: "Immediately." I received the impression that if we did not leave immediately we might not be able to get away for some time.

On my return to the aircraft I got into the right-hand seat and told Miss P. that the controller would like us to leave immediately. She was making navigational calculations using her map, a protractor and a flight-planning pad. She continued to do so. A short time thereafter a man came from the caravan to the right-hand side of the aircraft. I opened my door to speak to him. He asked us to start up immediately. I thanked him. He went away and I closed the door.

Miss P. then put away her map and flight-planning pad and said that she had not got her life-jacket on. She said that I had better do the take-off. I reached for her life-jacket, which was in the rear of the aircraft, and handed it to her and she put it on. While she was doing this I started the engine, switched on the radio and VOR and began to prepare for take-off. At this juncture the same man returned to the aircraft and indicated through the right-hand window that we should leave at once.

Soon afterwards the air traffic controller told us by radio that we were cleared to enter the runway and take off at once.

By now Miss P. was wearing her life-jacket and I asked her if she wished to resume control. She said that she did and took control. After a short time she taxied on to the runway, lined up facing west and began the take-off run. The time was about 15.05 local time. The weather was dry and sunny, visibility was good and the wind was blowing at about 15 knots from the south-west.

The aircraft seemed to take a long time to gather speed. At about 60 knots IAS, when the aircraft ought to have been airborne or nearly so, the nosewheel was still on the runway. However eventually we unstuck and climbed away. The aircraft seemed reluctant to gain height and I thought this was due to the flaps remaining in the take-off position. After a short time I pointed to the flap control, Miss P. raised the flaps and the aircraft then seemed to me to be behaving normally.

There was then a short radio conversation with the controller to confirm that we could turn out right to the north. Still climbing, Miss P. turned right until we were flying on an easterly heading about two miles north of the airfield.

When we were at a height which I estimate was about 1,200 feet AGL, Miss P. said that the left-hand door was not closed. I reached behind her seat with my left hand and pulled on the toggle. I attempted to close the door but could not. Then the door suddenly pulled out of my grip and went upwards, where it remained for a moment and then tore itself free, breaking off just outboard of the hinges.

I took control of the aircraft, made a radio call to St. Valery requesting clearance to return and turned the aircraft towards the airfield, where we landed a few minutes later.

In my opinion the cause of the door becoming detached in flight was that it had not been properly closed and locked before take-off."

The second report initially was very brief and occurred to the Jodel Mousquetaire:

"Report on How The Flap Came To Be Broken
I flew from Kiel to Groningen on the 22nd of August 1980: it was obvious that the wind was increasing in velocity on the starboard beam coming in to land at Runway 24. I was told there was a crosswind flow from 280° at 38 knots: I was not permitted to land on the grass into wind and just before touchdown the wind carried me across the runway to the point where my flap caught one of the upstanding runway beacons.

It was reported to the Air Traffic Police and the aircraft was inspected by the head mechanic, who pronounced it fit to fly, but foregoing the use of flaps."

Needless to say, the Committee would require further information:

"Thank you for your letter – it was a bad scene at Groningen: in point of fact I was on my way to Amsterdam but the wind and the rain grew so intense that my passengers started to become airsick and I decided to put down at Groningen which I declared an alternative airfield.

To the best of memory the wind was 30-35 knots from 280° on a runway of 240. I was not given the option of landing on the grass and when I took this point up with the Air Traffic Controller he told me his hands were completely tied by the Air Police who had pronounced the grass as being unsafe. He made the point that this tied the hands of the Air Traffic Controller who was ultimately responsible for safety and said, in point of fact, the grass was perfectly all right and had been used extensively by some Tiger Moths over the weekend when the Air Police were not present.

In point of fact, I fell into the hands of the Air Police and was interrogated as though I had committed some criminal act – it was a curious contrast from the feeling of the "safety net" extended upwards by the Air Traffic Controllers to help me to locate the aerodrome in very bad conditions of visibility and the bureaucratic arrogance of the Air Police."

The member then received a letter from the Club's Senior Check Pilot:

"Following the Committee's hearing of your incident with the Mousquetaire I have been asked to write to you. I don't think there is much to say; my appreciation of the facts suggests that you were the victim of circumstances which you were powerless to do much about. However, having said that, it must be remembered that as the pilot-in-command you were solely responsible for the safety of the aircraft and its occupants. To this end you had the power to take any action that you considered fit, and on this occasion had you declared an emergency (again by your report the situation was rapidly developing into one) then the controllers would have had no choice but to render every assistance with regard to the landing area, without fear of a comeback from any third party.

The Committee felt that in this instance it was unfair to pronounce a verdict of bad airmanship upon you, but in view of what I have said they considered it reasonable to ask you to cover the cost of the repairs to the aeroplane, an account for which is enclosed."

This elicited still further information:

"Thank you very much for your kind letter and succinct statement about responsibility for safety in the air. I found it very helpful and would add that I would like to see more of this sort of authoritative statement in the Tiger Rag. I find there is too much emphasis on the hairy side of aviation and it tends to overlook the need for real professionalism amongst private pilots if we are to survive against the sort of gestapo Air Traffic Police such as I met up at Groningen.

I am also extremely pleased to be exonerated in this instance. As a matter of fact there was a bit more going on my end than I have actually reported, e.g.:

1. *As I crossed to Jutland, so weather conditions deteriorated, wind rising and rain coming down.*
2. *The mounting turbulence caused both my passengers in the rear seat to threaten to be sick.*
3. *The rain was not just coming down – it was actually coming in, thus adding to the general discomfort.*
4. *As we passed over the Groningen radio beacon my navigator announced he had lost any control of his hands. I have never come across this symptom before but I imagine it was a function of nervousness.*
5. *The rain was so bad at this moment that it was impossible to locate Groningen visually and I personally found some difficulty in coping with the acute psychological problems within the aircraft, locating the aerodrome and actually getting onto the runway.*

It transpires later that whilst all this was going on there were various alarms and excursions going on at Groningen caused by the Swedish pilot making a precautionary forced landing some 10 miles short of the aerodrome.

All in all I think I did quite well to get us down in one piece!

The point of this long dissertation is that you are now inviting me to pay for the damage. I would do this cheerfully as the price of valuable experience but I would really like to understand the principles behind your request. . . ."

This now required a further letter from me:

"The Committee did not hold you negligent or responsible under the Club Rule which provides for cases of bad airmanship and therefore there is no 'legal' obligation on you to pay a 'fine.'

However, they did note that it was a case of 'poor airmanship' and following an unwritten convention it was considered reasonable to ask you to pay for the repairs in view of the fact that they were of a minor nature and that it would be, as you say, a 'price for valuable experience.'

There is also a Club Rule XXVI which allows a self-imposed 'fine' to be donated to either the Prize Fund, the Hospitality Fund or the Legal Fund, and if you would like the matter dealt with under this heading, please advise. But please rest assured that, if you do not wish to pay either for the repairs or a fine, that wish will be respected and understood.

From a personal point of view, I was very relieved that the matter was not more serious (and it might well have been) and in this connection I would like to take the matter up with the Dutch authorities because it is only by doing this that 'interference' with the pilot's responsibilities is avoided in the future. However, I will only do this with your permission."

This produced a third and final letter:

"I am quite disarmed by your letter of October 21st and suggest we pay up. I enclose my cheque accordingly.

I am not in fact enthusiastic about pursuing the Dutch Air Traffic Control people: as you say it was a case of 'poor airmanship' and I do not feel exactly bombproof."

All in all 1980 had been another successful year for the Club and the Redhill problem perhaps should not be unduly exaggerated. In fact, during July I even managed to get away for three weeks to take part in the Round Britain Yacht Race.

At the beginning of the year Norman Jones had agreed that it would be a good idea for the assets of the Club to be owned by a Limited Company and so The Tiger Club Ltd was formed with my father, myself and Mavis Harriott as the shareholders. In 1980 a small profit was achieved and flying hours, despite the looming economic recession, were only slightly down on 1979. One member, Paul Hinkley, flew a record 229 hours during the year, mostly in the RF.4 and taking advantage of the rebates on offer for 'over 50 hours' and midweek.

Don Henry wrote from Florida that he would like the name of his trophy for aerobatics, the Henry Trophy, to be changed and called in future the G-B trophy; we agreed with pleasure and the competition is now part of the British Aerobatic Association annual programme. A British team consisting mostly of Club members had been to Oshkosh to take part in the world championships.

All the events and activities during the year had gone well, displays, F1 racing, foreign touring and glider-towing. We even managed to stage both the Precision Flying Championships and, for the 11th year in succession, the Hamilton Trophy at Redhill.

Perhaps the star of the year was the Sea Tiger G-AIVW which, through the efforts of Tom Freer and Keith Sissons, flew a record 87 hours during the season, so that there were now 12 members with seaplane licences. Jonny Seccombe described his experiences in the *Rag*:

Was it Rattie or was it Toad who said something to the effect that there is 'nothing, absolutely nothing like messing about in boats'? Of course neither of them had wings, nor did Grahame say anything about aeroplanes or even Tiger Moths in his stories, but for those whose attention is divided between boats and aeroplanes, where does Mike go on those weekends away from Redhill? Might find it interesting to combine the two. I have always had a desire to fly up the fjords of Norway in a floatplane or amphibian, so as the

85

first step in that venture I found it irresistible this summer to drive down to Rye for long weekends to learn to fly a floatplane.

Anyone who suggests that a Tiger Moth has sluggish controls, a slow roll rate, a stiff rudder and less than sparkling performance, plus a continuous need to be looked after and administered to, has obviously never flown a Sea Tiger. It is a terrible aeroplane in the air; ailerons are totally ineffective, you need both feet on the rudder bar to shift it either way and all the speeds are the same, 65 knots. On the water it is fun, *real* fun!

My first day at Scotney Court it was blowing a stiff 25 knots, enough to ground all but the most intrepid flyers at Redhill. The seaplane was in its element. 'Swing' turns could only be performed by the most skilful, while 'hump' turns, when you reverse the normal weathercocking characteristics, were the order of the day. Long periods of taxying, porpoising and skipping were interspersed with short circuits for a little relaxation, eventually culminating in that extra little rating on the licence.

And so plans for Scotland were made. The car had to be serviced and new road maps purchased. Somebody else was bound to have a 'half mil' you could borrow, but woe betide if the arrival party lost its way. Memories of batting over the plain behind Blackpool at 500 feet to reduce the headwind, and skimming over the waves across Morecambe bay at 50 feet will always be with me. Tom Freer taking control and diving across the hills into a cloud-shrouded Windermere was a moment that could never be experienced in a landplane. As long as you can see water, you're going to be OK in a seaplane. Who ever heard of flying round a cloud-infested lake at low altitude unless you were tired of life?

Have you ever spent two weeks on a flying holiday, camping beside the tailplane and covering hundreds of miles without seeing an airfield or another aircraft apart from low-flying jet trainers? Have you ever wanted to see the Lake District or the Scottish Lochs from close quarters without infringing the 500-foot rule or wondering about the ditching characteristics of your aeroplane? Have you ever thought what it would be like to sweep past a 1930s lake steamer on the step of a 1940s Tiger? Have you ever turned onto finals knowing there was absolutely no need to look up long finals to check there was no cross-country circuit merchant about to slice into your wingtip?

'VW may be slow on floats, she may be more in her element on wheels during the winter, but as Toad said (or was it Rattie): 'There's nothing like messing about in boats.'

There was a lot of enthusiasm around!

CHAPTER 5

1981

One piece of unfinished business left over from 1980 was our small mobile fuel bowser. We had brought this back into use to stock motor fuel, which the CAA had now agreed could be used by certain light aircraft engines. In common with many other flying organisations we were becoming very seriously alarmed at the rocketing price of Avgas. The fuel bowser had been used in the past for many years to stock a second grade of Avgas.

Possibly as a reaction to our forceful attempts to get our lease issued, Mr Dalrymple now refused to give his permission for the bowser to be parked on a few square feet outside our hangar next to our main underground tank, and at the same time complained to the local council that we did not have the necessary licence – which we could not obtain because we did not have his permission! At the same time he instructed his solicitors to issue a second writ for forfeiture on other totally absurd and trivial grounds – such as that Rollason staff were working in the hangar and even that the Tiger Club Ltd were in occupation without his permission! However the licence for the fuel bowser was a serious matter because there is nothing that local bureaucrats like better than to prosecute on the slightest pretext people who supply petrol from a pump. My father, who was now busy down at Rye supervising the production of new Turbulents, replied to the writ in his usual disarming fashion:

"At my age (over 75) I am retired and hoping for peace, but I am in close touch with my son, Michael Jones, who is responsible for the carrying out of our side of my lease at Redhill. . . .

The name of your firm, Beaumont and Son, reminds me that I was a friend of a Major Beaumont in 1925 at the London Aero Club at Stag Lane. He advised me then on aviation matters. Was he the founder of your firm?"

Much to my relief, and probably to his, not long afterwards I received a private and personal letter from Peter Martin informing me that he was leaving Beamont to work for another firm . . . To cut a long story short, after weeks of frustrating correspondence including letters to our other local MP (we were lucky to have recourse to two local MPs because the actual constituency boundary went right through the airfield) Mr Dalrymple eventually agreed to give us the necessary permission, denying at the same time that his original refusal was in any way intended to be harassment!

During this time I was pleased to hear that we were receiving a certain amount of help behind the scenes from an organisation known as the Air Squadron. The Air Squadron had some time ago promoted and sponsored an aerobatic competition and quite a few of its members were also members of the Tiger Club; one leading light was James Baring, another was Tom Storey (who was on our Committee as the person responsible for the Club's Legal Fund) and another was Simon Ames, the manager at AOPA, who was the Air Squadron's Hon. Secretary. James was at this time living in the south of France but went out of his way to circulate the people who were both members of the Tiger Club and the Air Squadron as follows:

"As you can see from the attached list I am writing to you as a member of the Air Squadron and the Tiger Club. The former (being an association of friends interested in aviation who meet from time to time to discuss matters of mutual interest) would seem a suitable body to consider the matters raised in the following pages; and as members of the Tiger Club a proper solution to the problems that have arisen concerns us directly. I know you are all very busy, but please read it all very carefully. I can't underline the important bits, as it would mean underlining practically every word, but I would like to add that, in spite of the difficulties surrounding every branch of aviation today, the Tiger Club has never been in better shape, its membership never higher or more loyal and its value to the national and international community of aviation enthusiasts never greater.

However, as far as the Club's operation at Redhill is concerned the waters are exceeding troubled and I think it is up to us to shed some clarifying light and pour the necessary oil. The Club is not asking any favours, as you will see from the following summary of the situation. It is more a question of trying to avoid a confrontation which would cause severe damage to all concerned.

We of the Air Squadron, on the other hand, have recently been requested by Prince Philip (a T.C. member of long standing) to do our best to promote and publicise the Tiger Club's Dawn-to-Dusk competition. This excellent event has produced some really great efforts outside the Club. Now, unless matters improve, it is quite possible that next year's entries will be unable even to set off. . . .

The initial purpose of the present letter therefore is:
1. To inform you of the position at the moment.
2. To get your reactions and comments.
3. To ask if you have any information that might be illuminating.
4. In the event of a consensus of opinion, to attempt some joint action to defuse the situation.
There is, as you can imagine, a certain amount of detail and general background not covered in the enclosed bumf for good reasons. Time is precious in this situation."

Quite what influence the Air Squadron was able to bring to bear on our landlords I was never able to establish, but possibly the situation did slightly improve during 1981, although by this time the Club was, so to speak, becoming anaesthetised to the problems. Some considerable time later I was extremely flattered to be told that I had been put up for membership of the Air Squadron but that, not surprisingly, my candidacy had been blackballed by Anthony Cayzer, a director both of British & Commonwealth and Bristows. As for the Dawn-to-Dusk, early in 1981 Prince Philip graciously agreed to host a reunion party at the Royal Aeronautical Society for all past competitors in the event's 19-year history, and including future entrants. He also agreed to present the awards for 1980. It was an occasion much enjoyed by everybody and gave a very welcome boost to the competition.

On the social side 1981 was the Club's 25th Anniversary year, and to celebrate the Silver Jubilee the annual Ball was moved from the Arts Club to the Royal Garden Hotel in Kensington. Council member Bev Snook and Royal Aero Club Chairman Ian Scott Hill were the guests of honour. The attendance was slightly disappointing, probably due to the recession and a hefty increase in the price of tickets. There were also some grumbles. Fred Marsh wrote to the *Rag*:

Having attended the 25th Anniversary Dinner plus Dance last week I think the organisers deserve high praise for a really splendid piece of work.

The new venue was excellent: it was comfortable and even car parking was without problems; the food was the best I have had at a T.C. 'orgy' for many a year; the band too struck the right decibel value and rhythm.

Even Bev's speech was both short and to the point: wonders will never cease, although it is a pity that neither Bish nor G-B were mentioned, but then one can't have brevity and all the names.

One item, however, was missing on Friday night – the Club spirit! Although everyone seemed to be enjoying themselves with plenty of good food and wine and women, there was no SONG.

In spite of increasing membership, is the Club in decline? I do of course appreciate that many of those (if not all) who joined the Club during the 50s and early 60s are now broken old men (not the women of course), no doubt as a result of professional and business exertions and pressures, BUT let it be remembered that they were young and most lively ONCE UPON A TIME. Could it be that later vintages progressed too rapidly from a retarded adolescence to premature middle age? Could it be that the Committee has become too moribund, senile and self-satisfied and is in need of a blood transfusion or a night of the long knives?

In the 'good old days' Norman in periods of intuition brought some new blood on the Committee: is similar intuition again required before the Club spirit disappears completely and we become yet just another Flying Club, albeit with a glorious past?

Whether Fred was right or wrong there was still a very full programme of events and activities in 1981 – racing, aerobatics, displays, foreign touring, glider-towing and the rest. Maybe he was forgetting the recession and, as I pointed out during one Committee meeting, it was now cheaper to fly by Laker to New York than to take a Stampe to Little Snoring for an aerobatic competition. However there were also other signs of restlessness. A member wrote in anonymously:

Letters in the *Rag* have opened up a debate on the Club, its existence, activities and future, giving food for thought.

The consensus of opinion appears to come down on the side of the argument that there is a substantial lack of spirit, drive, leadership – call it what you will – within the Club.

The high standards of team spirit set by Norman and Bish and followed by many appears to have evaporated into individual groups with solo interests and no overall sense of direction. Almost like lemmings we seem to plunge downhill with eyes tight shut.

The Tiger Club still has much to offer. It is unique and, if it disappeared, the world would be a much worse place. To sit and grouse is one thing, but to do is quite another. Therefore, here are some suggstions for the Club's future:

1. Have we and can we investigate replacement aircraft? Some of those which are still on the fleet should be put out to grass. . . .

2. The Club is ruled by autocracy. In Norman's active times that was a fact of life but in today's situation it might not be the best for the Club. Members pay substantial entry and annual subscriptions but there is no say in the running of the Club, which has gone through many changes in recent years. Members should have a right to elect members to the Committee annually. Looking at the membership book there are currently 23 Committee members, but how many of them actually turn up to take an active interest, contribute to the Club rather than to themselves and – perhaps of significant importance – represent the true interest and opinions of the members? It is time for change, an annual General Meeting or Extraordinary General Meeting, proper representation, elections and clarity of leadership.

3. Norman, bless him, has guided us for many years but, living afar from Redhill, there must be less and less that he can undertake as against the great works he did in times gone by. Might we realign the heirarchy and ask him to become our President?

4. The Tiger Club is represented on many Aviation Committees. Why don't we hear what is going on? Are the reports made and never reach the *Rag* or do our representatives operate as the Redhill Mafia?

5. The dispute with the aerodrome owners goes on and on. There are two sides to anything but are we doing enough? Have we the right man in the right place? Full details may not be available although the membership has a right to know – we are paying.

These suggestions and criticisms may be rejected and possibly may never see the light of day. If so many more of us will be convinced of what we hope is not happening, that is to say the Club is being run by a few for their own benefit and the "I'm alright, Jack" attitude which so many now fear is a fact of life.

To the credit of this writer – and to this day I still do not know who was the author of this letter – some of these ideas were eventually put into practice and the Club became more 'democratic.' Maybe at the time both Benjy and I were at fault, and although Norman was receiving regular reports, his presence was missed. Benjy was also away quite a lot and I was probably doing too much sailing.

I was also in the process of getting married. Quite by chance I had met Norvela at a restaurant in Victoria where people used to gather after the monthly Committee meeting. It was called the Maple Grill; the food was good and inexpensive, and it was run by some very friendly Italians. Norvela was there having a meal on her own. Although I had known Norvela through sailing for several years, it had been some time since we had seen each other. It was a very happy coincidence; she was looking for a partner and so was I: she was still a keen sailor and so was I. In 1979 she had been elected as a Conservative MEP for a marginal seat in Birmingham and her candidacy had been proposed by Sir Geoffrey Howe. Although I was not an over-enthusiastic Conservative supporter, I was a very keen 'Europhile.' Norvela also ran a very successful industrial consultancy business with an office in Buckingham Palace Road. She was a keen golfer and I was willing to learn. Her support for me and the Tiger Club over the ensuing years was like a bright light in what seemed at times like gathering darkness.

In 1981 the Club elected two new Honorary members, Prince Bernhard of the Netherlands and Hector Monro MP. As with most Clubs, people were invited to become Honorary Members for two reasons: first, because they had performed a very significant service to the Club in the past and, second, it was hoped that they would do so in the future. In 1981 we had 27 Honorary members on the list including all the founder members and of course the 'Royals.' The rule was that Honorary Members had to complete the normal application form and might be asked to transfer to ordinary membership. Prince Bernhard was the first foreign 'Royal' to become an Honorary Member and we were delighted when he accepted the invitation. It came about because he had let it be known via his old friend and Club member and former ATA pilot Diana Barnato Walker that he was in current practice on the Tiger and he would welcome the opportunity of flying one on his visits to England. Proudly we asked Diana to let him know that we already had 10 Dutch overseas members. Hector Monro was an active and enthusiastic private pilot and the current Minister of Sport; we hoped that he could be of help in the future.

As a response to complaints that there was a certain lack of Club spirit at this time and also to moans that there were too many cliques at Redhill, Benjy launched the idea of a new function, Duty Host, and asked Terry Dann to organise it. Terry wrote:

The Role of DUTY HOST

Function
♦ *Generally to promote contact and friendship between Club members.*
♦ *Primarily achieved at Redhill during weekends by a Duty Host who will help members mix and make them feel part of the Tiger Club.*

Duties
♦ *Welcoming members not familiar with Redhill, showing them around, introducing them to other people present.*
♦ *Have available lists of local pubs, hotels, members who can provide accommodation, details of Club social activities, Club aircraft etc. and discuss these with interested parties.*

Organisation
♦ *A rota of volunteer Duty Hosts will be maintained.*
♦ *The Duty Host will attend between 11.00 and 16.00 on any one weekend day.*
♦ *An armband will be provided similar to Duty Pilot and there will be a Duty Host book containing the lists etc. mentioned above.*

Qualifications
♦ *None – apart from plenty of Club spirit!*

Unfortunately the idea was not a success. You can't win 'em all! Terry later wrote to the *Rag*:

"Many thanks for putting my letter concerning Duty Host in the last *Rag*. I'm sorry to say however that it has provided absolutely no reaction, and that despite extensive efforts on my behalf I have been only able to raise four volunteers for the post, including myself.

The Duty Host function was carried out quite successfully on four occasions, operating as an adjunct to Duty Pilot. Many longstanding members that I contacted felt in fact that the Duty Host's functions were quite firmly included in those of the Duty Pilot. Perhaps if nothing else this exercise will have served to clarify that point.

I hope that the lack of support for Duty Host does not reflect an apathetic situation in the Club but rather that the time is not right at present for an additional post."

By 1981 the microlight movement as a development of hang-gliding was becoming popular, probably as a reaction to the ever-increasing costs and over-regulation of normal powered flying. The Club was committed to 'providing its members with good sporting flying at the lowest possible cost' and microlights could be just the answer. Jonny Seccombe, who was a microlight enthusiast, was invited to join the Committee and to organise a microlight section. He lost no time in introducing a machine one weekend at Redhill:

The *habituées* of the Tiger Club hangar were treated to a rare sight during a recent weekend when Jim (I'm a Company test pilot and I'm insured for millions of pounds) Bowyer arrived with the latest product of the British Aerospace Industry roped firmly to the roofrack of his well-travelled Volkswagen. The long sausage revealed a Vulcan hang-glider, and the tubes and wheels were unfolded to take shape as the first production version of the Hiway Mk. 2 Skytrike. Surreptitiously the aircraft was assembled inside the hangar, away from critical gaze, and the regular discussion developed, commonplace to the hang-glider pilot: "WEEEEL, I suppose it's flyable, let's go and have a feel of the wind."

Close examination of the machine resulted in the general consensus that it was extremely well engineered, Structurally there didn't seem to be any problem although there were some design details that broke new ground. Mike was interested to know if the sail of the wing could be put to nautical use, Jim is working on fitting the recoil pull-start to the Turbulents, one member was fascinated by the apparent control reversal (although I am sure Neil Williams would have explained that it was all perfectly simple if you imagined yourself sitting on top of the sail and using the King Post as a joystick), and a number of hardened Tiger pilots were delighted to find that there was no rudder on the machine, although there is a foot throttle to keep idle feet out of mischief.

Jim, having been fully briefed on the surrounding aeronautical hazards, ventured to start the inverted single-cylinder two-stroke engine, which emitted a discreet growl on the second attempt. First problem is solved – noise level is acceptable. After a brief pause spent strapping into the comfortable cushioned seat and adjusting the venturi of the ASI – the only instrument installed, but still an optional extra – it was off to the peri-track on the way to the threshold of one westerly runway. The sight of the trike buzzing along reminded one of a demented go-cart trying to leap into the air.

After lining up into wind, a take-off roll of 40 feet culminated in an abrupt rotation that launched the kite into the air. As it climbed determinedly into the stiff breeze the spectators were impressed but somewhat awed by the degree of control available in the admittedly turbulent conditions ('CDC was grounded but 'IVW did carry out a short flight later). After a few tight circuits

Jim cut the throttle and the kite descended almost vertically to land on the left-hand side of the runway. A long taxy back to the hangar was interrupted by a sudden gust that placed a severe negative load on the sail. Two loud clunks announced the departure of a few 'mil' of the prop-tips against the rear flying wires and a disconsolate Jim steps out of the seat. (Will Geoff please pay attention to the taxying mode in future!) A further question and answer time follows, interrupted by the urgent ringing of the telephone!

The sight of the Stampe being started for an aerobatic sortie galvanizes Jim back into action and without further ado the kite is back at the threshold. The Stampe offers pride of place to the Jungmeister, carrying out its first flicks and graceful slow rolls since being rebuilt, while in airspace all of her own the Vulcan is thrown through a sequence of wingovers, downwind dashes and upwind hovers. An abrupt fuel starvation results in a premature but totally controlled vertical to *terra firma* and there is much talk about pre-flight checks. A slight contretemps with a gust while stationary facing downwind on the peri-track results in a brief interlude of semi-inverted manoeuvring, but no damage is done and we sit down to discuss a day's flying.

What are the lessons? Microlights are fun, cheap and practical. It's a totally different form of committing aviation. It is not a substitute for other aircraft but complements them by opening up new fields of aviation while using otherwise useless pieces of airspace. It's cheap, less than £6 per hour, and it costs very little to train and keep current. It is practical because it's inherently safe. The days of high thrust-lines and human undercarriages are over. The technology is well proven in the hang-gliding field, nor is the noise level any longer offensive.

What of the future? Roll on the two-seater! Please send one to us as soon as possible. Thanks to Jim Bowyer for putting up with all those questions, flying well and sensibly in almost marginal conditions and taking the trouble to drive all that way for the benefit of the Tiger Club.

Jonny also wrote a letter to the *Rag* seeking help for his Dawn-to-Dusk project:

"I am taking the unusual step of publishing my objective in this year's Dawn-to-Dusk competition because its success will be based entirely on the amount of help I can muster from the membership. Basically the aim is to visit as many homes of Tiger Club members during one day as possible by air. An accelerated Dawn-to-Dusk "Bunberry" if you like. The aircraft type chosen for this venture will be a microlight Skytrike which has the fortunate characteristic of having a take-off roll of approximately 80 yards in still air and naturally a reduced landing roll. It has an additional advantage in that, if by some misjudgement the landing area will accommodate a landing but conditions restrict the possibility of a successful take-off, the aircraft can be easily folded up and taken to an adjoining field for take-off. (I'll have to check the competition rules on that one: how far does the aircraft have to be flown during the day as opposed to being driven around on the roof of a car?)

I am therefore appealing to all members of the Club who have a nearby field or large lawn with unobstructed approaches to contact me as soon as possible. Naturally all prospective sites will be visited from the ground first and local requirements noted to avoid unpleasant incidents on the day. As yet I have not decided upon a suitable method of recording the fact that I have visited those homes that are shown in the log but I am open to suggestions! As the Skytrike has a very reduced cruise speed I do not anticipate venturing far from southern England and this makes it even more important to contact as many people in that part of the country. If you have a microlight landing strip with easy access to your home please contact me as soon as possible."

Unfortunately the microlight movement never did take off at Redhill; the aircraft were almost immediately banned by Mr Dalrymple from using the aerodrome. To the customary threatening letters Norman replied:

"Thank you for your two letters of 29th June.

We have had a number of microlights down here (at Rye) and there is really no reason why they should not be treated like any other aeroplane provided of course that they conform to proper aerodrome practice.

One really cannot start banning one or other type of aeroplane just because one happens to dislike it."

But this was one battle which the Club was not prepared to fight. Perhaps we should have done. But some members were sceptical. With hindsight they might have been less sceptical if they had been able to forsee the subsequent development of microlight aircraft. After all a Turbulent now qualifies as a microlight and fortunately Mr Dalrymple had not yet found a way of banning Turbulents.

A major change which took place in 1981 was that Benjy handed over the editorship of the *Tiger Rag* to Charlie Shea-Simonds; Charlie was well qualified for the task since he had previously produced the British Parachute Association magazine – *Sport Parachutist*. The character of the newsletter now changed and, as many thought, not before time. For years it had been laboriously typed on stencils by two charming and devoted ladies running a business called the Reigate Typewriting Agency. They really enjoyed the task and were sorry to lose it. The *Rag* was now to benefit from modern technology; it appeared in print, on glossy paper, with a coloured masthead and with photographs and cartoons. It was a welcome change and most members approved, but the production costs meant that the frequency of the publication had to be reduced. A few people disapproved, particularly two American members.

Tom Foxworth wrote:

"This will acknowledge yours of 17 May regarding my expressed displeasure with the *Rag* in my brief note to Michael. I apologize first for the tardy reply: I was busy checking out as captain on the L-1011-500 Tristar which I'm now flying (mostly to Rio). And I also apologize for the fact that my criticisms didn't seem constructive. I'll concede they were not specific.

Obviously the Tiger Club is fortunate to have willing volunteers to undertake the work involved in producing a *Rag*. Inevitably your own style will influence the outcome, irrespective of the character of the Club as others may know it. It's also obvious that your intent is to be slick, modern, magazine-perfect.

But to me this represents the Tiger Club as something it isn't – or wasn't (at least, to me). The *Rag* I'm receiving is no longer cozy – warm – or intimate. It no longer fits like a well-worn slipper or old friend. I don't recognize it. Instead it's pretentious. Even forbidding. I don't trust it like I used to.

Moreover, layouts are, in a word, dreadful. I can't even follow it.

In short, I have in my library every copy of the *Rag* printed (mimeographed) since I joined the Tiger Club in 1966. But I somehow don't have the urge to save it any more.

Are these comments constructive? Maybe not. Subjective? Yes, perhaps so. Helpful? I don't know. Obviously you won't unscramble your egg. And what you are doing with the *Rag* no doubt reflects changing times. . . .

But to me the Tiger Club is and always has been an anachronism, and you fail to capture that. It appears to me that instead you are trying forcibly to drag it into the here-and-now of the 1980s. Yet for almost 20 years what I always loved about it (and maybe there are still a few out there like me) was that a visit to the Tiger Club was a trip backwards in time, an escape to a haven of nostalgia that nurtured ever since I saw my first picture of a biplane . . . for each visitor, a different haven maybe, but each one real nevertheless. So I view your effort as a tug in the wrong direction . . . and essentially destructive. To touch and feel and smell the Tiger Club's vintage aeroplanes (like 'CDC) is to step through the picture frame on the museum wall and come out whole on the other side.

God, and there you were . . . free! With a special, glorious kind of freedom. Radios and technical regulations and paraphernalia spoil that. Certain kinds of ambition spoil it too. The Tiger Club celebrated the primitive. That's what I loved about it.

I have my *Sport Aviations* and other modern magazines. They often have token mentions of 'quaint' oldtimers, especially if anybody has built a replica or refurbished an original. They usually look too good to be true. The Tiger Club, on the other hand, was *real*. Their aeroplanes were unostentatious (which could only happen in England, anyway) and above all, always working. Five biplanes wing-to-wing – and all working! *That* was the indelible, unforgettable realization left with me on my first-ever visit to Redhill. The old *Rag* somehow enhanced that special feeling each issue. The new *Rag* doesn't do it. Slickness ruins it."

And Carol Nelson followed up:

"This letter is to say I was struck to write in sympathy with Tom Foxworth's comments on the *Tiger Rag*, especially in the sense that I too was surprised at the change in tone that the new *Rag* conveys. The old 'chattiness' is gone and in its place is more of a <u>newspaper</u> than a friendly newsletter with some humor and sense of closeness. But, I suppose nothing stays the same – and the photos are a nice touch. . . ."

This was the first time that I had read of the Club being described as an anachronism. But it was not to be the last!

We had three Committee members looking after the display scene – Pete Jarvis, Robin Voice, and in 1981 a newcomer to run the Turbulent team, Neil Thomason. It was a very busy year, particularly for shows abroad. The dividends to the Club's finances were better than usual and people were beginning to entertain the idea that we just might be able to stage a full show at Redhill. 1981 was also the International Year for Disabled People and there was a holiday home for disabled people in South Nutfield.

We received some nice letters, including one from Dick Nesbitt Dufort. Dick was a disabled ex-Army pilot now working for the CAA. He kept his own specially modified aircraft at Redhill. He was to receive later in the year an RAeC silver medal for his pioneering work on behalf of disabled pilots:

"May I on behalf of all those present at our fête on Saturday – guests from Crabhill, the public and members of our Committee – thank you for arranging the display of Turbulents and a special thanks to the pilots who took part.

It was was really exciting for us, greatly enjoyed and appreciated.

A magnificent contribution to this the International Year of Disabled People.

Just a line to tell you that I have had glowing reports of the flypast which you arranged for the Crabhill fête – I really do mean a very very big thank you and I do hope that all those who took part enjoyed it as much as the spectators on the ground.

Sadly I was unable to be at the fête and I gather that it was in an enormous field which made the attendance look a little low, but I was assured that those who were there thought it was marvellous. Perhaps as it has been such a success you might consider doing it again.

Dennis Oakley, the local Treasurer of Crabhill House, is going to contact you, mostly to thank you. He is a great admirer of old aircraft and has on occasions dropped into the Tiger Club in the hope of seeing some interesting planes. He is also a good friend of various people at Bristow's. So may be one day the three triangles can get together and achieve an air display – it would be terrific!"

There were also several other charity shows and flights. Robin Voice carried out a successful standing-on-the-wing cross-channel exercise. This was not the first time that the Club had performed this stunt; Barry Griffiths and Alanah Campbell had done it in 1963, but it was a first flying both ways.

Robin was persuaded to put pen to paper:

One of the joys of T.C. is the people you meet. I often fly the Girl-on-Wing Tiger; you get to meet interesting people doing that too. Well, 1981 was the year for the disabled and this super girl set up a couple of sponsored flights. The first was at Jock Maitland's Liverpool show. He was getting a free act so he was happy; all went well so Gail was happy. She is blonde and charming – Jock offered to pay for her to come to his future shows.

The next trip was to be a celebration of the Moth etc. etc., and X-Channel! Well, I explained how difficult, how expensive, about the rescue services, and told her father it was a foolish idea. It didn't do any good so I played my trump card and introduced her to Michael. He thought it was a good idea. One used to be able to rely on Michael.

So off we went for lunch in France. Talked to Le Touquet. Talked to CAA. Talked to Wissont. Decided to use Manston so as to make friends with Kent Radar. Spoke to Invicta who were friendly and later waived their £17 fee, spoke to about 15 assorted air force officers and it was all set.

Came the great day, meet at Redhill (station) at nine. Thos Cook staff refuse to open their door until 09.01 despite the queue from 08.40, suspect – at 09.20 – that Gail may be at aerodrome, of course she'd been up and walking across London since 06.00. Fit portable radio in Tiger, surprised as always to find it seems to work. Fly to Manston in reasonable weather, use the 'gap' between Challock and Ashford, good weather at Canterbury and follow wrong railway towards Dover. Kent Radar awake enough to 'check my heading.' Find the thing like the Thames estuary isn't, it's Manston runway, about 2 miles long and half a mile wide. Land on runway opposite taxiway, so far so good.

Taxy instructions "proceed 1,000 yards west, turn north, and follow northern taxiway." Do this and find I'm back touching the northern edge of the runway, get back to starting point and ask why? Told this vast acreage of concrete unstressed for aeroplanes, wonder about fire trucks and Tiger Moths. Head towards Invicta, only half a mile away on a pleasantly scenic route via parked aeroplanes on hard standings and a meandering taxiway, DOWNHILL, take to the grass. Tower ask why? 15 all.

Get to Invicta, nice people. Meet Customs officer. Gail says passport at Redhill because "no pockets in her flying suit." Customs officer discusses publicity with local papers. *Daily Mail* haven't turned up. Customs officer takes photos for Press.

Nearest French aerodrome at Wissant so, off we go for lunch in France.

Tell Kent Radar we're at 800 feet AND WON'T DESCEND UNLESS IN EMERGENCY. Messages of good wishes heard and appreciated. Get to mid-Channel and call Calais – usual silence. Return to Kent Radar, reach Cap Gris Nez and land before anything goes wrong. Ask CFI to close flight plan, explain that M. le President had agreed the trips with the Customs. I'd agreed everything with Le Touquet. Check time, 14.15 local, too late for lunch. Shelter from cu-nim. Walk to café for sandwich. Return to aerodrome and interview Laurel and Hardy policemen sent by Calais. I hadn't told Calais. Interview local Mayor, also sent by Calais. Explain that flight plan and Customs agreed by Le Touquet. Find birth certificate, show police. Cu-nim has got bigger – seems to extend from London to Paris. Gail says return trip must be on wing and today. Cu-nim and low stratus don't matter. Decide I wouldn't even walk to the aeroplane in this weather. Policeman takes statement. Persuade him to drive me to café, telephone Le Touquet to cancel return trip to Manston. Policeman listens in. Le Touquet says how nice to hear from me and agrees to call Manston etc. Policeman relaxes and buys me coffee. Return to aerodrome and interview Customs officers who have arrived from Calais. Gap appears in cu-nim. Get airborne to file flight plan via Le Touquet, low stratus covers land, vis out to sea not impossible, file to Lydd who are apparently open until 6 pm local, land while still winning.

French policeman takes photos for Press, set course for Lydd, in drizzle, Gail looks happy as can be. Gap in cu-nim seems to extend to England, stay out of real rain all way across – curious radio effect, Lydd can hear me but not me them; usually it is the other way around. Reach UK coast, moderate rain, Gail looks very happy. Lydd helpful, curious that, arrive on finals at same time as C.150 – he is asked to overshoot, just as well as I hadn't seen him. Land and taxy in, meet the friendly Meerhallen, interview the rude Customs man, he doesn't ask for passports. Meeson arrives in new Pitts; Stratton Richey arrives in Islander G-HMEG and gold braid overload. Persuade a reluctant Gail to use the front cockpit, no need to refuel, and fly home in sunshine.

Did someone say next weekend is Inverness?

Neil Thomason described a typical weekend in the life of the Turb team leader:

There were two shows to do – Sunderland and Church Fenton, both on the Sunday afternoon. The first problem was finding pilots for such a venture. Various problems arose at the last minute with team members suddenly finding they had to go to work in various parts of the world – Singapore, New York, Brixton, Old Warden (to work?). The team was still only three right up to the Friday evening before the show. Then John Marten-Hale, who is a merchant seaman, was about to board a 737 at Heathrow bound for his ship at Nice when he was paged. There was a message for him which simply said: "Don't get on that plane." His ship, apparently, had been arrested in South America, so it didn't need its crew just then. Instead John became the 4th Turb pilot.

Departing Redhill on Saturday afternoon the four Turbs left for Fenland, a friendly place which always welcomes Tiger Club members. On this occasion though, someone struck the wrong chord with the leader by announcing: 'Four Turbulents, eh! I didn't think you had that many left; didn't you leave most of one amongst the cabbages last year?' On the Sunday the plan was for the Turbulents to display at Sunderland, leave while airborne after the show and head for Church Fenton. 'TLB had come along too to carry the poles from Sunderland to Church Fenton. Dave Wise would pick them up in it after the first show and was due to rendezvous with the Turbulents near Church Fenton so everyone could go in under radio control.

It seemed a good idea to drop in to Church Fenton on the way up on the Saturday to refuel and to have a look at the display site. This would also be a good practice for the rendezvous.

The Turbulents left Fenland 10 minutes before the Jodel, all bound for a disused airfield south of Church Fenton, to meet at 1,000 ft. Everyone arrived at the specified time at the specified place, but could not find each other. The Turbs gave up the search first and went into Church Fenton non-radio, followed shortly afterwards by the Jodel. The Radar Controller at Church Fenton was most amused, having seen everyone roaming around in the same spot. Dave Wise in the Jodel had had a clever idea and arrived at 2,500 ft so as to get a better view. As a result he had flown directly over the top of the Turbs many times without seeing them. The Turbs, needless to say in a tight formation, were too busy watching each other to notice anything else.

The route from Church Fenton to Sunderland has the Yorkshire Moors in the middle, just at the point where a complaint known as "Turbulent bottom" begins to set in. If you've sat in 'PNZ for a couple of hours at a stretch you'll know what this is. A bit of fun seemed appropriate to divert the mind, and the Moors are just the place. . . .

Sunderland was well organised, with a hangar expecting the aeroplanes, and a hotel expecting the pilots. The next morning a quick practice with the four aircraft went OK, and the team was ready for a hectic afternoon.

When G-ARBZ at last agreed to run, after 10 minutes' winding up, all seemed to be set. The Turb slot came, and as the leader taxied out for take-off a great roar came from the crowd; you could hear it above the engines. Now the team's display is good, but not that good, and certainly not before they've even taken off. Alas, the star attraction was 'SAM, nose in the ground and tail in the air. Well, one has to stick to one's slot times in the display business, so the crowd could only be treated to a three-ship display in the air. All the same they had their money's worth – exactly the same happened the next time 'SAM tried to go!

The rendezvous at Church Fenton worked this time, with everyone at 800 ft, and the depleted team arrived together. This was certainly an improvement over two weeks previously when 'TLB got lost between Blackpool and Barton, eventually arriving 30 minutes after the Turb show had finished. The pilot in question, more used to flying Stampes inverted, claimed he couldn't navigate the right way up.

The RAF were well organised as always and after fuel, tea and a personal briefing another three-ship display went off well. Apparently it raised some eyebrows, scooting around the station's buildings, but that's probably what we were booked for. When the question of the fourth promised aircraft came up, they were very understanding when told it had gone "unserviceable." 'SAM wasn't actually damaged, but went straight home, just in case.

The team took part in 12 displays this year, including two in Belgium. All the shows were well received by the paying public, albeit amidst cries of "shambles" from Tiger Club members watching.

The routine used lasted about nine minutes from take-off to landing. It consisted mainly of formation flying and tail-chasing. Many observers have commented: "That looked fun, but how was it supposed to go?", so a description will appear in a subsequent issue of the *Rag*.

In 1981 the Sea Tiger had another successful season; the highlight was an invitation from the Greater London Council to take part in Thames Day ('81). Tom Freer and Sue Thompson landed the aircraft on the Thames (incidentally, should it be 'on' or 'in'?) between Westminster Bridge and Lambeth Bridge. Roger Sherron then taxied up and down between Waterloo and Vauxhall Bridges and finished with a short display flight landing on Nine Elms Reach. Somebody remarked that he was probably the first American to land and take off legally in the middle of London . . .

Although we were faced with a major recession that year and aircraft utilisation was well down, Club membership actually increased and people were busy with all the other customary activities: foreign touring, glider-towing, aerobatics, precision flying and air racing (both handicap and Formula 1). Since these three latter disciplines were now run by their own respective associations, the achievements of Club members did not always receive the recognition they deserved in the *Rag*. One exception was a letter from David Hamilton:

"You may be interested to know of the Tiger Club's involvement in the IVth World Precision Flying Championships held in August at Tollerton. The Championship had its problems but we finished and had a result, and our little Association can at least boast of holding and running a World Championship.

Anyway herewith the names of Tiger Club members who were deeply involved and these are as follows:

1. Myself – Contest Director
2. Dick Barnby – Airfield Director
3. Ian Hewitt – Treasurer
4. Sven Hugosson (overseas member) – Chairman of International Jury
5. Arve Caspersen (Norway) – Chief Judge
6. Nick Carter – Deputy Chief Judge and British Judge
7. Erica Griffiths – Secretary

Participants
1. Arne Nylen (Sweden) 4th
2. Jorma Halle (Finland) 10th
3. Neil Thomason (UK Reserve) 12th (non-counting)
4. Helge Holmedal (Norway) 17th
5. Dick Nesbitt-Dufort (UK Reserve and Team Manager) 30th (non-counting)
6. David Timmis (UK Team) 35th

Throughout the year, needless to say, we were in almost continuous negotiation over our lease. Now that the airfield regulations had more or less been agreed, our landlords started to focus on the landing fee question. Barry Smith, who chaired the Club's aerodrome Sub-Committee had already had a full and frank meeting with Mr Dalrymple and Mr Fry, and had reported on the outcome both to me and the Committee.

His conclusion was: "I think the Club has to recognise reality and organise itself accordingly."

One point that did emerge was that our often-repeated requests to hold an air show at Redhill could be favourably considered.

The problem for them was that the original lease, which had been granted to the Club by the previous aerodrome owners, not them, quite clearly stated that the Club would pay all landing fees on a *per capita* basis for all its members, regardless of whether they were flying Club aircraft or not and regardless of whether they were visiting the airfield or flying an aircraft based there. This part of our lease had never been challenged – not even during the court case when our lease was renewed in 1974. Was there not room for compromise, particularly if we could obtain a legal agreement giving us the right to hold an annual air show?

On the question of members' aircraft based on the aerodrome, whether in our hangar or not, I believed I could sell to them a reasonable annual block fee arrangement which would be optional. All of them understood that times had changed and they were all highly valued as Club members.

In fact it was soon pointed out to me that, of the 70 or so fixed-wing aircraft now based at Redhill, there were only half-a-dozen or so which did not belong to Club members. When I put the proposals to the landlords, they agreed in principle subject to suitable safeguards, such as maximum all-up weight, the aircraft not being operated by more than three members and carrying no advertising etc.

I then suggested to them that we could double the *per capita* fee, which at a shilling (5p) per week per member was now absurdly low bearing in mind the current inflation. They had no difficulty accepting this. However on the subject of visiting members being charged they were adamant. These people could be offered a discount but that was as far as they would go. I discussed the situation with Barry, who agreed to circulate a paper to the Committee. It was a very long document, and to be fair to Barry he set out the arguments on both sides very fairly. However he hinted that we might be best advised to make yet one further concession on this final point. He wrote:

"It is abundantly clear that Redhill Aerodrome Holdings regard the landing fee issue as fundamental. For them it has the symbolism of representing a demonstration of their right to run their own aerodrome. . . . It is my view that a failure to agree on this issue will mean a return to the courts. . . . On the other hand assurances have been given that the settlement of the lease will result in a reasonable atmosphere for the continuation of the Club's activities: aerobatics in the ATZ, gliding, special events such as spot landing and precision flying competitions will not be threatened and there will be no return to 'petty harrassment' (my words, not theirs, but I think I am fairly reflecting the tone of their assurances). There has even been mention of T.C. displays at Redhill. . . . In addition we have a definite assurance that if visiting members do pay landing fees they will attract a substantial discount which will not be available to anyone else. . . ."

I did not agree and neither did the Committee. We had already made very substantial concessions on the whole question of landing fees. Why should visiting members, many of whom kept their aircraft on nearby strips, be charged a large sum of money, albeit with a discount, every time they visited their Club by air? We also distrusted 'assurances.' As a result the negotiations broke down. The endless meetings, correspondence, the exchanges of solicitors' letters – and solicitors' letters are never short – came to nothing. The landlords issued their third writ for forfeiture of our lease on the same spurious grounds. All we could do was to threaten a renewal of our proceeding for contempt of court.

Barry later resigned from the Committee. We had agreed to disagree. I thanked him for the enormous amount of time and effort he had devoted to the problem – and he lived a long way from Redhill.

I wrote:

"The Club cannot survive in any sense without the support of a large and enthusiastic membership, and to deny to numbers of members the expectation of reasonable access to their home airfield will be fatal to the future of the Club. . . ."

The Committee then appointed Neil Jensen, who already owned two aircraft based on the airfield – including a Jungmann – in his place.

In this gloomy situation there was one ray of sunshine. During the year Benjy had floated the idea of a Tiger Club 'Rally.' The Committee seized upon it with enthusiasm and the following announcement appeared in the *Rag*:

Summer Garden Party 1982

This Rally next year on 19/20 June is really taking shape now. It's going to be the biggest Tiger Club event ever; the entire Club might be there. We'll be taking over an airfield for the whole weekend to do everything we've always wanted to. There will be spot landings, Turbulent races, handicap races, microlights, gliding, parachuting, aerobatics, balloon bursting, flour bombing, navigation courses, treasure hunts, huge formations and more. Nothing will be compulsory – everyone can do just as much or as little as they like. 'CDC will be pounding the circuit all day (yes, all 16 hours) with a different pilot each time. That should break some Guinness record. Make sure you take part in it!

In the evening on Saturday there will be a barbecue and ball. If anyone just wants to drop in for that, the Garden Party will be a valid finishing point for a Dawn-to-Dusk entry on the Saturday, and perhaps a starting point on the Sunday.

This is going to be an event for the whole Club. We hope every member will join in the fun. Note the date now, but find an aeroplane too – most Club aircraft have been snapped up already. (There is a rumour that some members will be resorting to Spitfires and a B-17.)

The Summer Garden Party Sub-Committee would be interested to know what else you would like to do on this extraordinary weekend away. Please call Jonny Seccombe or Neil Thomason with any ideas, especially if you would like to organise an activity.

We had something to look forward to!

G-AWEF, the last remaining Club Stampe. Over the years at Redhill the Club operated seven Stampes, which flew in total over 13,000 hours. Photo: Jim Alderton.

TOP: The old RAF Control Tower stands forlorn in the rain, waiting to be removed. Photo: Graham Plumbe.
BOTTOM: Wing-to-wing: five serviceable biplanes outside the hangar in 1983. Photo: Mike Peare.

1982

Towards the end of 1981 it became apparent that John Dalymple and George Fry were anxious to reach a final agreement on landing fees. The differences between us were narrowing and the discussions becoming more friendly. We were also now on first name terms. On the 30th December I received the following letter from George Fry:

"Dear Michael,
Thank you for your letter of 8th December. John and I have carefully considered the notes which you sent and I am enclosing with this a summary of our own comments.

At this stage it seems to me that it is probably right to arrange one more meeting in an attempt to reach the agreement which has so far eluded us. . . .

Since time is short, I am sending this across to you by hand and would be grateful if you would telephone John or myself as soon as possible as to whether you would like to go ahead with such a meeting.

Yours sincerely,
George."

We had made one final concession on the thorny question of members arriving in their own aircraft; they would only be entitled to one 'free' landing per day and they would only be eligible for that if they were flying a light aircraft, i.e. one under 1,300 kg auw. The suggestion was accepted and a few weeks later I was able to circulate the following letter to owner members:

"As you are already aware, the question of additional landing fees for members operating aircraft not belonging to the Club has been a major issue in a long and costly dispute we have had with our landlords for a number of years. . . .

During the last few months there have been intensive consultations and time-consuming negotiations with Redhill Aerodrome (Holdings) Ltd and others to reach a satisfactory solution, and I believe that we have now reached a fair compromise which, although adding an extra financial burden on owner-members, will enable the Club hopefully to improve its relations with its landlords, look ahead and at the same time give reasonable protection for the future. . . .

I am therefore setting out, as an attachment to this letter, full details of the arrangements for landing fees which will now apply. . . .

I would also like to add that as part of the whole package the Club has agreed to increase the existing block fee we already pay by way of landing fees, the position of visiting members has been suitably protected and Redhill Aerodrome (Holdings) Ltd for their part have agreed to allow the Club to hold a flying display at Redhill on an annual basis, and every opportunity will be given to suitably qualified members in acceptable aircraft to participate in this display if they so wish.

Finally, I appreciate that this agreement will not suit everybody, and that you may as a consequence feel that it is necessary to reconsider your membership of the Club and make your own arrangements with Redhill Aerodrome (Holdings) Ltd. . . ."

It had been hoped that we might have been able to hold a display at the aerodrome in 1982, but it would take several months before the solicitors could agree on a lease which we could sign and seal, and the prospective show did not take place.

There was also one large fly in the ointment. Mr Dalrymple was now putting pressure on the new arrivals in the neighbouring hangars to fit their aircraft with VHF radio; in fact he was going so far as to threaten that they would have to remove their aircraft from the aerodrome unless they did so. There were complaints from members but it was difficult to intervene. All we could do was to record the following minute in Committee:

'Committee disagrees with the attitude of Redhill Aerodrome management regarding compulsory carriage of radio in members' aircraft and confirms policy that carriage and use of radio at Redhill must be a matter solely for owner and pilot.'

It was a storm cloud on the distant horizon.

At the beginning of the year Brian Smith sent the Check Pilots his customary newsletter:

As some of you may have gathered there have been some recent changes in the hierarchy of the Club. Norman has become our President, Benjy has taken over the Chairmanship and I have replaced him as Vice-Chairman. Consequently this is the last newsletter you will be receiving from me, and so I would like to take this opportunity to thank you all for your support and dedication to the job over the last seven years. During this period our accident record has never been better and it's due to your professionalism towards the job; long may the circumstances continue.

My successor is Pete Jarvis. Having now been relieved of several grown-up daughters and settled down to a fixed base at Gatwick, Pete will be able to play a more active role at the Club from now on; with his long experience as an instructor in the Service, plus his active membership of the Club since the mid-sixties he's the obvious candidate for the job.

Pete Kynsey has been appointed Deputy Chief Pilot, the position having been created to provide adequate admin. cover with the membership now standing at over 800. Again, Pete is an experienced instructor as well as being a very active Club pilot and will fit in perfectly with the job.

My parting shot has been to appoint Brendan O'Brien and Roger Graham as check pilots, so no doubt we all extend them a warm welcome with many happy hours of being bounced around the airfield.

The changes were overdue since Benjy had now been our *de facto* Chairman for some years. Brendan O'Brien was also invited to join the Committee, eventually to take over the organisation of the annual ball from Ian Hewitt.

Brendan was a colourful and extrovert character who, when he first joined the Club in 1973, had caused a few headaches in matters of flying discipline. Now he was proving a considerable asset. He was essentially what the French call an *'animateur'* and was later to become both an accomplished display pilot and air show commentator. He livened up the occasion at the Tower Hotel with some original innovations, suitably described by Benjy in the *Rag*:

This year's Dinner had got to be different from the last few. Not that they hadn't been successful, but it didn't need Fred Marsh to tell us that some of the early spirit had been missing. With this edict in mind Ian Hewitt, aided and abetted by Brendan O'Brien, quietly organised some surprises. The venue was attractive, modern, and the big welcoming bar was soon a hubble of noise. Strangely clad folk mingled happily. A dancing clown sold raffle tickets and a helmeted Red Baron was there to perk up any spirit that might have been down . . . it was then I began to get the feeling that this was to be no ordinary night.

Our MC for the evening was Brendan, elegant in his white dinner suit. As I write this some weeks later I'm sure an incongruity arose, for his bow tie kept lighting up, but then so much began to happen the moment we moved into the ballroom for dinner that I'm fuzzy over details. Shouts of delight broke out as guests entered. From the ceiling hung big model aircraft and hundreds of balloons, and on every table – except the top one (come on, we aren't that stuffy) – clustered distractive goodies like model gliders to pilot around the place and streamers and aerosol cans of plastic spaghetti, and guests didn't wait to be invited to play. Things happened promptly, just like they used to. I thought the staff were wonderful and served throughout the cheery pandemonium with broad smiles.

Greatest innovation of all, though, was the picture shows. Vast screens covered opposite walls on which one could either enjoy a non-stop film show – all flying, of course – and a non-stop coloured slide show. Silently the same events returned to the screen again and again. When later I got up to speak not only could I not read my notes – I must get my eyes checked – but out of the corner of one eye I was disconcertingly aware of a younger me making a fool of myself standing on the wing. I may not have said anything coherent at all, for if all that wasn't bad enough someone had brought that laughing doll again.

Our Guest of Honour was member Sir Hector Monro and as an experienced MP he was no way put out by all the fun. I can't recall a more popular speaker; his jokes have been going the rounds ever since. Informality has always been a feature of our dinners, and the two short speeches and the Toasts (the Queen, the Club, the Guests and Absent Friends) were soon over and Brendan O'Brien in unabashed form led unerringly into the prize giving, a performance worthy of an old-time MC presiding over a Theatre of Varieties.

Music broke out and we danced till after one. What more to say?

The food was excellent, and the company of good friends made the evening memorable. Everyone would want me to thank Ian and Brendan and their many helpers. I think Michael's comment to Charlie Shea-Simonds after the Dinner sums things up nicely.

Said Michael, who was presumably still in shock: 'Next year, either everyone will be there . . . or no one!'

Charlie and I share the view it'll be everyone.

Although Hector Monro had just lost his job in the Thatcher government as Minister of Sport, he now joined the very considerable lobby to persuade the Treasury to do something about the price of Avgas. At this time, wearing my Rollason hat, I was on the council of the General Aviation Trade Association (GAMTA), an organisation which had been founded by Rex Smith, a long-standing honorary member of the Club, the boss of CSE and former chairman of the British Light Aviation Centre. I can well remember the feverish campaigning which took place. Owing to the small demand and the cartel which supplied it, the price of Avgas was way up on the price of motor fuel, and why should we pay the same rate of duty when we did not receive the slightest benefit from the tax we paid? The Chancellor got the point:

Many members will have read with delight and pleasure that the duty on aviation fuel was substantially reduced in the Budget in March. Although it will not be possible to reduce the Club flying rates as a result of this, it will at least guarantee that the existing rates will remain the same and give much needed relief to the finances of the Club which have been under some strain recently as a result of continued poor utilisation. The Club is proud to have been associated with the successful campaign to reduce Avgas tax to levels comparable with other European countries and although there were clearly many factors involved in this decision our particular thanks must be paid to the Chancellor of the Exchequer, who just happens to be our Member of Parliament!

Nearer home there was another small success on the political front. At least one tiresome stop and exorbitant landing fee at Lydd could now be avoided:

After years of patient effort the Club has at last succeeded, through the good offices of George Gardiner, MP for Reigate and Redhill, in obtaining a concession to allow Club members to clear direct outbound from Redhill on *bona fide* Club flights for a 12 month trial period.

The essential features of this concession are:

1) 24 hours' notice of estimated time of departure must be given, or in the case of weekend or Monday departures before 1600 hours on the Friday before.
2) It is only a clearance outbound. The inbound clearance must be obtained from a normal Customs airport.
3) No duty-free fuel or stores may be shipped.
4) Passengers and crew must be British Nationals and must carry passports or proof of identity.
5) Members will be liable for payment for official attendance, but if the Customs Officer has not arrived 30 minutes before the notified time of departure the aircraft can be cleared for departure without him. . . .

On the subject of the Club's finances, Brian Smith, now that he was Vice-Chairman, considered it appropriate to issue Mavis Harriott and me with a longish paper containing a detailed analysis and a large number of recommendations. In an attempt to improve utilisation the Club was now operating only 15 aircraft compared with 18 the year before, but the total hours were still on a downward trend and the situation was worrying. Some of Brian's suggestions were helpful but his conclusion was that to break even we needed to achieve at least 3,000 hours a year. The last year we had done this was in 1973 although we had come near to it in 1979. The Club now needed to rely more and more on income derived from activities outside the direct hire of its aircraft – both social and flying.

Nor was it exactly helpful that 1982 was an *'annus horrabilis'* as far as accidents were concerned, and our three Tigers, G-ACDC, G-AOAA and G-AIVW were all involved. 'CDC and 'OAA were both badly damaged in precautionary landings caused by worsening weather: 'CDC, just back after an expensive C of A, during the very early morning leg of a Dawn-to-Dusk flight – and this was not the first time that a Club aircraft had come to grief in this way, – 'OAA hurrying to get to a display commitment in Scotland. Both aircraft were easily repaired but, worst of all, 'IVW in its floatplane role was totally destroyed stalling into the sea off Rye following a slow turn at 500 feet The occupants were rescued by the inshore lifeboat, and luckily no one was seriously hurt in any of these incidents.

Fortunately we still had G-ASKP resting in reserve, but the loss of 'IVW and its floats was a grievous blow; in 1982 it had only been converted to floats for a very short season and now it was most unlikely that there would ever be another Tiger on floats. Over the years the Club had operated no less than 14 Tigers and, although a few had been sold, at least five had been written off. The aircraft were becoming precious and Rollasons were running out of spare parts.

Charlie Shea-Simonds raised Club spirits in the *Rag*:

Every great institution has its setback or two and I'm sure we are no exception, but out of it will emerge a stronger and more proficient organisation. Such is the Tiger Club.

The Chairman was a little more specific, and issued the following notice to flying members about 'CDC:

'*Until further notice this aircraft is restricted to local flying. . . . Members will appreciate that in order to help preserve such a valuable and now rather lone aircraft, some limitations on its use must be made.*

G-ACDC, again until further notice, may <u>not</u> (1) land away (2) do aerobatics or any display or any demonstration flying.

In spite of these not unreasonable limitations we do hope that Club members will continue to enjoy flying this magnificent aircraft but do so with great respect to her age and uniqueness.'

Also during the year there was a rash of minor incidents requiring the Committee to issue reprimands and fines in accordance with Club rules: a forced landing in a Stampe – albeit successful – because the pilot had misread the fuel gauge, a Turbulent on its nose through being started without someone in the cockpit, and other stupidities. We were going through a bad patch.

On the other hand the Club's inaugural Garden Party was a great success. The *Rag* reported:

The Garden Party at Middle Wallop was held in excellent weather over the weekend of 19/20th June. Neil and Jon had organised every form of fun competition and these light-hearted events kept all the Club aircraft flying constantly over the two days.

Over 40 aircraft were present during the weekend, from which the Super Tiger, 3 Stampes, a Jungmann, the RF.4 and three Turbulents produced the Balbo. The social side of the weekend revolved around an excellent barbecue and disco held in a marquee on the Saturday night.

The whole weekend was such that it will inevitably become an annual Tiger Club event.

As for the catering, Erica Griffiths explained:

At last, I can find enough time to sit down and concentrate on a report on the Tiger Club Weekend Rally!

I think it must have been some six weeks before the event that I was asked if I would look after the catering, a task willingly accepted. Little did I realize what I was letting myself in for. . . .

When I started finding out just how much it would cost to have caterers look after the food for us, I decided it would have to be a 'homegrown' venture and set about contacting people who could help. I found three very willing helpers at a place called 'The Well' opposite the Victoria Coach Station where the British Precision Pilots' Association holds Committee meetings. People who attended the weekend will remember the cheerfulness and willingness to help of Sheila Grimmant, Jenny Harding and Mary Atwill, without whom I could not have managed. . . .

I found caterers, wine merchants, hire shops, food stores, van hire (and loading and driving): all came within my sphere. Fortunately, on the day of the event members were around to help sort out the barbecue itself.

Next year, though, if we repeat the exercise, it might help if the helpers are actually on site to prepare breakfast for dawn-patrollers. Mind you, we stayed in a delightful bed-and-breakfast in Middle Wallop that I can thoroughly recommend.

But next year I will know how much telephoning is involved with organising things like the marquee. Did the Army say they would provide one? Yes. Only later do we find it's the standard Army tent that you can hardly stand up in. But half the fun was in setting up and taking down the Big Top, and wiring in the disco (I think I must be getting old – I found it far too loud, I couldn't talk with people for the volume, and I don't think I was alone in that, so it can't have been age!).

On the Sunday, there were more people wanting lunch than I had anticipated, but not many more. . . .

It was a delight for the three helpers to be taken up in the Jodel and flown around, an experience they are still talking about. And for them to then see the sort of flying display of so many Tiger Club aircraft, and a few strange visitors, not to mention the Harrier showing her paces. It was magical. That's what our Flying Club is all about, flying and sharing that camaraderie.

And for the young lady who didn't know why the Tiger Club bothered having passenger members, I would like to say that, until the blessed day arrives when I can finally afford to do something about learning to fly, it's wonderful for me to be 'only' a passenger member, and do what little I can to help maintain the Club spirit. . . .

Some 100 people turned up to enjoy themselves on that huge expanse of well-mown turf on Salisbury Plain and the Army Air Corps were the perfect hosts, letting us do exactly what we wanted. It was a welcome relief from the pressures at Redhill.

Another somewhat smaller social event, but no less important, took place later in the year. Benjy produced the report:

Proof of the close Tiger Club relationship with the Osnabrück Flying Club was very apparent during our latest 'At Home' to them over the second weekend in September. No less than 10 aircraft arrived at Redhill on the Friday afternoon, carrying some 30 guests.

Just how long our two Clubs have been visiting each other's airfields is a bit in dispute. It is certainly 16 years, possibly 18. Somehow we have got into the comfortable routine of alternating visits. But whatever the period, the friendship goes from strength to strength. Wynn Evans, the current Touring Secretary, was responsible for this most successful get-together. Although some of our visitors stayed with Club members, most stayed at the revamped and most comfortable Croydon Airport Hotel, where on the Friday evening over 50 sat down to dinner. Amid cheerful speeches in abandoned English we were presented with a magnificent cuckoo clock. (Incidentally it now hangs in all its music box glory on the Clubroom wall – listen out for it. Much to Michael's disgust that's just what everyone did whenever it chimed. It was like a two-minute silence on the hour every hour.)

Saturday dawned as lovely a day as any during this Indian Summer. David Timmis bravely drove a bus load to Penshurst Place whilst others selected to 'do' London, and for preference the British Museum. Personally speaking I haven't enjoyed my task as guide so much for ages, but I looked in vain for much that was British. There's more here from Germany, said one bemused but happy visitor. It was true. But all agreed it was the finest museum they'd ever visited.

A long and delightful weekend came to an end with a send-off from Redhill that will take some beating. Adrian 'Dev' Deverell – our tame Chief Engineer – and his friends put on their now celebrated Cowboy & Indian Show. Amid the sound of quickdraw ·45s and Winchester repeaters and Dev dressed overall as the most authentic Indian Chieftain ever, our guests flew off happily but somewhat prematurely – alarmed into an early departure by the information that Customs at their designated airfield (from which to leave the country) closed at 1 pm – and another closed between 1 pm & 3 pm.

Unreasoning bureaucracy apart, this year's 'At Home' must be voted the best occasion for many a long year. Already some of us are planning the return. We do hope more members will join us for our visit to Germany in '83. Our friends there make us most welcome and if you share an aircraft – as most of us do – then the costs become positively attractive. Nor need you worry if you've no previous experience for we usually fly in company, when the collective experience makes the formalities easy, leaving you wondering why you hadn't gone foreign before. . . .

On the aerobatics front, John 'Harpo' Harper was at this time our Committee member representing our aerobatic enthusiasts and our liaison with the British Aerobatic Association.

I knew John well. Going back a bit, I used to share a large rambling 'mansion' flat in Barnes, West London with Bill Goldstraw, who at the time was the Club's senior Check Pilot. In fact the flat used to be occupied from time to time by other Club members stuck for accommodation. Bill had decided to emigrate to Australia and John, who had just recovered from a bad accident he had had displaying a Turbulent at Shoreham, decided to take over Bill's old room. John was a BBC cameraman and a vegetarian. A quiet and modest – but very determined – flyer, John was now a top exponent of Pitts aerobatics and competing on the international scene; he was soon to give up his job with the BBC and become a full-time display pilot. He reminded members to sort themselves out ferrying the Stampe to competitions:

In June 1974 five Stampes could be seen at Snoring for the McAully and three were from the Club. Even were that possible again it would not happen for a competition; ferry costs would see to that. Once or twice over the years the Club has not been represented at contests because the ferrying could not be sorted. Now, almost without exception, pilots practise in order to compete, so to spend good money in the slot and then find oneself unable to attend – whilst surely a hazard of the sport – is bad for one's aerobatic health. So get together and make it work, and those that fly pay more for the privilege. The anger of others after a late arrival can make this a rather dubious one, but the flyer is the boss – angry words leave less impression than strato-granite.

The season has begun and when you are away competing fly with your head as well as with your hands. We know we are good, others are not sure. The national pastime is picking holes – don't make any.

Earlier he had also reminded the Club that a replacement for the Stampe should be on the agenda:

Whilst the Stampe can no longer be regarded as an Advanced aircraft, it is a great aerobatic trainer, strong and forgiving, an excellent bridge between Intermediate and Advanced levels. Pilots tend to be attracted to aircraft of greater potential, and for those at the Advanced stage this is understandable. For basic, Standard, Intermediate, and simple Advanced manoeuvres, the Stampe is – arguably – the best trainer and competitor available. Rather like the Tiger, it teaches you well and most aircraft seem easier afterwards. With more advanced, more powerful mounts as standard trainers, the trap is to run before refining the walk – basics become too easy and may be dangerously overlooked in attempts to progress. . . .

Pilots – some from scratch – are being lured by the prospect of hiring aircraft capable of higher levels. Is the Tiger Club in danger of entering the aerobatic doldrums? Should we consider the use of more advanced aircraft, or should the Club rest on the past and assume that those who wish to progress will do so regardless, *après* Stampe?

The CAP.10 was the obvious answer. It was being built at Bernay in the premises where the SAN Jodels used to be produced and had already replaced the Stampe in France as an aerobatic machine both for training and competitions. I used to visit Bernay regularly to pick up Jodel spares which were still being supplied there and I was familiar with the factory and had met its boss, M. Mudry, on several occasions. The CAP.10 was an attractive aircraft which could also be used for touring and its noise level was acceptable. With the benefit of hindsight we should haven taken the plunge and bought it; I believe now that the cash both could and should have been found. But there was a fierce loyalty towards the Stampe in the Club and Rollasons had, long before, acquired the spares and drawings from the Belgian production line. Perhaps it was this and the fact of our unsettled and precarious position at Redhill which tipped the balance against the investment.

It is of interest that now, almost 20 years later, the debate over a Stampe replacement is still raging in the Club!

At the beginning of 1982 there were worries about the Turbulent team and Neil Thomason issued the following note to the Club's officers and prospective team members:

The object of this note is to outline the plans for Turbulent displays this year and to document certain concerns of which I am aware so that these can be resolved to ensure another successful season, which will enhance the Club's reputation at home and abroad.

Concern has been expressed over the lack of experience of some of the pilots who flew in last year's shows. These pilots had had a fair amount of practice and had demonstrated a reasonable ability at formation flying during practices of the simplified sequence used last year. However, during the displays certain incidents occurred which are cause for concern to other team members. To ensure this year's displays are impressive and, more importantly, safe, we are introducing a new system. In future only those pilots who, after an adequate number of practices (including full practices over the airfield), are considered by three leaders independently to have reached a standard compatible with the Club's excellent reputation and safety record will be permitted to fly at air shows.

Despite widespread publicity within the Club of our need for more display pilots this year, very few members have shown the enthusiasm and ability necessary to join the team. However I am confident that with a few more practices Jim Green, Bob Grimstead and Bob Downing will be able to demonstrate their competence at flying this year's more complicated routine to the high standard required, as will Colin Boardman after some additional general practice in three- and four-ship formations. Along with Jon Marten-Hale, these pilots will probably make up the full-time members of this year's team.

Last season problems frequently arose as a result of pilots scheduled to fly a display cancelling at only a couple of days' notice, generally because of having to work. However on one occasion the pilot concerned, using this pretext, actually spent the weekend at a Fly-In instead. Whilst it is understandable that some pilots may find it difficult to predict when they will be required by their employers, I hope that full-time members of the team will be able to honour all the commitments they make to fly this season. I have prepared a list of reserve pilots who may be approached at short notice should the need arise however. These are those pilots who have considerable experience from previous seasons . . . If not enough of these pilots are available for a show this year, it will have to be flown with less than four aircraft or be cancelled.

If any events occur this year that cause concern, please air the matter immediately, informing any other pilots involved, the leader and me directly what the problem is or was.

The team has recently been relying on privately-owned aircraft to make up the required four. This has worked reasonably well but has potential problems:

♦ Owners may wish to sell their aircraft during a season or use it elsewhere themselves on a display date.
♦ When damage occurs the position of the pilot vis-à-vis the owner is not always clear.
♦ Landing fees are now payable at Redhill by pilots using the aircraft (other than three named pilots).

I feel that while we could continue as we are, the availability of four well-maintained Club aircraft could solve these problems. . . .

Would all pilots please let me have a one-page autobiography including a synopsis of your job (real or imaginary) and how you learned to fly, as commentators invariably request these.

I enclose a few diagrams outlining this year's routine which will be the same as that devised by John Taylor for 1978. A 'pilot's eye view' description should appear in the next issue of the Tiger Rag.

One of the former leaders of the Turbulent display team, Pete Channon, had now retreated to his native Cornwall. He had acquired a 50-year-old

Comper Swift and proposed by way of celebration a repeat of Charles Butler's flight to Australia in a Comper Swift in 1932. It was an ambitious project and, faced with bureaucracy in the Middle East and jails in Iran, Pete was reluctantly forced to abandon the flight. Quite how the Club became directly involved I had no idea but we received a letter of complaint from the Director of Civil Aviation in the Syrian Arab Republic stating that Pete had diverted off the 'standard route' and had flown over prohibited areas without permission. On his behalf I sent a humble letter of apology and promised that he would be suitably advised of the seriousness of the situation on his return. It was my private belief that it was now infinitely more difficult to fly oneself to Australia in a small single-seat aircraft than it was in 1932. Such was the progress of sporting aviation.

The lease was finally granted and signed on 29th September 1982, more than seven years after it had originally been ordered by a court of law; it was due to expire on 25th December 1987. The date for the first rent review – December 1979 – had already passed and the second was due in December 1983. We paid over large sums of money in back rent and other charges which up till now had been refused. The lessees were now the Tiger Club Ltd – not Norman Jones – but inevitably the landlords insisted on personal guarantees, which I was happy to give. Apart from this and a minor amendment that we now had a obligation to supply fuel to all fixed-wing aircraft on the aerodrome which might reasonably demand it, nothing had changed. We still had a licence to use the airfield and a positive covenant to run a Flying Club as well as hangaring and maintaining aircraft. We also had a covenant not to run a flying school and not to permit flying by any person except 'pilots of experience.'

The landlords could still make aerodrome regulations (reasonably) and still had the power to define 'dangerous flying' (reasonably). Why had the work of a couple of days by a junior solicitor taken seven years to complete?

The compromises over landing fees and the permission to hold a flying display which provided substantial extra revenue to the landlords could have been achieved at any time after the lease had been issued. It is a question to which I still do not know the answer. Maybe it had something to do with big business which I did not understand, and the phrase "the unacceptable face of capitalism" kept running through my mind.

Anyway for the moment all was sweetness and light. Our leaking hangar roof was repaired. All the writs and threats from both sides were withdrawn and I wrote to our solicitors to thank them for their efforts and to inform them that it was probably now time for us to make a change.

I also wrote to Tom Storey, the trustee of the Club's legal fund, giving him a report on the Club's legal costs in obtaining our lease, which had amounted to the modest sum of £3,600 and asking him for the donation which had been agreed by the Committee. Tom replied:

"Thank you very much for your letter of 15th December 1982 setting out the costs incurred by the Club in its legal wrangles with the landlord. I am sure it must be a great relief to you now that the lease is finally signed. I enclose my cheque for £1,000 made out to Kennedys as you requested.

I will write a short summary of the matter for the Rag *which may help to remind people of the existence of the Fund.*

On a completely different tack you may be interested to know that I have got hold of a pair of Edo model D1070 floats. These were originally used on a 40 hp Cub; they have been stored since 1938 but appear to be in good condition. I have written to Edo to determine if they may be used on any other Cubs and await their reply. . . ."

Some wrangle, I thought! And now let us get our priorities right – another seaplane was on the agenda!

Meanwhile we had asked John Dalrymple and his wife to be our guests at the forthcoming annual Ball, an invitation which he accepted with pleasure. Benjy wrote to Norman to say that now the lease was signed he hoped that the landlords would now 'unwind.' Unfortunately they wouldn't!

CHAPTER 7
1983

In January 1983 there was a longer than usual Chairman's letter:

"Writing the Chairman's letter this year has proved an intriguing exercise in balance. The irrepressible note of optimism for the future of our Club has had to be tempered with the sobering facts that during 1982 we have had to cope with three serious accidents to our Tiger Moths and that recession is still with us.

Yet on the other hand we finally managed to secure our lease at Redhill after much long and contentious negotiations; the controversial issue of landing fees has been settled and, although this has been achieved at considerable cost, it is acceptable and hopefully relations with our landlords will now be improved.

Enclosed with this letter is the usual subscription reminder for 1983 and the list of flying rates. The flying rates have not been increased since 1981, thanks largely to the fact that the inexorable rise in fuel costs has at last been reversed. Needless to say other costs have been rising and consequently we have found it necessary to increase the rates on a few of the aircraft – in particular the Tiger. Generally, however, in an effort to check the decline in utilisation that has occurred over the last two years, flying rates will continue to be held to the existing '81 levels. New ways of increasing utilisation on some aircraft are also under active discussion.

As for subscriptions, which essentially have to meet the overheads of running the Club, we regret that further rises are inevitable. One innovation is that we have had to introduce a subscription on the members of the Club who are in the category of spouses of existing members. We hope that they will understand and continue to give the Club their support.

Another more welcome change is that we have introduced an Associate (joining) rate at a reduced level for new members under the age of 28. Although the membership is now almost at its highest level ever, it is still vital to attract the right type of new member, and we hope that prospective younger members will be encouraged by this. Finally, may I assure you that the Club and the Committee will continue to promote all its aims and objects in the field of sporting flying in the coming year, and in particular I would like to take this opportunity of reminding you of the three outstanding events in the Club's calendar in 1983: first, of course, the Annual Ball on 12 February; second, the Garden Party, to be held again at Middle Wallop on 25/26 June, and, finally, our very own Air Show at Redhill on 11 September. I look forward to seeing you at all these events and, in the meantime, best wishes for safe and successful flying in 1983."

The discussion about new ways of increasing utilisation on some aircraft had been going on for some time, and at the end of 1982 the following circular was sent to Committee members and all Initial Check Pilots:

It was proposed by the Chairman at the last Committee meeting that the Club Rules on acceptance checks on Tiger Moths should be amended in the light of changing circumstances, including the need to encourage prospective new members, to improve utilisation on other types of aircraft and to lighten the existing burden on Initial Check Pilots.

The proposed amendments are as follows:

<u>Club Rule II</u>
Delete   *'take a dual acceptance flight in a Tiger Moth aircraft.'*
Substitute   *'take a dual acceptance flight in either a Tiger Moth or a Jodel, Condor or Super Cub aircraft.'*

<u>Club Rule XII</u>
Delete   *'a new member is required to fly a minimum of three hours in Tiger Moth aircraft before converting to other types.'*
Substitute   *'a new member is required to carry out a type check on a Tiger Moth with an Initial Check Pilot before converting to the Stampe or any single-seat type.'*

Since this proposal is likely to be controversial, please would you let me or the Chairman have any comments, preferably in writing, on these amendments before 15th January. The matter will be discussed at the Committee meeting on 19th January and a decision reached one way or the other for 1983 at that meeting.

The amendments were indeed highly controversial and produced numerous letters, some of which were long, closely argued and passionate. The great majority of the Check Pilots, including those on the Committee, were firmly against:

'It would produce a two-tier Club,' they said, *'and the whole character of the Club would change.'*

'If people wanted to fly a Jodel, Condor or Cub they could go somewhere else.'

'It would be a downgrading of skills.'

'The Club would be devalued.'

'Most people joined to fly the Tiger.'

'The Club is a unique institution.'

'I view with grave concern any proposal that seeks to make flying membership easier.'

'Those who are unwilling or unable to fly the Tiger are not the sort of people we want.'

'The membership is quite large enough.'

These were a cross-section of some of the comments received. The debate in the Committee was unusually prolonged and the decision was postponed till the next meeting.

Many people wanted to know more about the 'changing circumstances.' The Chairman and I explained that there were currently nearly 50 new members in the process of trying to pass the initial Tiger check. We now had 650 flying members flying the same number of hours as were flown in 1960 when there were only 170. We did not want to lose members or their subscriptions. If the amendment produced only a marginal improvement in utilisation it would be worthwhile.

When the Committee met the following month, there was a small majority, including the Senior Check Pilot, in favour. One or two people had changed their minds as a result of another amendment, which was that to become a full member of the Club it was essential to pass the Tiger check; if one couldn't, or wouldn't, one remained an Associate Member. As Benjy explained in the *Rag*:

During the February Tiger Club Committee meeting it was decided to vary the rules in order to recognise a changing emphasis in our approach to Club flying. It was an important decision, embracing as it did the long-held principle of an initial checkout in the Tiger Moth as a prerequisite to membership.

Our Club was formed at a time when flying Tigers was the rule and not the exception. Nearly 30 years later the position has been reversed, and the relative rarity of the Tiger outside of the Club now presents something of a quandary in familiarisation. Whilst, on the one hand, we in the Tiger Club are jealous of our high standards and are, if necessary, still willing and able to continue with initial checks on the Tiger, yet on the other hand we are all too aware that, without sufficient tailwheel experience, the head-on 'or else' introduction to a Tiger and to the Club can be a daunting, even off-putting, experience to a newcomer, a state of affairs that was never intended all those years ago.

So to ease that encounter it is now proposed to allow new members to take their acceptance check to the Club in a choice of aircraft: Condor, Jodel or Super Cub as well as the Tiger. It is hoped that the subsequent run-up to the fun of Tiger flying and, via the Tiger onto the Stampe and the single-seaters, will be through the easy stages of unrestricted flying for the Associate Member on a whole range of tailwheel aircraft.

Nor is there any time limit on the Associate Member to qualify on the Tiger, for we feel that, at his own pace and without pressure, the new member will not only enjoy the challenge in doing so but will welcome an easier introduction to the good fellowship of our Club. Full membership will now only be open in future to members who have passed their type check on the Tiger, and this recognition will continue to be awarded after a year or so with, of course, the usual provisos.

The decision to change our rules wasn't either an easy one or, for that matter, unanimous. The main concern against was a fear that there would be a lowering of our standards of airmanship. Most of the Committee however felt that this wouldn't prove so. Our overwhelming concern is to the membership and their freedom to fly. Norman put it in a nutshell 27 years ago at the Club's first annual dinner:

'The Club exists to promote the enjoyment and to elevate the standard of private flying, at a reasonable cost, and to **spread around** some of this enjoyment.'

He got it right then, and we believe we've got it right now.

In 1983 there were some changes in the Committee. John Stewart-Wood, our enthusiastic handicap racing spokesman, was killed practising for a race in his own aircraft. Wynn Evans was seriously ill and handed over foreign touring matters to Don Lovell. Neil Thomason resigned because of pressure of work and Pete Kynsey was invited to join as a stand-in for Pete Jarvis, whose attendance at meetings had been somewhat infrequent, one of the most important people at Committee meetings being the Senior Check Pilot. There was even a rumour circulating that Brian Smith would have liked his old job back. David Timmis took over the responsibility for the Dawn-to-Dusk competition from David Hamilton, who was concentrating on Precision Flying.

Another newcomer was Jeanne Frazer, who volunteered to take on the heavy task of organising the Redhill show. She had joined as a passenger member and had then upgraded via the Condor scheme to full flying membership; she had worked for a time in the Club office but, more important, she knew all about sponsorship, promotion and publicity and ran her own business called Avalanche Promotions. Even *more* important, she had a winning smile and warm personality, in fact just the right person to handle all the inevitable little problems and conflicts which would arise.

Benjy wrote privately in one of his letters to Norman:

"I have a feeling that we have struck lucky in our choice of display chief. She doesn't lack in tact either. It would seem that she has won over the airfield manager by the simple expedient of talking about the 'Redhill Show' instead of just the 'Tiger Club Show.'"

Jeanne was soon busy explaining things in the *Rag* and getting Club members 'on side':

After all the excitement of the Annual Ball, I'm sure everyone connected with Redhill will be looking forward to the air show to be staged there on Sunday 11th September.

Having made the decision and approached the Ministry of Defence to see what we can obtain in the way of military participation (we are hoping for the

Red Arrows, BBMF Spitfire & Hurricane and perhaps one other), we are about to get bogged down in the trivia of such necessary evils as portable loos and drainage, public catering, car parking, traffic routing, fencing, printing, etc.

Obviously the Committee will agree a budget for the event, but before we commit ourselves to spend any part of it we would like to hear from any members who think they may have a useful contact with an outfit who could supply any of the above-mentioned services. . . .

We shall, of course, be appealing for volunteers to carry out a number of tasks at the event, not least for the inevitable 'FOD PLOD' to restore the aerodrome to normal condition after the public has dispersed. Watch this space in the next issue . . .

In the meantime, any suggestions for the show will be welcomed.

Jeanne also let everyone know that there were going to be plenty of other things going on besides the flying:

Firstly, a short explanation of all the enclosed paraphernalia relating to the air show. It might seem to some to be an overdose of paperwork; however, as it is a public event and one that demands careful planning, we are trying to cater as well as we can for both members and public and endeavour to stage a well-organised and successful event. So, please help us by applying for your passes on the forms provided and, of course, encourage as many of your friends and colleagues as you can to attend.

While we hope for a good public attendance on the day, we should like to ask for Club members' help in the following areas:

1. Trade Exhibition Space: Exhibition sites will be available in the public enclosure to any company or individual with merchandise to sell or promote. The sites are reasonably priced, so if you know of any likely takers . . .

2. VIP Hospitality Space: Alongside the Tiger Club area away from the public enclosure, we hope to encourage a small number of companies or individuals to entertain their clients or friends in style at the Air Show. The caterers can provide mobile units or marquees and provide menus to suit individual needs, with morning coffee, hot or cold luncheon and afternoon tea. The Tiger Club will levy a site charge and an allocation of guest tickets will be included. Catering charges would be separate and dependent upon menu requirements . . .

3. Printed Programme: We hope to produce an attractive and informative programme for public sale at the Show and will be making advertising space available in the form of full-page, half-page and quarter-page areas. As with the Trade and VIP Space, advertisers do not have to be connected with aviation, so if you have a good contact you think might

like to advertise please follow it up. Members are also invited to submit articles and black and white or colour photographs for inclusion.

So, if you think you know of anyone who would be interested in any of the above facilities, please try to help.

And . . . if you're not actually flying in the display, would you like to volunteer for a variety of tasks on Saturday 10th and Sunday 11th? There's plenty to be done, so leave your name in the office at the Club if you're willing to help out.

The venue for the Annual Ball had been changed to the Gatwick Hilton. The move out of London did not suit everybody but turned out a great success, with the attendance nearly double the previous year, and we were to continue to hold the event at the Gatwick Hilton until the Club finally moved from Redhill six years later. Brendan was again the master of ceremonies and had arranged for the dining room to be decorated with some quite superb model aircraft.

For the first time for some years we were able to record a reasonable profit and, thanks to several lady members selling raffle and tombola tickets, a useful sum was raised for the Hospitality Fund.

Our guests of honour were Sir Geoffrey and Lady Howe. Unfortunately Sir Geoffrey had been stranded at a finance ministers' meeting in Washington and could not make it, but Elspeth Howe, already a well-known public figure in her own right, made an excellent speech in his place. Sir Geoffrey sent a letter of apology:

"I was so sorry not to be with you all on Saturday night. As you will have gathered, I was at the time flying, some 11 miles above the earth's surface and at about 25 miles a minute, in an aircraft whose outside temperature was about 90 degrees Centigrade! But it was no more able to take off with 23 inches of snow on the runway than one of your excellent Tiger Moths. Hence the delay!

Thank you so much for looking after Elspeth so kindly: she much enjoyed the evening. And I much appreciate the Tiger Moth glass that she brought home for me."

Two other guests were Danny and Tasmin Foreman. Danny was the cheerful secretary of GAMTA, the GA trade association. Apart from the fuel tax lobby, I had worked with him and others the previous year to make banner-towing legal again in British airspace. Happily this campaign had also been successful and the Club had purchased the necessary equipment and letters to advertise the Redhill Show. Although strictly an aerial work exercise to be undertaken by commercial pilots – and there were plenty of these in the Club keen to experience a new type of flying – banner-towing, like glider-towing, had a vaguely sporting flavour. Needless to say we did not dare approach Mr Dalrymple for permission to carry out practice flights at Redhill with the Super Cub but Chris Freeman at Headcorn was as usual only too willing to oblige. Danny also sent a nice letter of thanks:

"I am quite sure that last weekend's Tiger Club Ball will prove to be a GA high spot for 1983. Tamsin and I were most honoured to be guests at such an enjoyable evening and I do appreciate the undeserved compliments contained in your speech.

The whole occasion possessed a tremendous 'ambience' and I fully realise that the Tiger Club is probably unique in this country in that it still captures the enthusiasm and 'joie de vivre' of the old-timers, plus the rather bright and shiny new aviators so essential to the health of our industry's future.

We both enjoyed ourselves enormously, from the impromptu speech given by Lady Howe to that smooth O'Brien compèring. It was also a pleasure to see Norvela again and we liked the idea of musical chairs on the top table."

The other big social event of the year, this time with flying included, was the Garden Party at Middle Wallop. Building on its success the previous year, no less than 250 members and friends arrived by road and air. The event made a small profit and plenty of much-needed aircraft utilisation:

By kind permission of Colonel David Mallam, Commandant of the Army Air Corps Centre, the Garden Party was held for the second year running at Middle Wallop. Jon Seccombe deserves considerable credit for laying on the whole affair virtually single-handed, and for his efforts he was rewarded with perfect weather for both Saturday and Sunday 25th and 26th June. Sunday was the best day with up to 50 aeroplanes in evidence, with many members travelling great distances to make it – the prize for the latter going to Don Henry who journeyed from Florida to be with us. We had six Tiger Moths at one stage, with the one and only Fox Moth, the one and only Arrow Active and the chunky frame of a fabulous Stearman. Even the Editor of *Pilot* magazine joined us, although one couldn't help feeling his all singing/dancing, bright and beautiful Wichita Wonder was slightly out of place – perhaps he even regretted for a few moments having parted with his lovely Jungmeister.

The Flour Bombing was by far the most popular event, with Jon Seccombe organising himself into winning it in the Super Cub with, at the other end of the scale, only a handful entering the Editor's challenging Treasure Hunt. Steve Thompson won the latter in a Formula 1 Racer whilst the gorgeous all-female Panel of Judges awarded Derek Piggott first prize in the Aerobatic Competition. Derek flew a graceful, imaginative sequence in a Motor Falke; Tony Baptiste was runner-up in the Stampe. Alex Wright won the Spot Landing in a 721 Glider (though there were mutterings about the use of air-brakes!) and Jon Marten Hale was runner-up in the Super Cub.

Throughout the two days there were plenty of amusements for all. Pete Jarvis was not allowed to step down from the Super Tiger until a large number of members had satisfied a strange desire to stand on the wing, whilst a few more had their first taste of gliding. A number of Army Air Corps pilots had their first biplane flights, whilst others stood in amazement at the spectacle of so much aviation going on in such a small corner of their airfield. It's worth recording at this point how welcome the Army made us – they really were the perfect hosts in every way.

The disco, superbly orchestrated (not really the right word but never mind!) by Jon Seccombe's brother-in-law persuaded most to take some late-night exercise, whilst some heavily-hung heads the following morning evidenced an above-average alcoholic consumption.

It was a splendid weekend and we look forward to returning next year. Our thanks to the Army Air Corps, Jon Seccombe and his team of helpers, particularly Roger Marson, Chris Donne, David Body and Geoff Masterton: without them it wouldn't have happened.

All the normal sporting activities were also in full swing that year. As far as F1 racing was concerned I had by this time more or less taken a back seat in FARA and the Beta *Blue Chip* which I used to consider my special prerogative was being loaned to various suitable people interested in the sport. Perhaps the machine was not as competitive as it used to be and to stay 'in the money' one had to spend a good deal of time and cash on modifications and refinements.

The racing in the UK and France was being dominated at that time by Steve Thompson, who had designed and built a new wing for the standard Cassutt. Steve, who had joined the Club in 1965 as a hangar helper, was another interesting product of the Tiger Club 'system.' After learning to fly at Sportair, he had acquired a degree in aeronautical engineering and then became an airline pilot with British Airways, taking the Hamble route. He would turn his hand to just about everything to do with light aircraft and a few other things besides; he even crewed for me from time to time on the occasional offshore race. His mastery of the technicalities of an F1 machine, both engine and airframe, was complete – he actually manu-factured his own propellers. In 1983, assisted by Tom Storey as his crew chief, he took the Americans on at their own game at Reno, the mecca of all pylon racing, and finished second in the final 'Gold' race. It was a quite outstanding achievement, and the Americans nicknamed his aircraft *The Empire Strikes Back.*

Around June '83 we British racers learnt that two of the French contingent were planning to take their Cassutts to Reno this year. This made me think hard about ways of doing the same because it would have been very poor if the French were to beat us to it. I found out that there was a chartered

Tristar flight to Los Angeles and contacted the charterer in LA to obtain his permission to take my Cassutt on his flight. This permission was given so the trip was on.

On September 6th Harvey Tring and I loaded the racer, Harvey having kindly towed the aircraft to the airport on Derek Wright's ubiquitous trailer. Customs proved to be no problem, the XS29 being sufficient to leave the country for Bangor, Maine, the first stop in the USA. At Bangor the Port Director of the Customs Service was most helpful and cleared the machine in as baggage so that leaving the USA would not involve me in any Customs at all. The flight continued to LAX, where I was delighted to find a FARA member, Bill Rogers, on the airport with a Renta-truck to move the racer to Torrance airport some 10 miles to the south.

I spent Wednesday, Thursday and Friday fitting the aircraft into a borrowed trailer for the 500-mile drive to Reno. John Parker, a former F1 champion at Reno, most generously loaned me both the trailer and the use of his hangar for any work I needed to do. Bill Rogers loaned me his son, David, who proved very good at lying in the dirt putting the nuts on eye-bolts. Friday afternoon we visited the *Spruce Goose* in its dome at Long Beach near the Queen Mary; the aircraft is most impressive with a tailplane span of 113 ft (about the wingspan of the B-17). Well worth a visit.

On Saturday 10th we drove up to Reno, towing the trailer with Carol Roger's camper van. It's an impressive drive, including one hill that took 5 gallons of fuel to climb. We took 11 hours and averaged around 8 mpg; pretty good considering the terrain, which took the road to over 8,000 ft at times.

On arriving at Stead Airport I felt rather depressed as the hangar seemed to be full of very sleek-looking racers. We retired to town for beer and burgers. Sunday morning we rose bright and early to get the aircraft assembled. More work than normal had to be done because I had disconnected all the plug leads and dismantled the fuel system while preparing the aircraft for the trans-Atlantic crossing. Also at this stage the engine and aircraft were cleared by the scrutineers, including measurements of valve lift and clearance and swept cylinder volumes. Carbs were visually checked also. Still we managed to get ready in time for a test flight Sunday evening, making mine the first F1 airborne in the week.

Monday 12th was the first of three days for practice and qualifications, so I practised in the morning on the wood prop, recording an unofficial speed of 210 mph. I then changed to a metal race prop and a different intake. All seemed to be well so I decided to qualify that afternoon, recording 226.961 mph. Qualifying continued until Wednesday night, so we amused ourselves with countless minor adjustments and improvements – we hoped. At the end of qualifying my aircraft was 7th fastest out of 24, putting me into Heat IC to be held on Friday 16th.

The objective in heat IC was to remain in the fastest eight of all the speeds recorded in the three groups in heat I, thus keeping a place in the Gold Final on Sunday. The start at Reno is done as a line of eight aircraft abreast, three on the runway and five on the ramp. This I found rather alarming as I was one of the five on the ramp and there were no lines painted on it. Actually there was no problem, the natural differences in acceleration of the aircraft providing the separation needed. Following the start lap I found myself in fourth place which I maintained to the end, behind Charles Wentworth, Ray Cote and Tom Miller, and just beating last year's winner, Jon Sharp. The British camp, now expanded by Tom Storey and Robin Voice, was well pleased with this and we retired to the usual cocktail party in very good spirits.

On the social front, I must say that we found the organisers and all the other crews most hospitable, the organisers even providing free rooms for us at Harah's Hotel and Casino and loaning me a car for the week. My recollection of events is now rather blurred but I think there was some kind of organised bean-feast on every night bar two, and we did our best to do them justice!

Saturday, the third of the public days, brought more racing, but no flying for me as the final was scheduled for Sunday morning. We concentrated on the great British art of psyching up the opposition by threatening international protest moves, but put in a little more time on the racer, removing what little weight was possible by taking out all unnecessary plumbing and instruments. I've never had such a good view of the spar before!

The final was started towards the east and I was placed on the runway, one of the three faster aircraft having elected to take the ramp due to its smoother surface.

After the 180° left turn to get back onto the course I was running fourth behind Wentworth, Cote and John Dowd in a slab-wing Cassutt. Flying high downwind I seemed to gain rapidly on Cote and lost sight of him after a lap of so; Charles Wentworth motored off into the distance as before, leaving Dusty Dowd about 50 yards in front and below me. We flew nine laps like this but finally I just managed to creep by him, dive down and finish second.

First five results were:

Charles Wentworth	7.48.42	239.016 mph
Steve Thompson	8.17.94	224.846 mph
John Dowd	8.19.42	224.180 mph
Ray Cote	8.20.08	223.884 mph
Jon Sharpe	8.24.08	221.108 mph

Sunday afternoon we furiously dismantled the aircraft and drove back to LA on Monday. By Thursday evening I was home again and a terrific holiday was over. Two weeks later I raced at Duxford in pouring rain and finished fourth. Back to reality!

Prospective entries for the 1983 Dawn-to-Dusk were promising but we were worried that other organisations were getting in on the act. I wrote to David Timmis:

"Further to our telephone conversation, I would like to confirm that there is serious disquiet in the Committee about the continued association of the Club with the G-NAV commercial promotion. I appreciate that this association only takes effect at the time of the reception and prize-giving and that it is obviously too late, once again, to do anything about it this year. We also very much appreciate the work you are doing and have done to organise the Dawn-to-Dusk competition.

However, as you say, this situation must be resolved once and for all this year and to this end I suggest that we obtain an independent assessment of the G-NAV system of navigation from Wynn Evans, who entered the competition last year, and Tom Freer who is a member of the Institute of Navigation. If these reports confirm the verbal comments I have received we must immediately write to Wansbrough-White & Co Ltd, and formally disassociate ourselves. If the reports are favourable, we must then decide if we think that there are any benefits to the Tiger Club from a joint reception. Whatever the outcome I anticipate that we will have to make it clear to the Palace, if necessary, that we are not happy about the present situation.

Also, I do not wish to be oversensitive about this matter but I did notice that in the Press Release no mention was made of the Tiger Club!"

David replied reassuringly:

"I, too am very concerned about the Committee's attitude towards the reunion and the sharing of it with Gordon Wansbrough-White. I suggest that the event is carried out successfully on May 20th, and then we shall all have to consider the best course for the continuation of the Dawn-to-Dusk competition in the future. I suggest that uppermost in our minds should be the continuation of royal patronage for the <u>Tiger Club</u>, and the Dawn-to-Dusk competition in particular."

As for aerobatics, at the end of the season Tony Lloyd, a Club member and editor of the BAeA newsletter, sent me a very interesting report on the competition scene with particular reference to the participation by Club pilots and the Club's Stampes. After producing some statistics on the growing popularity of the sport over the last couple of years and pointing out that: *"generally pilots nowadays are doing more competitions than they would have done five or six years ago,"* he went on:

"On aircraft, there are developing trends to introduction of other aircraft, privately-owned Pitts, group-run CAPs and various miscellaneous aircraft which are now part of the general scene, where they would have been interlopers five or six years ago. Standard level in 1983 was just under 30% Stampe, 30% CAP, 10% Pitts, 30% various (Aerobat, BA-4, Nipper, Tiger etc.).

Tiger Club pilots have demonstrated that the Stampe is competitive with the CAP and Pitts at Standard level. The successes of John Allison, Keith Miller and Richard Pickin have proved this. There's no reason why a proficient Stampe pilot can't win at this level.

The problem comes when one has done all one can do and must move on to Intermediate or Advanced. The lucky ones have the resources to enable them to get a Pitts, either of their own or in consortium. The CAP.10 groups are a possibility, but quite frankly the two-seater is not adequate to see its pilot through to Advanced and Unlimited.

For most the answer has to be a Pitts or Lazer, and consortium probably the only way to go. I don't see there being too many Clubs able to put a Pitts S-2B or Zlin 50 on the flightline.

I looked at the 48 pilots who flew in 1983. These included 22 Tiger Club members, nine of whom flew the Club Stampe, nine others flew Pitts, the numbers made up by CAP.10, Zlin 526 and Pace Spirit.

During the year there were 14 competitions (including supporting features), 10 won by Tiger Club pilots. . . .

Let's hope there's still the interest from the up-and-comers to justify the Club's Stampes' continued competition – at Standard level at least it's still a winner – and it does seem that there is a significant proportion of the more successful who have done their apprenticeship on the Stampe or similar aircraft."

Back at the airfield the storm cloud was growing more ominous. As part of what we hoped would be a generally more relaxed atmosphere, Neil Jensen had volunteered to attend the Aerodrome Users Committee. This had been set up by George Fry as a sub-committee of the main Aerodrome Consultative Committee, partly, I suspected, to avoid embarrassing complaints about the management of the airfield being placed on the main agenda, to the irritation of local councillors and other environment representatives. Neil represented the Club and all its private owner members based on the airfield and, in addition to George Fry, John Dalrymple and one AFIS officer, there was one person from Bristows and one other person representing the four or five private owners who were not members of the Club. I mention this now because it was later claimed by the landlords that there was a 'majority' in favour of mandatory radio on the Aerodrome Users Committee!

Anyway, at an early meeting Neil suggested that the Club would like to do some night-flying and proposed the dates for the forthcoming Hamilton Trophy and, of course, the agreed Redhill Show. I immediately received letters from Mr Dalrymple to the effect that these matters should not be brought up in the Aerodrome Users Committee before he had given his formal agreement in advance, and incidentally he would require 72 hours notice if we wished to do any night-flying. It was not a good start.

More ominously he wrote to me again in connection with a Pitts Special G-BKDR based in our hangar and owned by Tim Barnby. Tim was one of our Check Pilots, an aerobatics enthusiast and an airline pilot and his father, Dick, also a Club member, was a former RAF instructor and had only recently retired from his senior air traffic control job at Gatwick. At his request I had included Tim's Pitts on the list for block landing fees for 1983.

Mr Dalrymple wrote:

"It is understood that G-BKDR is not equipped with any radio facilities whatsoever and . . . I am unable to give my approval for this aircraft to be operated at Redhill aerodrome. I have of course written to Mr Barnby direct."

Roger Graham then took up the matter on Tim's behalf and solicitors' letters were exchanged which resolved the problem. Roger then wrote to me:

"As I indicated to you on the telephone and no doubt you have already discovered from the Aerodrome Users Committee Meeting, Dalrymple is going to raise the subject of radio via the Airfield Regulations. At least the matter will be open for discussion and he will not be trying to achieve a result by the back door via pressure on individual aircraft owners."

Unfortunately the matter was not 'open for discussion' but at what point precisely the landlords had decided to make radio mandatory for all aircraft and make their full frontal assault upon the Club is not totally clear. In April I had received a long letter from Mr Dalrymple, obviously drafted by his solicitors, saying amongst a lot of other things that the landlords had "no wish to derogate from our lease" and in May he had written:

"You will note from the Users Committee Minutes of the 14th February 1983 that all Users representatives present at that meeting, other than your own representative, agreed with the Management's views that the mandatory use of radios was, having regard to the volume and variety of flying activities being carried out at the Aerodrome, in the interests of Aerodrome safety."

TOP: A 'Balbo' rehearsal for the 1983 Redhill Air Show. Photo: Dave Wise.
BOTTOM: Jodel DR.1050M Excellence, the Club's popular tourer and handicap racer, seen here with sponsor's stickers. Purchased in 1966, it was finally sold in 1989 just before the Club left Redhill.
Photo: Author's collection.

TOP: John Blake's cartoon published in the *Tiger Rag* illustrating the imposition of mandatory radio in 1984.
BOTTOM: Biplane Four with smoke at the 1987 Redhill Air Show – this time by *Le Tigri* from Italy. Photo: Author's collection.

On 27th June I was handed the new 1983 Regulations coming into effect on 1st July. They consisted of 10 pages, 16 paragraphs, 67 sub-paragraphs, and 33 sub-sub-paragraphs. In 1963 the Aerodrome Regulations had consisted of two pages, one for fixed-wing aircraft containing 9 paragraphs and one for helicopters containing 10 paragraphs, and then there was more flying going on at the airfield. Such was progress.

Obstructive as they were, we had already agreed to live with the 1980 Regulations. Now the 1983 issue contained two new paragraphs on which no further compromise was possible: one was that aerobatics over the aerodrome were banned and the second, even more fundamental, was that with effect from 25th December radio would be mandatory for all aircraft. On 28th June we had one final meeting in an effort to persuade them to negotiate, suggesting that they should hold a referendum on the radio question. This they absolutely refused to do but they did eventually agree to allow a one-hour aerobatic slot over the aerodrome on weekday evenings and on Saturday afternoons in the winter, providing of course the pilot was in radio contact with the AFIS.

The upshot of all this was that we would have to go to Court and this we proceeded to do. It would have to be a High Court action and would necessarily be very expensive – particularly if we lost. Via the *Rag*, Benjy sent an appeal to members, summarising the situation:

As you know, I wrote at the beginning of the year saying that the long and contentious negotiations on our lease at Redhill had been successfully concluded and that hopefully we could look forward to a period of improved relations with our landlords. In the last issue of the *Rag* it was explained by Tom Storey how these negotiations had progressed and how part of the legal costs which were associated with them had been met by the Legal Fund, and that as a result it was necessary to top up the Fund. Since then a number of contributions have been gratefully received.

However, unfortunately, the latest news is that the Tiger Club is now faced with a fresh attack upon its flying at Redhill and that I must now step up our appeal to all members as a matter of urgency.

A few weeks ago, the Club and its private-owner members were issued with a new set of Aerodrome Regulations. With the ink scarcely dry on the signatures to the lease and with the existing regulations agreed as part of the negotiations leading to that lease, our landords now seek to ban all flying at Redhill unless the aircraft is equipped with radio and the pilot is willing to use it, accept in consequence a degree of air traffic control and thereby inevitably compromise the 'see-and-be-seen' principle under which the Club has been operating without problems for 25 years. As if to add insult to injury, the signal square is to be removed.

Needless to say, we see this as an act of senseless provocation against the Club which amounts in effect to a notice to quit flying. We have sought top-level legal advice and this is that our landlords do not have absolute power in this matter and that they have a duty, having regard to the history and nature of our lease, only to issue regulations which are reasonable. We have been further advised to issue a writ in the High Court seeking a declaration that these new regulations (which incidentally include a number of other clauses which are wholly objectionable) are invalid and unlawful.

Our landlords, Redhill Aerodrome Ltd, are a wholly-owned subsidiary of a large organisation called British & Commonwealth Shipping Company PLC. A number of personal approaches have been made to the Directors of this Public Company – so far to no effect. Also notice has been given of the intention to raise the matter at their Annual Meeting, but whether anything will be achieved by this is doubtful; all we can hope for is that at least they will reconsider their present attitude, which in my view is neither correct nor proper. In the meantime we must seek the protection of the Courts, which inevitably will cost a great deal of money . . .

The Tiger Club is more than just a Club, it has become an Institution, and personifies the very word 'freedom' to pilots the world over. Its continuation is as important to the future of light flying as it is to its loyal membership. We cannot and will not submit to this harassment. Consequently I appeal to you to make a donation – no matter how small – to the Legal Fund.

One of the many people who responded to Benjy's appeal was founder member Jimmy Denyer, who was the director of Newcastle Airport. He enclosed a cheque and wrote:

"I am in receipt of the July/August 1983 Tiger Rag and note that the legal funds are getting a bit thin on the ground with respect to the Club's fight against the owners of Redhill. They appear to be attempting to force the Club to comply with a number of aerodrome regulations which I agree are totally unnecessary for the type of sporting activities that have been carried out for a number of years."

The landlords immediately retaliated against our legal action, seeking and winning injunctions to enforce the regulations until such time as the case came to court. In the meantime Neil had quite understandably withdrawn from the Aerodrome Users Committee. In retrospect it is still my firm conviction that the Club was absolutely right to go to court on this issue.

In my view there are four clear tests that should be applied to any proposal for a new rule or regulation:

♦ Firstly, the evidence for it should be seen to be overwhelming; in this case it was safety, and the evidence there as far as Redhill aerodrome was concerned was non-existent.

♦ Secondly, the motive behind it should be transparent, and the landlord's motives in this case were highly questionable.

♦ Thirdly it should be reasonably practical to implement, particularly on grounds of cost. On this test the practicalities were not insurmountable, although it was true that the supply and installation of radios would be very expensive. One of the problems was that the CAA in their infinite wisdom had recently allocated a new 720-channel frequency to Redhill, and Mr Dalrymple had insisted that this was the one to be used under the mandatory radio regime; this meant that the few sets that we did have installed in the Jodels would have to be changed as well. On the other hand new small fully-transistorised sets were just coming on to the market requiring only portable lightweight batteries rechargeable on the ground.

♦ But fourthly, the most important test is that the consequences of any new rule should be, on any reasonable prediction and in the long term, beneficial for those who would be required to comply. On this last test, I was in no doubt.

Not only would it be impossible to run a sporting flying club in any meaningful way but also, if a regulation such as this could be imposed at Redhill, a precedent would inevitably be set for the introduction of virtually any new restriction. In fact I knew instinctively that if they succeeded on this, then our days at Redhill would be numbered.

In connection with our lease I also had other things on my mind. Graham Plumbe, who was an honorary member and the Club's surveyor, had written to me suggesting that we should create some new shares in The Tiger Club Ltd. Why? the landlord's surveyors had started to focus on the rent review which had been due in 1979 and were now proposing an annual rent of £20,300 to be back-dated. We were currently paying £3,500 and in the run-up to the settlement of our lease I had received a letter from George Fry indicating that they would be prepared to accept £6,000. It was obvious that we would now have to go to arbitration on this as well and that, as guarantor, I was staring at personal bankruptcy. Once again the ethics of big business apalled me!

As for day-to-day Club activities during May that year there had been a couple of accidents.

An Auster belonging to a Club member had been parked on the grass outside our hangar and had been inadvertently started without chocks and without anybody in the cockpit. The pilot had been unable to prevent it careering into Tom Storey's Mew Gull and Ian MacClennan's Turbulent, causing severe damage. The pilot swore that the switches were 'off' but in the circumstances it was unforgiveable and he was asked to resign.

Another accident had occurred to the Club Turbulent G-APNZ touring in France. The pilot had landed on a small grass airfield which was waterlogged and had turned the aircraft on to its back. He phoned me to say that there was extensive damage to the fin, rudder and rear fuselage, and also the propeller was broken.

What was he to do?

I told him abruptly: "Get the aircraft repaired and don't come home without it!"

At most small grass airfields in France there was usually a workshop next to the hangar and a friendly crowd of homebuilders, and I had an idea that this airfield would be no exception. I was right. The repairs were carried out on the spot quickly and expertly and a week later the aircraft was back at Redhill with a borrowed prop. John Sarratt and Dev gave it a minute examination and could find no fault, and I don't think we ever did receive a bill from France.

After the Garden Party everybody was getting organised in earnest for the Redhill Show. A small Steering Committee had already been formed to assist Jeanne and deal with specific tasks. Brian Smith was appointed Display Director, to be assisted by John Taylor; Robin Voice and Neil Jensen would assist Jeanne with promotion and publicity and the ground organisation. Earlier in the year there had been some rumblings amongst some of the more experienced display pilots in the Club about where the 'profits' from the Show would go, and after discussion with the Chairman I circulated the following memo to the Steering Committee:

As you know one of the important aims of the Club is displays and another is to provide the members with good sporting flying at the lowest possible costs. In the past, to achieve this, we have run full Club displays using an outside organiser. More recently our efforts have been almost entirely confined to limited participation in other people's displays. The essential income to the Club from this source has never been large, averaging approx. £3,000 per annum. Last year this figure slumped disastrously. At the same time, for various obvious reasons, the main revenue of the Club, i.e. the hire of aircraft to members, has also declined by approx. 20% over the last two years.

Consequently, when after long and difficult negotiations a long-term agreement was secured to hold an Annual Display at Redhill, it was essential to treat this as an opportunity and a challenge to generate a fresh source of income to supplement the Club's revenue from this source and to make up the gap in hire revenue; our objective is therefore no more or no less than this.

Clearly we could continue the practice of the past and contract out the organisation of the Redhill Show to others, and there have been plenty of offers. However since this is not likely to be entirely satisfactory in terms of the potential income and other Club requirements, it has been decided, rightly or wrongly, to do the job ourselves.

The idea has been circulated that we are likely to make large profits from this enterprise and that we should therefore specifically commit these profits in advance either to various capital projects or various good causes, with the object of motivating some people. In reply to this, I have to say first that, since this is our first Show and we are relatively inexperienced, optimism on this score could well be misplaced; second, considerable financial risk will be incurred and, finally, the Club has urgently to generate new sources of income to meet its current liabilities, let alone entering into any new commitments, and it would be entirely irresponsible of me as a director of The Tiger Club Ltd. to suggest otherwise.

Therefore apart from the motivation of participating in the display and achieving something worthwhile, I can offer no further objective and if anybody continues to insist on more precise objectives than those outlined above, I cannot help and can only suggest that it would assist the project as a whole if such people would withdraw from active involvement at an early stage.

I hope that the above clarifies the situation and that members of the Steering Committee will communicate these objectives and policy to other members if and as required.

Amongst other detailed notes on the subject of budgets and administration the memo went on to point out that essentially this was a Club Show for Club members and that, as far as the flying was concerned for other than the Club's aircraft, priority should be given to members' aircraft based on the airfield or elsewhere "even if this might compromise the excellence of the Show overall."

As it turned out, eventually, everything went like clockwork and everybody, both in the air and on the ground, pitched in with enormous energy, enthusiasm and commitment. To add to the traditional Club display acts, Charlie Shea-Simonds organised the parachute jump, Philip Meeson the Marlborough aerobatic team and Keith Sissons the B-17 *Sally B*.

In addition the RAF turned up with the Battle of Britain Memorial Flight, the Vintage Pair and a Jet Provost, and the Navy with the Swordfish, and Chris Bellhouse organised sponsorship for a Formula 1 air race. Many members provided individual display acts and there was even a 'time of arrival' prize for members visiting in their own aircraft before the show began.

Neil turned up trumps, inviting the Veteran & Vintage Car Club and introducing the Club to Ray Chudley, an ex-policeman, who knew all about road signs, gates and the collection of the money.

Unfortunately on the day the weather was atrocious, raining most of the time and with a low cloud base and, needless to say, the size of the crowd was disappointing, but thanks to Jeanne's skilful and enterprising ground organisation, enough advance income had already been generated so that we were just able to break even.

More important, in the aftermath of the Show the local Press were enthusiastic and we received a great many complimentary letters. Also we now reckoned that we knew how to run an air show on our own airfield.

After the air show, we had to start preparing our case in earnest against mandatory radio. The hearing in the High Court had been fixed for 16th January 1984 and clearly there was going to be a lot of work and a lot of talking to do. In the first place our lawyers advised us to conduct a survey and a questionnaire was circulated to our flying members. Thanks to my wife Norvela and her business, which had all the facilities for producing reports, the results were collated into a full and very detailed document. The findings of the survey were published in the *Rag*:

Following the questionnaire which was recently sent out to 325 Members who have flown as pilot in charge of a Club aircraft at Redhill during the past 18 months, we are now pleased to publish the results.

In the first place there was a response rate of 73% which increased to 80% taking into account the replies received after the date due of 30th September. 80% of the replies added written comments.

To the question: 'In respect of your flying at Redhill Aerodrome do you consider that mandatory radio will result in an improvement to air safety?', 97% said 'No.'

To the question: 'Do you consider that, if some pilots use radio at Redhill and others do not, this is detrimental to air safety?', 81% said 'No.'

It was also apparent from the written comments that most of the small minority who replied 'Yes' to this question had a preference for no radio at all.

To the question: 'Would you personally continue to be interested in flying Club aircraft at Redhill under a system of mandatory radio?', 55% said 'less frequently' or 'not at all' and nobody said they would fly 'more frequently.'

Earlier this year a survey was also carried out of private owners based at Redhill and also of comparable aerodromes. 78% of the private owners objected to mandatory radio and only 6% were positively in favour. Also there is not a single grass aerodrome within 50 miles of central London which requires mandatory radio as a condition of use either for based or visiting aircraft. . . .

Some time later we produced a second survey of all aircraft movements at Redhill from the movement logs kept by AFIS. This showed that the actual total number of movements, including helicopters, had been on the decline since 1980 and that 92% of all fixed-wing movements had been made by Tiger Club members, who had already made their views very clear on the question. Both these survey reports were sent to Sir Nicholas Cayzer, who by this time had received a peerage, an award which some newspapers later claimed was not unconnected with the fact that British & Commonwealth Shipping PLC had been making large donations to the Conservative Party.

The response was not encouraging. In the first place, both Lord Cayzer and Lord Rotherwick had resigned as officers of Redhill Aerodrome Ltd and secondly, since it was us who had started the court action, they could not comment because the matter was *'sub judice.'* Anyway, as far as we were concerned at least we now had the evidence – or so I thought . . .

We had also been in contact with the CAA, or rather the National Air Traffic Services (NATS), with a view to obtaining some evidence of their neutrality. They spoke with a forked tongue. "No, they certainly had not influenced the aerodrome on the matter" and there was no automatic link between AFIS and mandatory radio but, if asked to comment, they could only say that "in their view it would be of general benefit to the safety of traffic on the aerodrome."

I then sent them copies of both our surveys and later they communicated their 'view' to the landlords. They made no comment on the surveys. Some neutrality! . . .

Meanwhile Norvela had bought a few shares in British & Commonwealth in order to be able to put down a question at the company AGM. Again the response was negative: "In view of legal proceedings we cannot comment."

We received basically the same reply from all the MPs we approached, including both the aerodrome's local MPs, Geoffrey Howe, who was now the government's Foreign Secretary, and George Gardiner. We had also written to Michael Colvin, the Chairman of the Conservative Aviation Committee with the same result; finally we tackled David Mitchell, the Minister responsible for aviation and to whom the CAA was in theory answerable. Surely, we said, the CAA is exceeding its statutory powers by saying that mandatory radio would be beneficial to safety when there is no legislation to that effect?

The Minister disagreed. In fact, on the political front we got nowhere.

It is always a highly convenient ploy for MPs and others when faced with awkward questions to quote the *'sub judice'* answer. Moreover some time before this I had read an article in the *Sunday Telegraph* with the headline: 'CASH MAKER CAYZER,' and underneath: 'Lord Cayzer, already one of the richest and most powerful men in Britain – he is a close *confidante* of the Prime Minister and senior Tories as well as one of the most eminent men in the City . . .'

I suggested to Norvela that perhaps it would be better if we approached MPs who were *not* members of the Conservative Party but my wife, being a staunch party member and a Conservative MEP, did not think that this idea would be appropriate.

Attempts were also made to secure a settlement behind the scenes and away from the lawyers. James Baring wrote a long letter from the South of France recommending this course:

"Under these circumstances I think it is time to realise that it must be in the interests of both parties to part company as soon as possible rather than continue what has become an unpleasant and increasingly unprofitable relationship. To this end I suggest that the Club offers to vacate the premises at the earlist possible occasion provided they can be given suitable financial compensation to afford them a chance of establishing themselves elsewhere. . . . Let's name the sum we need to clear off and ask them if they will pay it."

It was sensible advice. I discussed a figure with James and our professional advisors since the Club could well be out of action without income for a considerable time and there would be redundancies. In the event the sum was quite large by our standards but Lord Cayzer was not even interested. With the benefit of hindsight, it might well have been in the interests of his company's shareholders if he had been. Tom Storey was also in touch with Anthony Cayzer and had put forward a compromise proposal that the radio rule could be waived at the weekends, a suggestion which would have been acceptable. Anthony Cayzer wrote that the the the proposal was not a practical one; Redhill Aerodrome had been designated as an emergency landing area for the new East Surrey hospital and besides, there had been one case of a Piper Cub taking off on the wrong runway . . .

However, when it came to a question of the landlords' motives, we had a minor stroke of luck. We had already had reliable information that the Bristow helicopter training school would be closing in the new year. We now received a leaked letter addressed to the Department of Trade from Redhill Aerodrome Ltd and signed by John Dalrymple. He was replying to a Department of Trade Consultative Document – 'Facilities for Business Aviation in the South-East of England.' The letter was marked 'confidential' but perhaps we had at least one friend in the government.

Mr Dalrymple wrote:

"I believe that Redhill Aerodrome offers tremendous potential for expansion and if it were to be developed could have the effect of relieving Gatwick Airport of the movements of the smaller types of aircraft. . . .

In 1984 Redhill Aerodrome celebrates its 50th anniversary but remains very much as it was during the war years. I believe that now is the time to give due consideration to updating the aerodrome and to contemplate as to whether it could play a major role in aviation by becoming a satellite of Gatwick Airport in respect of general aviation activity. Development of this nature would not involve an excessive capital outlay and would certainly provide the relief sought. Redhill's runways are parallel to those of Gatwick and its Aerodrome Flight Information Service Unit could be extended to full Air Traffic Control."

We were right. It was not safety but the development of the airfield which was their primary consideration. In the light of this statement and in the run-up to the Court hearing, we wrote many more letters to Lord Cayzer and his acolytes. We also suggested one more compromise, which was to include in the regulation a recommendation for the use of radio but to require it only for touring aircraft and not for specialised racing, aerobatic or display machines owned by the Club or its members. This was also turned down by the landlords. Their solicitors wrote a final letter on 30th December:

"Merely requiring radios only for touring aircraft would not solve the problems with which our clients are confronted. As to merely recommending the use of radio rather than making it mandatory, that is unlikely to be successful either: we already have examples of Tiger Club members' aircraft fitted with radios but they are not used."

There was one more minor act of the drama to be played before the case came to court. The landlords' solicitors demanded security for costs and, if we could not provide it, our case could not be heard.

We managed to persuade a judge in chambers that the Club could meet its liabilities even if the verdict went against us; but privately I knew that if that were to happen there was no way that we would have the funds to appeal.

During 1983 in the euphoria following the Falklands war, the Conservative government was returned to power with a greatly increased majority. In our current situation, I was somewhat dubious whether that would be to be to the benefit of the Tiger Club. On the other hand, despite the recession and the ongoing conflict at Redhill, there had been plenty of excellent sport flying carried out during the year and much had been achieved. Also the Club's membership stood at a record level.

CHAPTER 8

1984

For the first time ever the Club was closed over the Christmas and New Year holiday. The dreaded mandatory radio regulations which were due to come into force on Christmas Day had not been withdrawn pending the trial of our case on 16th January, and we were advised by our lawyers that our aircraft should remain grounded until judgement was delivered. The private owners also went along with this decision. In a sense it was a relief that the whole business was going to be finalised one way or another during a time of the year when anyway there was not much flying to be done.

Also many people were looking forward to the Annual Ball which was due to take place at the Gatwick Hilton on 11th February. The big attraction this year was that Prince Andrew had accepted our invitation to be the Guest of Honour. Also, Christopher (Superman) Reeve, a Club member, had promised to come along.

It was only the second time that a 'Royal' had actually attended a Club Dinner Dance and the Prince's equerry, Adam Wise, explained the protocol in a letter to the Chairman:

"I know that Prince Andrew is looking forward very much to this evening and to meeting your members. He is quite happy for you to state on the invitations or any other material to be issued to members that he is to be the Guest of Honour.

However, I would suggest that in order to keep the occasion as informal and private as possible, we do not give any advance publicity to the fact that Prince Andrew is to attend, other than to the membership of the Club itself. To this end, I do not intend to include this evening in the list of public engagements which Prince Andrew undertakes; there will simply be an entry in the Court Circular the next day to say that he attended. There is no need to be secretive about it, but if we make the engagement a public one, then the Press will require facilities and will turn the place into a circus. . . .

If you wish Prince Andrew to speak at the Dinner, perhaps you would be kind enough to give me any help that you can with suitable subjects which he might discuss, and achievements and personalities of the Club which should be commemorated. . . ."

It was a hugely successful occasion, as much enjoyed by the Prince as by everyone else, and there was a record attendance of over 320. Once again the event was brilliantly masterminded by Brendan with an enthusiastic team of helpers. One highly popular innovation designed by Andrew Chadwick was a menu which, if you followed the instructions carefully, could be ingeniously converted to an all-flying aircraft. The Ball produced

144

a handsome profit, and also from the raffle and tombola a four-figure sum for the Legal Fund. Maybe in all the fun our members had not totally forgotten the impending crisis!

Although the High Court case had finished on 23rd January after a hearing lasting five days, for some unaccountable reason we had to wait for the verdict, which we were told was going to be delivered on 22nd February, nearly a month later. Some people, fearing the worst, said that this was deliberate so as not to put a dampener on the Tiger Ball, others that the judge was privately and discreetly taking soundings amongst the political establishment and the CAA.

Whatever the reason, the delay was very annoying and this was not the only thing. On the question of publicity our lawyers had told me that in no circumstances were we to seek publicity for our point of view; it would upset the judge and would be in contempt of court and so on. This was very frustrating; we had already received reasonable coverage in the local papers and in the light aviation Press. We needed to bring the matter to the attention of the national Press. It was not, after all, a criminal case and our opponents were actually employing a public relations firm. Also, literally hours before the hearing opened, I was told that the detailed survey reports which we had produced both on aircraft movements at Redhill and on the answers to the questionnaire could not be produced in court – not even the signed and completed questionnaire forms! The judge would not even look at them unless each and every person who had contributed to the survey appeared in court and testified on oath that this was their answer and opinion on the question. In this way the evidence of 230 experienced pilots, of whom over a quarter were holders of professional licences and which included the statements of several air traffic controllers, went by the board. We would have to rely, to use the legal jargon, on the evidence of two 'expert' witnesses. Again I was indignant. In retrospect, perhaps we should have sought an adjournment and arranged for a couple of hundred people to queue up in the Strand; maybe that would have brought us the publicity we needed . . .

There were also several other things about the trial and the way our case was conducted which worried me. Our advocate, Patrick Ground, was now a Queen's Counsel and he had also been elected as a Conservative MP in 1983. He was totally familiar with the philosophy of the Club and had visited the airfield on several occasions. He had advised us in the past and had recommended the action we were now taking. However, in my view he did not plead our cause with the passion and conviction that was required, which essentially was a struggle for long-established tenants' rights and the personal freedom of many people. In particular, for some reason, he had decided not to question the landlords' motives with the necessary rigour nor to expose the deeply damaging actions that had been taken against us in the very long process of getting our lease renewed.

145

By the strange – some would say anachronistic – convention whereby a leading counsel has to be assisted by a junior barrister, we had the services of Mr Graham Stoker. He had represented us at the preliminary hearings; he had also visited the aerodrome and had actually flown an aerobatic sortie in a Stampe with Roger Graham. Perhaps he would have handled our case better; at least our costs would have been substantially reduced.

As far as the judge was concerned, someone had already warned me that High Court proceedings were all very well providing one gets the right judge: unfortunately, as far as we were concerned, the Hon. Mr Justice Mustill was the wrong one. Hardly had the case been opened when, on hearing that the defendant's parent company was British & Commonwealth PLC, he said *sotto voce* – but perfectly audibly to everyone sitting in the front of the court – that in that case he did not want the matter to go to appeal!

Perhaps he knew something about the reputation of B & C PLC as litigants and, whatever was intended, it was a depressing comment. It was also a mystery why the case lasted five days when it had been originally estimated to take only three. Although there were several witnesses on both sides, the judge took very little notice of any of them, although he did finally concede as a result of the evidence given by Pete Kynsey that the landlords "should think again" about the use of radio while a pilot was practising aerobatics over the aerodrome.

For the landlords, apart from Mr Dalrymple the witnesses included a director of Bristows, Mr Alistair Gordon, who described the Club's activities as "silly," the secretary of the Aerodrome Owners Association who were one of the sponsors of the AFIS idea, and the owner of Denham Aerodrome which already had a hard runway, a Cessna flying training school and a mandatory radio regime. They had also subpoenaed a gentleman from the CAA who repeated the line already taken in correspondence.

One other surprising witness for them was a Club member and experienced ex-RAF pilot Dick Millward; he used to run a Group with a Chipmunk at Biggin Hill, and some years back had offered the aircraft to the Club on lease and for displays providing he could have hangarage so to be able, as he had put it, to fly from a delightful grass airfield. Unfortunately hangarage for a Chipmunk was not available and as a result Mr Millward must have harboured a grievance against the Club and, so I was told, had actually complained to the CAA about something or other at the aerodrome.

For us, our 'experts' were Maurice Looker from White Waltham, a 'radio-free' grass airfield west of London with similar 'landlord' problems, and Harold Best-Devereux who was, at any rate by the size of the bill he eventually presented, a professional court expert witness. Neil Jensen gave evidence for the Club and in particular for the large majority of private owners, and I was questioned interminably, particularly on the subject of the cost of fitting radios to the Club's aircraft. As I struggled with the answers I distinctly remember being more concerned with the cost of the proceedings if we lost the case.

Anyway we all trooped back to the High Court in the Strand on 22nd February to hear Mr Mustill's decision. We were still mildly optimistic. Patrick Ground had scored a final point when he had asked Mr Dalrymple if Redhill Aerodrome Ltd had held a directors' meeting to approve the new aerodrome rules and regulations, and was there a minute to this effect? George Fry and a colleague hurriedly left the court and returned shortly afterwards clutching a piece of paper. They had been to Cayzer House, the head office of B & C PLC, situated in the City only a stone's throw from the Strand, to fetch the document. It was read to the court. Yes, there had been a directors' meeting held at Cayzer House on 27th June and it was minuted that, after careful consideration, it was in the interests of the company to adopt the new regulations with effect from 1st July. The approval had been given only four days before the regulations were due to come into effect and nothing was said about safety! As far as we were concerned, it was the final piece of evidence we needed to demonstrate that 'safety,' whilst it might have been the pretext, was not the motive for the imposition of mandatory radio.

Mr Mustill read out his judgement in a slightly faltering and somewhat inaudible manner. He said that the problem was one he found very difficult to resolve but we had lost our case. The judgement was contained in a 16-page document, and reading it then and reading it now some 17 years later it seems to make no more sense now than it did then. Briefly, he accepted that the basic safety case had not been proved. He disagreed that the CAA had not been neutral. Inexplicably he concluded that the landlords had acted in good faith but he agreed that there were no potential benefits to the airfield users. He admitted that the introduction of mandatory radio would cause the Club hardship but he suspected that only a few would give up membership. Finally from all this and with the usual legal meanderings he concluded that if Mr Dalrymple, Mr Fry, Lord Cayzer and their friends thought that mandatory radio would make the airfield safer, they were entitled to have their view enforced.

Immediately after the case, as the responsible director of The Tiger Club Ltd, I had to consider the options: one was to keep the aircraft grounded, continue to refuse new members, disband the Club and pay our now massive legal bill from the proceeds of aircraft sales. Although we still had four years of our lease to run and still a covenant to run a flying club, we could probably just manage to pay our way by hangaring and overhauling aircraft and the Club could be a moribund organisation possibly operating a single aircaft. No doubt such a course would have suited Mr Dalrymple but was unthinkable as far as I was concerned. It would all depend on the attitude of the membership not only to find the cash for the radios but also to fund the legal costs.

As far as these were concerned and jumping ahead a bit, the landlords' solicitors were not slow in presenting their bill; it came to the grossly inflated sum of £35,000. Fortunately, there is another legal convention whereby one's opponent's costs can be 'taxed' by a 'taxing master' providing that the taxed bill is paid immediately. Fortunately as a result of this process, their bill was reduced to £18,000. Needless to say, our own costs were a good deal higher and the final account for the whole exercise came to near enough £50,000. It took quite a time to pay our own solicitors but eventually we managed it, the final payment being made from the proceeds from the sale of a single aircraft.

The Committee meeting which took place at the Biggles Wine Bar on 28th February was inevitably a crisis one and there was a record attendance. Some members were looking for scapegoats and both Benjy and I came in for a certain amount of criticism. Although I said that our case had been well presented, I knew this was not so and I felt personally responsible for the disaster. Consequently I had already privately decided to waive the small salary I was receiving from the Club as my own contribution to the legal costs. After some discussion it was agreed to put the affair behind us and to impose a 'once off' levy on members' subscriptions as a contribution to the legal costs – £50 for flying members, £25 for non-flying. Mavis Harriott, the Club's Treasurer, who very rarely attended Committee meetings, brightly suggested that this had to be the minimum and would be some small compensation for all the subsidised flying that members had received in the past. It was also agreed to send out two letters immediately, one from me explaining the situation and one from the Chairman rallying the Club. In fact Benjy had already drafted his:

"Michael Jones has just told me that we have lost our High Court action. As I replaced the telephone and pondered this appalling news, I suddenly recalled an earlier case and looked it up.

Some 20 years ago, our then Chairman Norman Jones had written:

'There are sad hearts and aching pockets to be found in the Tiger Club. We are licking our wounds after our first battle with the law. The sad hearts we do not expect to last long, but the aching pockets may take longer. The law looms very large in the life of the private flyer – and a law which is made and administered by those who have no practical knowledge or experience of our difficulties.

But it is a poor faith which fails at discouragement. People may measure themselves, not by what is done to them, but by what they do to others. That we should use this case to try and get a square deal for private flyers in the future is right and wise. But to allow it to discourage us or, still worse, for it to give us a 'chip on the shoulder' would not be in the Tiger Club spirit.'

I can do no better today than to commend his words to you for he counselled wisely.

Much will have to be done, and much faced, and I will keep you fully in the picture as it develops.

Of one thing I am sure, the Tiger Club's strength is well founded in the beliefs of its membership. And I know with a total certainty that our Club will continue and will grow even stronger, for that is the sort of Club we are."

My letter, together with a separate letter to all the private owner members, went off in the same envelope and was a good deal longer:

"As you will have appreciated, we have delayed sending out subscription reminders this year pending the results of the High Court action which we felt obliged to take against our landlords on the issue of mandatory radio. The hearing took place during the week beginning 16th January and judgement was delivered on 22nd February. Unfortunately we lost the case and the judge ruled that all aircraft using Redhill Aerodrome must in future be in communication with Redhill AFIS on 123.225 at all times in the circuit. Since none of the Club's aircraft can comply with this regulation, it follows that they must remain grounded until further notice.

Whatever you may think of this amazing verdict, it has now to be accepted. The upshot of it was that all flying is dangerous but mandatory radio is 'better for safety' and that it was reasonable for the regulation to be imposed. Unfortunately, although the CAA professed neutrality and agreed that the safety record at Redhill was excellent, this seems to be in line with their current thinking. . . .

Copies of the detailed note that we have made of the Judgement are available on request; there will be a report on the case in the next Rag. *I would like to take this opportunity of thanking all those members and others who supported the Club in court and during the recent months, which have been a very worrying time.*

Needless to say we are now faced with quite horrendous legal costs, and the sums that have already been so generously donated to the Legal Fund, much from outside the Club, will in no way foot the bill. However, I make no apology for the stand we took on what was a very important principle. We obtained the best advice available, our case was well presented and I can assure you that the outcome surprised many of the people who were closely involved. We sincerely hope that the decision will not have wider repercussions for other aerodromes.

As you know, we recently carried out a survey of the regular flying members to put the question, amongst others, of whether they would be interested in continuing to fly at Redhill under a mandatory radio regime. The result showed that a considerable number of members would continue to fly, albeit less frequently. Therefore we will now as an urgent first step fit up two or three of the biplanes with the appropriate workable radio and change the existing equipment on some of the touring aircraft. However, this again is a very substantial capital cost, not to mention an ongoing new annual commitment for maintenance, depreciation etc., but it will at least be business as usual as soon as and as far as possible.

As a result of all this, subscriptions for 1984 have had to be very substantially increased and details are contained on the attached form. In essence we are asking for a once-off minimum levy to the Legal Fund, reduced in proportion if you have already contributed to the current appeal, together with a normal but increased subscription; for the sake of simplicity again as a once-off exercise in 1984, there will be only two classes of membership – flying and non-flying – based on your existing category.

With relatively little flying activity being possible in the short term, some current commitments and overheads will have to be temporarily reduced. The essential thing will be to preserve the assets of the Club and its associated engineering back-up as far as possible for the future. However within these limitations we shall continue the existing facilities at Redhill for members and keep other ancillary activities going.

It is fully understood that all this may place considerable hardship on the membership of all types and some strain on your loyalty. I hope not, but I have to face the situation with realism. The short- and long-term future of the Club, particularly in relation to the possibility of finding a freehold site for our more important flying activities, must depend on the response received.

I will keep you fully informed as the present situation clarifies. In particular, notice will be given of flying rates and the availability of aircraft immediately after the Budget in a week or so.

On this occasion of crisis in the history of the Club, the Chairman has written a separate letter to you which is enclosed. I fully endorse his message and his optimism for the future. In the meantime I would like to thank you for your understanding and patience."

Regrettably, two members of the Committee, together with one other person, decided to send out their own private circular on the future of the Club without consulting the rest of the Committee. Although the letter raised several interesting points, it was discourteous and its timing was unfortunate, and the signatories subsequently resigned from the Committee. One further proposal was discussed at the February crisis Committee meeting, which was that there should be more democracy in the running of the Club and that Committee members should in future be elected instead of being appointed by the Chairman. It was generally agreed that this was an opportune moment to put the necessary procedures in hand and hopefully everything would be finalised by the end of the year.

When the Committee met again in April, we knew that we still had a Club since by then 179 members had renewed their subscription and paid the levy, providing the Legal Fund with what was now a reasonably healthy sum. Also three aircraft now had the required radio. However, to say the least, the financial position was still precarious and it was decided, since new members could now be accepted, to introduce for the first time in the Club's history a membership entry fee.

Also Tom Storey, being a chartered accountant, was asked to produce a report on financial options for the future. The Club's 1983 accounts had already been produced and so he had all the information he needed. His report was predictably gloomy but contained some useful suggestions for raising further finance, including the issuing of shares to prospective investors. The 1984 flying rates were sent out in late April with the first *Tiger Rag* of the year which was something of a crisis issue. I produced an article explaining what I thought were some of the politics behind the High Court disaster. Pete Jarvis produced the necessary notes from the Senior Check Pilot and Benjy displayed his usual refreshing optimism. Some extracts are worth repeating:

The other power in the land from whom we sought assistance was of course the CAA, or rather the National Air Traffic Services and the government department to whom they are politically accountable. Their attitude was that it was none of their business, but they then proceeded to undermine this apparent impartiality by assertions from their ivory tower to anybody who was willing to listen that in their view mandatory radio at an aerodrome where ground radio was installed was generally a good thing, and that Redhill was no exception, and this in the face of all the evidence of the near-unanimous views of the people flying there. Unfortunately our landlords were willing to listen, and it is a well-known fact that there has always been a strong lobby in NATS who, for obvious reasons, hanker after mandatory carriage of radio by all light aircraft. This party's views were roundly defeated in 1975 and also in 1978 at that time with the assistance of politicians who were then in Opposition rather than in government. It is my belief also that at that time there was a more liberal climate within the CAA.

In 1977 the then Chairman of the CAA wrote:

'World aviation is probably more subject to rules and regulations than any other industry. The need for safe aircraft, sound maintenance and expert pilots is self-evident and the record of British Aviation is good . . . In all its regulatory activities, I believe that the Authority's objectives should be to promote safety standards, service to the customer, and economic health in Civil Aviation, in the simplest and least burdensome manner possible . . .

Above all we must not arrogantly assume that the regulator always knows best or that regulations can never be streamlined or cancelled. In a world already overwhelmed with rules, the CAA must not shirk its often unpopular tasks, but it must always aim at a light touch if possible!'

Well, times certainly seem to have changed again and there is no doubt that the High Court ruling, despite the judge's careful assurance to the contrary, adds powerful weight to the mandatory radio lobby in NATS; perhaps someone might be able to persuade them to make an ex *gratia* contribution towards the costs; that might at least assist us in the considerable capital expenditure required to equip and re-equip our aircraft with new radios, which in the case of many can be fairly said to be intrinsically worthless.

Anyway, as has already been stated elsewhere, the decision has been made and has to be accepted. We must live with it as best we can, at least for the time being. Redhill has now become radio-active and we await the consequential fall-out with curiosity and apprehension. . . .

So what's new? Nothing much! The Club is still at Redhill, with some old biplanes and the weather is still the same . . . changeable! The only difference is that we will have to obtain essential pre-flight information with the aid of modern electronics instead of the Mark I Eyeball . . .

No, Big Brother will not be watching over us from the lofty, corrugated edifice called 'The Tower.' He will be a member of the non-flying fraternity and, as an 'Aerodrome Flight Information Services Officer,' will be on call to offer you information as to current airfield conditions, as he interprets them. Such information must be accepted at face value until you can confirm it yourself. The AFISO cannot exercise control over aircraft reporting to him but can offer advice as to the last-known position of aircraft whose pilots have been in contact with him. Your responsibilities remain the same as they always were. Do not allow the use of radio to detract from those responsibilities.

This is a new, but not impossible, situation that Club members will have to accept in order to continue enjoying the pleasurable facilities of Redhill, its fine situation . . .

We have had to change, modify or reduce our operations and techniques many times in the past to accommodate (appease) various factions, and the enforced use of radio on the spurious grounds of safety is but a minor, albeit expensive, hindrance. . . .

The judge, Mr Justice Mustill, deferred his judgement until the 22nd February, at which time he found against us. Quite how he arrived at such a decision is beyond me, an opinion shared by all I have spoken to.

However, there is no profit in looking back and it was in such a mood that the Committee meeting on the 28th February began to review the

Club's future. The 'one-off' call for financial help was approved, and if you haven't already renewed your subscription I do urge you to do so as soon as possible.

Naturally, we will continue to fly at Redhill as fully, and with as good a heart, as the circumstances permit. Since the new regulations we were opposing included the necessity of 720-channel radios, these are now being fitted initially to two biplanes and two Jodels, but these are very expensive and will take a little time to install. By the time you read this we'll no doubt be flying again. It was so that we covered the Club's direction in the short and medium term. Nor did we overlook the need for everyone's support for the forthcoming Summer Rally at Middle Wallop and hopefully the Autumn Air Display at Redhill.

In discussing the longer-term future the Committee was unanimous in agreeing that, although we still have some four years to run on the current Redhill lease – in spite of everything the place is still dear to us, – it would be more in keeping with our free spirit to seek a new home. One this time we can buy outright. Putting together a practical package is going to be quite a challenge . . . but one everybody felt would be hugely worthwhile. We agreed that no time should be wasted in commencing this project. These are early days yet, but with everybody's help – for instance you may know of a suitable site, or have valuable contacts – the idea will firm up and the Tiger Club will again be in the business of providing the sort of sporting flying that has become legend.

The support of the membership during this difficult period has been magnificent. My phone hasn't stopped ringing with offers for help. The unity within our Club set me thinking . . . how best can we recognise that huge potential of goodwill and ability? Last night I suggested the formulation of a system of voting for places on the Committee, and so induce everyone to feel that much closer and responsible for the running of our Club.

The Committee to date has perhaps been chosen in something of an autocratic manner, but the criteria of its membership have never varied. If we felt someone had something worthwhile to contribute then they were snatched in, and during the Club's long existence no one ever refused to serve! I'm sure the forthcoming elected members will continue that long tradition of unstinted service to our great Club.

The first 'fall-out' was that the planned 1984 air display had to be cancelled. We had already had discussions with the editor of the local paper – the *Surrey Mirror* – who was most anxious to co-operate with the project. In fact the aerodrome and the future plans of its owners were now receiving regular press coverage in the paper. In the circumstances we decided to issue the following Press release:

Although the Tiger Club has an agreement with Redhill Aerodrome Ltd to hold an annual air display until 1987, it has been decided with great regret not to stage the event in 1984 provisionally fixed for 16th September.

Despite the atrocious weather last year, the air show at Redhill was judged a great success, if not in financial terms, by participants and spectators alike, and a repeat display was planned for this year.

However, following a High Court ruling early this year enforcing new aerodrome regulations imposed by the aerodrome management and opposed by the Club, the Tiger Club is faced with a severe curtailment of its activities both in terms of membership and aircraft utilisation. In fact a number of its aircraft still remain grounded. It has also been made clear to the Club by the aerodrome management that some negotiations will in effect be required to obtain the necessary modifications to the new regulations to enable the Show to take place.

In light of these problems, a major sponsor has pulled out, and the Club at the present time is not able to provide the considerable and essential financial backing for a successful show to be staged.

The Club bitterly regrets this decision which, it feels, will be a great disappointment not only to its many members who voluntarily supply their time, energy and skill to the organisation of the show both on the ground and in the air, but also to thousands of potential spectators and local supporters.

However in the prevailing circumstances it is felt that the decision is a sensible one. Hopefully, if the 'climate' improves over the next few months and the full co-operation of the aerodrome management can be secured, it will be possible to hold the event in 1985, probably earlier in the summer.

The Aerodrome Consultative Committee, which represents not only the users of the aerodrome but also local authorities and conservation groups, was informed of this decision at its meeting last week and expressed its support for an Air Display at Redhill in 1985.

On the other hand, the Garden Party at Middle Wallop organised by Jonny Seccombe in perfect weather again went well although numbers were down on the previous year. A new feature was a breakfast patrol on the Sunday morning to that other huge grass airfield on Salisbury plain, Netheravon, where Charlie Shea-Simonds just happened to keep his newly-acquired Tiger.

Also by this time flying was slowly picking up at Redhill. The Turbulent team had started putting on displays again and were arriving and departing Redhill by cleverly using one hand-held radio between the three or four aircraft. There were now six Club aircraft fully operational, but with such a variety of different radios and installations that I thought it helpful to publish a suitably humorous article on their use in the *Rag* under the title "Mandatory Radio – the Lighter Side":

I am indebted for part of the title of this article to Geoffrey Tait's excellent little book *Redhill at War – the Lighter Side*. I hasten to explain that his book has nothing to do with recent difficulties but with some of the more amusing goings-on at the aerodrome between 1939 and 1945. The object of this particular exercise is to try and explain very briefly what radios we have now fitted and how we are going to live with them without losing our sense of humour.

For the technical aspects I am more than grateful to Paul Hill; Paul is our long-suffering member who is the expert on radio communications in light aircraft; his patient advice and a great deal of his spare time has been cheerfully and freely given over the last few months, not only to the task of installing radios in the Club aircraft but also to quite a few members who found that their aircraft were grounded on 22nd February.

To begin with, two Club Jodels have been fitted with the Narco Comm 120 and hopefully the third will follow soon. Bearing in mind that our Jodels are the only Club aircraft which have actually been designed to take radios, it was thought sensible to replace their previous and faithful Narco Mark 12s (360 channels) with the up-to-date 720-channel version. Although on the expensive side, they are excellent sets with no problems, and whoever designed them thoughtfully provided for a large and complete display of the six-figure digits now required in order to make them the more easily readable. Unfortunately, unlike the Mark 12, there is no integrated VOR capability so the aircraft concerned have lost the navigation aid, but these will be restored at some future date when funds permit. Incidentally, if anybody has a use for some second-hand Mark 12s and VORs, the Club has a number available for sale; they will probably fetch £25 to £30 compared with around £1,000 for their replacements: so much for enforced obsolescence!

The next radio in the popularity stakes seems to be the German-manufactured Walter Dittel FSG50 and this has been fitted to the Club Fournier. Affectionately known as the 'little Dittle' it is particularly suitable where space is a problem. The set has a 'liquid crystal' frequency display which disappears when it is switched off – a useful reminder to do this when leaving the aircraft since in the Fournier there is no battery master switch and no charging system. Another interesting feature is that you will know when the battery is on the way out if the frequency numbers flash off when you press the transmit button or flicker when the set is switched on. The set has one three-way switch, 'off, 'on' and 'squelch.' It works best in the 'squelch' position although for longer range but with more interference switch back to the 'on' position. Setting aside its long-term serviceability, which is an unknown factor, the main snag with the set is the fact that the liquid crystal numbers are difficult to read in conditions of strong sunlight. Also, although the size of the numbers is again not a problem, it is slightly irritating that only five numbers are actually shown. One is expected to know, for example, that 123·22 equals 123·225.

The Tiger we now have flying, G-ASKP, has been fitted by Geoff Masterton with the British-made Ash 720, which now supersedes the Ash 360, which in its turn was developed from the popular McMullin TM360. Incidentally the Club has two of these sets on lease and we have been promised 720-channel replacements for them 'shortly.' The Ash 720 is strongly built, suitable for rechargeable battery operation and has all the usual trimmings, including an intercom facility, which is, of course, essential in the Tiger. The 25 kc frequencies are selected by a switch marked ·025, so to dial 123·225 you set 123·20 and switch over. Apart from a tendency for occasional breakthrough between channels, the major snag of this set, which needless to say has been referred to the manufacturers, is that the intercom when fully turned up causes a deafening high-pitched whistle in your headphones. Therefore do not set the intercom too high. The equipment which takes the normal RAF jacks is also more sensitive to dirty plugs and faulty helmets than Arthur Tyrell's indestructible intercom boxes, so make sure that your jack plugs are cleaned and polished.

As for the two Stampes, we were fortunate that these aircraft were from time to time in the past fitted with radios for formation aerobatics. These sets, battery-operated and known as Pye Bantams, have now been pressed into permanent service and by a lucky chance were capable of being modified to take the single channel on 123·225. Obviously, since they are only single-channel and have no intercom, they will only be a stop-gap solution but, considering they were manufactured in the early 70s, so far they have proved remarkably reliable. However the lack of intercom is a real problem because it is necessary to unplug your headphones from the set and replug them into the intercom box using a different lead. Consequently intercom can only be used outside the air traffic zone when the radio can, mercifully, be switched off, but to do it easily does require a certain amount of dexterity and preparation in an open cockpit. . . .

Finally the Club has acquired one portable radio of what is known as the 'hand-held' variety. This is self-contained with its own internal battery, a plug for a normal helmet and microphone and a 'rubber duck' aerial. It has been used by the Turbulents and I believe that with the engine throttled back and with a reasonable degree of interpretation by the gentleman at the other end it has occasionally worked. However to operate the transmit button a 'third' hand is required and in a Turbulent on a gusty day its use is definitely not recommended on the final approach, and I regret that I still subscribe to the view of the CAA that certain 'hand-held' sets now on the market, however technically advanced and alluringly priced, are not suitable where there is a mandatory requirement for the use of radio, a point which is doubly important in Tiger Club aircraft which have to be flown rather than driven round the sky.

Next, a brief word on helmets and headsets. Broadly speaking, two types are in use: the telex type with boom microphone and twin jack plugs for the cabin aircraft, and the normal helmet and oxygen mask microphone for an open cockpit. In the latter case, if you dislike strapping a piece of rubber to your face, throat mikes are an alternative option. This equipment can be readily borrowed from the Club but, since its use is now obligatory, it is probably best to invest in your own, although unfortunately it is not cheap. One good reason for this is the simple one of hygiene; although we still have a neurosurgeon on the Club books, we are short of an ear, nose and throat specialist! Some other important points in this connection: first, it is sensible, especially in the open-cockpit aircraft, to check with the tower that the whole set-up – helmets, microphones, and radio – is working before you strap in and have the engine started. Secondly when you disconnect yourself after the flight, do not pull at the wire leads of the helmet or headset but do so by holding the plug, and in the Stampes do not pull out the aerial connection! And remember to *switch off* the radio.

Finally, now that the High Court has given its ruling and the prescriptions and advice of the CAA have to be complied with, it is probably worthwhile to conclude this article with some brief points on procedure. The radio licence is regrettably now an essential and if you haven't got one you will have to get it and it does cover most of the details; there are various organisations at Biggin Hill who will oblige for a small fee.

First, when you are ready to taxy, you must establish communication with Air Taffic Control – sorry, the Aerodrome Flight Information Service Officer – and request permission to taxy, at the same time giving the necessary information if you are landing away etc. (Incidentally the movements book has now been removed from the hangar office since it is now superfluous.)

Having received his reply, including the ritual information on QFE, QNH etc. and having commenced to taxy, may I remind you that it is still necessary to look where you are going, e.g. weaving the nose of the Tiger and Stampe is still an absolute must. Having reached the take-off point, it is normal to announce when you are ready for take-off and you will probably receive the reply: 'You may take off at your discretion.' What the precise meaning of this expression is or the importance you should attach to it would probably exercise the mind of a linguistic philosopher but under no circumstances does it excuse you from making absolutely certain that the approach is clear of a landing aircraft. When you leave the circuit, it is normal to make a call to say that you are doing so and then, if you wish, you may switch the radio off and that will certainly help to prolong the life of most of the batteries. On returning to the aerodrome, now that you are equipped with radio, it is a legal requirement that you call the tower before entering the ATZ. You will then be given the landing direction etc., and it's no use looking for the signal square because it has been removed. After a standard rejoin (please) you will then probably be asked to call 'downwind' and 'finals,' after which you will receive the 'land at your discretion' reply, which again does not excuse you from giving your undivided attention that it is clear for you to do so. After landing turn left off all runways except 26 where a right turn is now required. Technically you should then call the tower and request permission to taxy back to the hangar but in my experience this does not seem to be asked for.

This then briefly sums it all up. For more detail, please read the book of Aerodrome Regulations which is available in the Flight Office. So far things have gone relatively smoothly, and if you can endure the radio interference, the aerodrome is still an enjoyable place to fly. Admittedly things have been rather quiet of late. The helicopter training school has closed down, probably to most people's relief, although we have been informed that fixed-wing *ab initio* training is to start soon, which is certainly a turn-up for the books. The glider has departed for sunnier climes, the Formula I racers have left for radio-free fields and aeros over the aerodrome can no longer take place on Saturday afternoons, and even when they are permitted other aircraft are not allowed in the circuit, which slightly dampens everybody's enthusiasm. Certainly there have been no reports of our friends in the tower falling off their chairs with the excitement. However we are now at least considering the formidable task of fitting radios to the remaining eight Club aircraft which are languishing in the hangar. The Super Cub, which is completing a major overhaul, is next on the list.

Finally may I reiterate the words of our Senior Check Pilot in the last *Rag* that the Mark I eyeball is still the overriding order of the day if the false and dangerous sense of security which mandatory radio induces is to be avoided.

At the time I underestimated the contribution that Paul Hill would make to solving the problems of installing radios, not only to all the Club's aircraft but also to those belonging to members. Paul used to run Bristow's radio department and had been a Club member since 1970. It is no exaggeration to say that without his expert and untiring help the Club would have had the greatest difficulty, both financially and technically, in getting all its aircraft flying again at Redhill by the end of the year. Tragically he was killed in 1987 while aerobatting a Slingsby T.67 but his wife Angela and son Matthew remain two of the Club's staunchest supporters. Paul's help was just one example of the remarkable solidarity shown by very many members in solving the crisis. Countless letters were received, many of which were published in the *Rag*. One in particular came from James Baring:

"Dear Fellow Members,

You have no doubt been following with concern the latest developments in the difficulties besetting the Club in connection with the terms of our lease at Redhill and our relations with the landlords. It is, I am sure, clear to all of you that the Club stands now at a crisis point in its history. Many of you may have differing opinions as to how we have arrived at this point, what the reality of the present situation is, and what should be done next.

I would most strongly recommend that in these circumstances you should place the utmost confidence in, and give all your support to, our Chairman, Lewis Benjamin, and our Secretary & Manager, Michael Jones. I have known them both intimately since 1958, and over the past 25 years have shared many a hair-raising, complex and worrying situation with them – both in connection with the Club and in other matters.

The Club's problems are, as you must realise, a microcosm of wider problems which afflict the country and the world. It is vital for our survival that we exhibit patience, goodwill and unity, without which all will be lost. The Tiger Club is much more than a flying club. Even its charter and stated aims do not fully encompass our real identity, a legacy built on the generous vision of Norman Jones, and by members past and present. Any attempts to write the Club's history leaves those tempted to do so lost for words or reduced to uncontrollable laughter – or tears.

We are going to go through a very sticky patch, and each one of you will have to make up your own mind what the Club means to you. Without being melodramatic, it is true to say that there are many powerful, ruthless, misguided and even malevolent forces stalking the stage these days. There are many who would rejoice at the demise of our association, and will exploit any disunity in our ranks to bring this about. On the other hand, we have many friends. Our enemies can be found on the right, on the left, at home and abroad, in all walks of life, at all levels. So it is with our friends.

So let the cynics, the self-interested, the bored and those who don't understand what the hell I am talking about depart without further ado. The rest of you, please write to Michael or Benjy with your ideas, your hopes and fears, your subscriptions (if not already paid) and your donations to the Legal fund if you feel so inclined.

James Baring,
St. Remy en Provence, France."

In fact, by the time the Committee met in July, the crisis was virtually over. True, there had been 100 resignations and nearly 200 responses were still awaited, but over 500 members had renewed, many with donations in addition to the levy. Two members I was relieved had not renewed their membership were George Fry and Dick Millward! One member we had been sorry to lose was a Conservative MP, John

Wilkinson. An ex-RAF pilot, he had been a keen Club flyer in the past, displaying both the Stampe and the Beta. Who knows? Maybe he did not consider that his continued membership of the Club would advance his political career . . .

Talking of politics, my wife Norvela lost her seat in the June elections for the European Parliament where she was representing a Birmingham constituency. It was highly marginal and she was expecting to lose. In a way I was sorry, because on quite a few social occasions I enjoyed meeting her colleagues, who were usually on the left wing of the Conservative party. But in fact I think that she was quite relieved because it meant that she now had more time to run the consultancy business as well as listening to my worries. I spent a few enjoyable days canvassing for her in Birmingham and arranged for Brian Bateson, who came from Blackpool and had pioneered the re-introduction of aerial advertising in Britain, to tow a banner in her support.

The Club, so to speak, still had one representative in the European Parliament, our founder member Peter Vanneck, who had managed to hang on to his seat in the north-east of England. Anyway, by the time August came round Norvela and I decided to take a sailing holiday on *Mowgli*, and after Tom Freer had helped us to get the boat down to Falmouth, we spent two weeks cruising in south-west Ireland. It was a welcome break.

One event which took place while we were away was a reunion of some of Redhill Aerodrome's pioneers organised by Geoff Tait, the airfield's enthusiastic historian. His book on the wartime history had already been published and the reunion was to celebrate the opening of an exhibition at the East Surrey museum. Benjy of course was there, as well as Geoffrey Last who had selected the site from his Gipsy Moth based at Croydon; so was Diana Barnato Walker. The main participants were Graham Douglas and his former wife Anne Welch, now a Vice-President of the FAI and author of several books on gliding and microlights.

Graham Douglas had bought the site, started the original Redhill Flying Club and had run the airfield during the war. It was said that if the Surrey Gliding Club had not been removed from the field after the war, Lasham would never have started. Mr Douglas had granted our original lease in 1959 and had offered the freehold to Norman Jones before it was bought by the Cayzer family in 1968. In retrospect, we were now truly paying the price for that missed opportunity . . . We used to have occasional spats with Graham Douglas and his airfield manager, Stanley Kerridge, including one serious dispute over landing fees, but I always felt that they both respected and appreciated the Club's achievements.

To complete the story we were sent a cutting published in *Popular Flying* in 1932, and also I looked up an extract from a 1959 Club newsletter:

TOP: Middle Wallop Garden party 1982: Brendan O'Brien with very senior member David Phillips. Photo: Lewis Benjamin.
BOTTOM: Watching themselves on video: Ian White, Mike Cowburn, David Keene and Neil Thomason in the hangar 'office,' with members' board in the background. Photo: Author's collection.

The gathering with Redhill's pioneers to celebrate the launching of Geoff Tait's book *Redhill At War: The Lighter Side.*

162

TOP: Fun and games at the 1984 Tiger Ball with our Chairman, Lewis Benjamin, and Prince Andrew.
BOTTOM: Succeeding Chairman Neil Jensen, on his feet at the 1986 Tiger Ball.

TOP: Prince Bernhard of the Netherlands with Benjy at the 1985 Tiger Ball. BOTTOM: The author with Founder Member and Chairman of the Royal Aero Club Bev Snook on the occasion of the 1985 Redhill Air Show. Photo: Lewis Benjamin.

A NEW AERODROME FOR LONDON

The chain of aerodromes round London, situated outside the area where fog is most prevalent, will be greatly strengthened by the addition of one lying two miles from Redhill and south of those hills which are an obstruction to aircraft when approaching London and flying under the clouds in conditions of bad visibility.

The application to develop the land for the purpose of an aerodrome was opposed by the Rural District Council of Godstone but, on appeal to the Ministry of Health, it has been decided that the aerodrome scheme may proceed subject, of course, to detailed plans being approved by the authorities concerned.

A Public Inquiry was conducted by an inspector from the Ministry of Health, evidence being taken from the local Council, the owner of the estate, the neighbouring residents, Mr G.C.H. Last, managing director of British Air Transport and the prime mover in the scheme, together with that from experts in aviation matters, including Sir Alan Cobham and Major R. H. Mayo.

It is hoped to have the aerodrome ready for use by the late spring or early summer of next year. When completed, an area of more than 100 acres will be available, giving landing runs in every direction of at least 700 yards.

Although we thought that we had publicised the matter fairly well, it does not seem to be generally realised that the TIGER CLUB now operates from REDHILL AERODROME, Surrey and its aircraft are available at that spot on all seven days of the week.

Ever since the Club came into being nearly four years ago it has been looking for a home airfield of its own, one that is outside the London Control Zone, one at which flying can be carried out with the maximum freedom that can be had in these restricted times, and one at which our fleet of 16 aircraft can be utilised to the full. To all intents and purposes this want has now been satisfied and we are now all set to go ahead with our training programme for next year's displays. . . .

We now had to set to work in earnest to produce the necessary changes in the Club Rules to allow the Committee, including the Chairman and Vice-Chairman, to be democratically elected. Already there had been some changes; Don Lovell had come back to take over foreign touring again following Wynn Evans' death from illness. Poppy Body had replaced Margaret Burgess to look after the Clubroom catering and Bob Grimstead was now representing displays, in particular the Turbulent team, instead of Neil Thomason. There was a vacancy for the *Tiger Rag* because Charlie Shea-Simonds had decided that three years was enough; he was out of touch, he said, and now that he had his own Tiger he was not going to incur the expense of fitting a 720-channel radio just to visit one airfield. In the meantime, until another volunteer could be found, the *Rag* was being produced from the Redhill office.

David Hamilton produced the first rules draft, and after some discussion with him and others a second draft was typed up and circulated to the existing Committee acting in a steering capacity. In fact the procedures for the election followed normal Club practice, with maximum and minimum numbers to represent both flying and non-flying (associate) members carefully defined. The relationship between the proprietors of the Club, the limited company and its directors with the Club was spelt out, together with the number of *ex officio* and co-opted members who could be appointed to the Committee from that source. The Chairman and Vice-Chairman would be elected by the Committee at its first meeting following its own election, and there was a rule that the Chairman would not hold office for more than three years without a break.

The precise powers of the Committee were set out and there were new rules providing for the expulsion of members and the use of Club premises; these had been lacking from the previous constitution. Finally the aims of the Club were updated to include touring as a specific objective, and a fourth principal aim was added, which was "to co-operate with other organisations working in the field of general aviation and sporting flying."

After a few helpful comments and some minor amendments, the Committee agreed the changes. The only serious objection came from Neil Jensen, who thought that things should be left as they were with a 'benevolent dictatorship,' Benjy should be persuaded to carry on as Chairman, and why should we appease a small minority of malcontents within the Club? Probably he also subscribed to the view:

"On forms of government, let fools contest
Whate'er is best administered is best."

But having already announced to the membership that changes would be made there was no going back. Consequently in October the Chairman circulated the following historic letter to members:

"Following my letter to you earlier this year after the outcome of the High Court action and subsequent announcements in the Tiger Rag, *the existing Committee acting in a steering capacity has now finalised a new constitution including procedures for elections to the Committee.*

These changes have been incorporated into revised Club Rules and a copy of these is enclosed herewith. They will come into effect immediately.

The constitution of the Committee and procedures for election are covered in paragraph V. If you wish to stand for election, please study this carefully. The date of the postal ballot has been fixed for 11th December, so nominations must be received by the Secretary not later than 11th November.

The remainder of this document to a large extent reflects existing Club Rules and Regulations but there are a number of essential additions and changes, so if you are considering offering your services to administer the Club – and I do hope many will – please do read the whole document.

It is recognised that this development is a small but important step in the history of the Club and to some extent is a leap in the dark. However, I remain firmly convinced that these changes are vital and necessary in order that we may all face and secure our long-term future with confidence."

In fact, in the way that these things turn out, an election never did take place because, although nine nominations were duly received, they were only sufficient to fill the required vacancies. Most of the existing Committee carried on as either elected unopposed or as *ex officio* or as co-opted. The new Committee would be the same size as the old. There were four new faces: David Body came back to be responsible for the Garden Party instead of Jonny Seccombe and also to replace John Harper in representing aerobatics; Dennis Hartas, one of our real 'golden oldies' who had joined the Club in 1957, returned to represent air racing, particularly the handicap variety; Harvey Tring, a new and very keen member came in to take over from Ken Smith who was standing down from the job of looking after the Clubroom and film shows; and Martin Evans, another comparatively new member, was co-opted to the editorship of the *Tiger Rag*, mainly because he had access to the necessary production facilities.

Meanwhile, back at the aerodrome, the predicted planning application had been made to develop the airfield; new airport-type buildings and a concrete runway were proposed. The Committee had already minuted that the Club, if asked, would oppose the hard runway as detrimental to our interests; but there was no way that we would either take the lead in or help to finance any official campaign. Another development had been the arrival of a flying training organisation from Biggin Hill with Cessna 150s and operating under the name of the reborn Redhill Flying Club. Although rumoured, it was still a surprise, because we had always been told in the past that *ab initio* training could not be allowed because of the aerodrome's proximity to Gatwick.

With all this going on, the *Rag* was now publishing a regular column under the heading 'Aerodrome News':

The Tandridge District Council at its Planning Committee meeting on 18th December turned down the application for the concrete runway but gave the go-ahead for the terminal building, new control tower, offices etc. – a slightly strange outcome which seems rather like giving a theatre company permission to stage *Hamlet* without the Prince of Denmark. Presumably British & Commonwealth will now appeal against this decision and the matter will be referred to the civil servants in the Departments of Transport and the Environment and probably also their political bosses. Whereupon, no doubt, democracy will be seen to move in its mysterious way, its wonders to perform. Presumably also a Public Inquiry is on the cards, but in the meantime it will be interesting to see whether the new buildings will be started without the runway.

In the midst of all this excitement, no doubt in an effort to be seen to be doing something, the aerodrome management moved the windsock from its time-honoured place where it could be seen from every approach to all landing and take-off directions to a new position opposite the control tower where it was immediately invisible to aircraft using the prevailing east-west runway. Representations having been duly made through the appropriate channels, it has now been moved to yet another position on the NE side of the field, and at the time of going to press that is where to look for it.

New ordinances recently added to the aerodrome regulations are: first, charges of an indeterminate sum for any landing made a minute or so after the aerodrome is officially closed, and second, the limited amount of night-flying the Club was officially allowed to do during the winter using its own goose-necks has now been effectively stopped by a charge of £25 per hour for the 'services' of 'air traffic control.' So members wishing to keep their night ratings current on Club aircraft have a problem.

The regular 'Club News' feature in the *Rag* was getting back to normal:

Under the enthusiastic guidance of Poppy Body, renovations have recently been carried out to the kitchen area of the Clubroom at the back of the hangar; these include a new sink unit, some new cupboards and now, thanks to Harvey Tring, a permanent supply of hot water. Quite how Harvey managed to arrange this we don't know but, as someone remarked recently, when Harvey is around we mere mortals had best keep quiet. We've also got a new carpet so, all in all, things will be more comfortable during what could be a long winter. Incidentally, many of these improvements have been financed by some welcome profits that Poppy has been able to generate from the catering ably provided by willing volunteers.

On the aircraft side, the Super Cub is now flying again after a long-overdue overhaul. It has been on one glider-towing expedition and the Club's syndicate glider has put in a welcome reappearance at Redhill using a portable radio. The Cub has been much in demand for visits to adjacent strips which seem to be springing up in greater abundance now that members are actively concerning themselves with alternative flying grounds. One in particular has emerged the other side of Merstham named Downlands – phone Chris Donne for details.

David Shepherd has found a pair of floats in Switzerland made to measure for the Cub, which he delivered to the hangar recently. It is planned to operate the Cub on floats for a limited period next summer. Members who are interested in float-plane flying are urged to contact Tom Freer in order that the demand can be assessed. The Committee at its last meeting expressed reservations about the wisdom and economics of this new seaplane project but they felt that encouragement should be given as far as possible to what has been part of the Club's activities for as long as most of us can remember, and the Cub should be somewhat more practical than the Tiger.

The three-seat Jodel, 'TLB, has at last received its new radio and this now brings the Jodel trio up to strength for touring. Stampe 'WEF has been retired for a C of A and its dual controls are being replaced. Finally, the Fournier has recently completed a C of A to allow it to operate a few more weeks until the aerodrome gets too boggy or frozen for its rather delicate undercarriage.

As far as new flying sites are concerned, there is still nothing definite. As already mentioned, a number of landing strips are on offer but the Club needs a little more than the average farm strip. However, we have recently received a list of 10 former grass airfields in Sussex, which at the end of the war each accommodated on average 90 Spitfires and Mustangs, and there were probably a similar number in Kent. All will be investigated to see if the owners, not to mention the planners, might be sympathetic. The challenge is being taken up but we will have to be patient.

The Downlands strip was also pressed into service as the venue for the 1984 Hamilton Trophy. I had discussed this with David and we were tired of trying to negotiate with Mr Dalrymple. It was a risky and slightly worrying decision but the Club needed a boost to its morale, and a little extra adrenalin flowing at Downlands would provide it:

Unfortunately, the aerodrome management refused to modify radio procedures to allow the annual Hamilton Trophy to take place as planned at Redhill. Consequently the contest was moved to the Downlands airstrip and was run in a somewhat revised form on 15th December.

The flour bombing and balloon bursting had to be dropped and a simple spot landing with power according to precision flying rules took place instead under contest director David Hamilton. 'Simple' is perhaps not quite the right word because the landing had to be made into quite a short and narrow strip and over some 100-foot-high trees. Therefore the emphasis was rather more on precision rather than a pure glide landing. The entries on this first occasion were restricted to Tiger, Stampe and Super Cub, but for some unaccountable reason the engine on the Cub decided at this particular time to play up (the fault was later discovered to be due to a loose exhaust box baffle), and so those pilots who had been assiduously practising on the Cub suddenly found themselves flying the Tiger or Stampe instead. Three full-stop landings had to be made (overshoots were ruled out) and penalty points were incurred in proportion to the number of metres one undershot or overshot the spot (higher penalties for undershooting).

After 11 pilots had flown three circuits each, it was found that Marcus Norman (Stampe) and Jim Alderton (Tiger) had tied for first place. A fly-off was then agreed with pilots swapping aeroplanes and with added penalties for every second in excess of a 1 min 30 sec timed circuit, after which Marcus emerged a narrow winner.

The competition was considered to be a great success and very enjoyable; Chris Donne and Harvey Tring organised an excellent barbecue and raised some cash for the legal fund into the bargain, and our thanks are due to 'Mac,' the owner of the strip, for his co-operation. It should be possible to organise similar events in the future and a modest aerobatic competition (Stampes only) is planned tentatively for the spring.

One distinct advantage is that, while the strip is only a few minutes flying time away from Redhill, it is outside the restrictions of Gatwick's airspace and so more height is available. It is also very well drained. On the other hand, flying into strips is an art with which not everybody is familiar and Downlands, flanked as it is on three sides by tall trees and on a fairly narrow ridge, could present problems. A look-see on the ground is still essential, and preferably get yourself checked into and out of the strip as well.

RESULTS

1. Marcus Norman	210*
2. Jim Alderton	210
3. Dave Keene	228
4. Phil Bolderson	293
5. Mike Dentith	306
6. Bill Browning	312
7. Brian Tapp	513
8=. Dave Body	585
8=. Howard Rose	585
10. Mark Ramsey	736
11. Martin Evans	886

* Winner after fly-off

By the end of the year we could look back and almost say that it was 'business as usual.' The Dawn-to-Dusk competition had produced a record entry and Prince Philip had again hosted the prize-giving and reception at the Royal Aeronautical Society. There had been a fall-off in entries by the Club Stampes in the national aerobatic contests, but this was due more to the fact that the experts had moved onto more advanced machinery, and although the performance of the British team in the World Championships had been disappointing, Pete Kynsey had carried off the National Championships.

The Formula 1 season had gone well although the Beta had not taken part due to a low priority as far as radio was concerned. All the other normal Club activities had taken place, albeit on a slightly reduced scale.

Inevitably, with half the aircraft grounded for most of the year, flying hours were well down. 'Almost' but not quite – Mr Justice Mustill had suspected that 'it will only be a few who will give up membership' (as a result of his decision). But at the end of the year we had lost more than a third of our existing members.

At one extreme there was a minority of people who would probably have cheerfully stood on their heads before flying a Tiger or Stampe if a High Court judge had ordered them to do so. On the other hand, there was a much larger minority for whom there was a limit to the price they would pay to indulge in their chosen hobby, a price that could be measured both in terms of cost and enjoyment. As one member put it: "the pain of flying at Redhill now exceeds the pleasure."

However there was another potential crisis episode now looming in the Redhill Saga, which was the rent review proceedings that were due to take place in 1985. . . .

CHAPTER 9

1985

The Committee duly met in January to elect the Club's new Chairman and Vice-Chairman. Neil Jensen was elected unopposed as Chairman and Don Lovell as Vice-Chairman after a vote. Also by this time Neil had accepted an invitation to become a director of the Tiger Club Ltd, as had Benjy and Tom Storey. Don Lovell had been a member of the Club since 1961 and had won the early Dawn-to-Dusk competitions twice flying his own Turbulent. He had already rejoined the Committee to run the overseas touring department, and of course his wife Tessa was still coping with all the paperwork in connection with the membership as well as organising a very successful bring-and-buy sale in the hangar to raise money for the hospitality fund.

Neil and Don, who had both been RAF-trained, and who both lived close to the aerodrome, came, so to speak, from the private owners' wing of the Club. Besides his Jungmann, Neil had owned at various times vintage Miles and Percival aircraft and Don was a Jodel enthusiast. Neil was also widely respected in the Club for his enthusiasm for aerobatics and formation flying. Much to my relief, he readily accepted the task of trying to deal with Mr Dalrymple, not only on the Aerodrome Users Committee which we had now reluctantly rejoined, but also in the vital matter of the 1985 Air Show for which plenty of delicate negotiations would be required. He soon wrote to John Dalrymple:

"I explained to you when I saw you the other day that I have been elected Chairman of the Tiger Club and I have chosen to make the holding of a regular air show one of my main objectives. It is something that the Club does well, even when the weather tries to interfere as it did in 1983, and I believe it to be a function that benefits the aerodrome as a whole and is good PR with the local residents. . . .

If I may end on a personal note, I believe there could be no better way for the Tiger Club and Redhill Aerodrome Ltd to demonstrate the will to co-operate amicably with each other (which incidentally is another of my aims) than for us to work together to ensure the success of a 1985 Tiger Club Air Show. So let us do just that. It has got to be to our mutual advantage."

Benjy as the outgoing Chairman presided at the February Tiger Ball. He had not offered himself for election. He had served the Club continuously as Chairman and Vice-Chairman since 1971 and the Committee unanimously voted him Honorary Membership. Later in the year a Committee Dinner was held in his honour as a token of the Club's gratitude and appreciation.

The Ball had already been a sell-out well before the due date. Brendan was again the popular compère and another substantial sum was raised for the Legal Fund. Our guest of honour was another 'Royal,' Prince Bernhard of the Netherlands, who proved to be a delightful and charming guest. He had flown over from Holland for the occasion and was staying up the road from Gatwick with Diana Barnato Walker.

"That will save you a hotel bill!" he cheerfully told Benjy.

In January there was serious damage to Tiger G-ASKP following an engine failure on take-off. It was the first such accident to a Club aircraft on the aerodrome that I could remember and it was reported in the *Rag*:

What lessons can be learnt from this sorry affair? The pilot escaped with only very minor injuries but the aircraft is in a terrible mess. The radio and some of the screened ignition harness survived and this has now been installed into G-ACDC which is now filling the breach. In the manner born, G-ASKP will be rebuilt again in a long due course. The purists will know that it is actually an older aircraft than 'CDC.

The event was witnessed by many and the pilot's report confirms the salient facts: it was a freezing, cloudy morning with a warm front approaching, very cold surface air and frozen ground. There were flurries of snow. The aircraft had flown half an hour before without trace of engine trouble. It was observed to taxy out and take off normally going east on a shortened runway. At approximately 50 to 60 feet the engine failed and the nose was lowered immediately to land, probably successfully, in the runway overshoot. At what appeared to be the point of round-out the aircraft climbed again and a turn was initiated to starboard. The engine then failed again and the inevitable stall and nosedive to the ground ensued from about 50 feet, narrowly missing the blister hangar on the SE corner of the airfield.

The technical causes of the engine failure have not been established with absolute certainty. One theory supported by some evidence is that it was a freak and unheard-of case of carburettor icing and, as a result, modifications to the heating of the induction pipes of the other Club Gipsy engines have been made. It's easy to be critical of the decision to turn; but it's easier to criticize the decision to continue the take-off. The answer, as we know – and as the pilot would probably admit – would be at the first sign of trouble, having first lowered the nose, to cut the switches, turn off the fuel and close the throttle, and take one's chance of rumbling gently into the far hedge. However, these decisions and actions in the critical half-seconds in which they have to be made are not necessarily instinctive or automatic. The real lesson must be constant awareness of likely disaster. There is a lot of truth in an old flying saying: 'You should be surprised if the engine keeps going – not if it fails!'

Early in 1985 the arbitration proceedings in connection with the rent reviews came to a head. Graham Plumbe and his assistant Chris Dawson had already done a great deal of work on the case but the landlords had been pressing for an immediate and formal hearing and it could now be delayed no longer; in fact, the hearing had originally been fixed for November 1984, but Graham had been ill and it was postponed to February 1985. The issues were highly technical and very complex, involving planning, the Club's finances, comparables, our covenants and everything else besides. Early on Graham volunteered to handle our case before the arbitrator both as advocate and expert witness. The landlords, in addition to their own surveyor, had instructed a firm of City solicitors and a barrister.

The Arbitrator appointed by the Royal Institution of Chartered Surveyors was a Mr James Baker. Graham's decision was brave, but was one which I very happpily accepted, not only from the point of view of our own costs – I could hardly expect the Legal Fund to come to the rescue again – but also by this time I was becoming fed up with lawyers! Also I had absolute confidence in Graham; he had saved the Club from financial ruin during the renewal of our lease in 1975 and he was now highly knowledgeable on all the legal aspects of rent reviews. Furthermore I had a feeling that we might stand a reasonable chance in a formal hearing in front of a 'judge' who was neither appointed by nor paid by the Government!

In the run up to the hearing the landlords had been persuaded to reduce their demand for the 1979 review to £15,000 but maintained their figure of £19,000 for 1983. Both sums were miles above the rate of inflation and, of course, both would be backdated.

It was now time to write what are called Calderbank letters; these are sealed offers to be opened by the Arbitrator only after his award, to be used by him to determine how the costs of the case, including his own, would be apportioned between the parties. The hearing lasted several days and Graham decided to inject some passion into his arguments and question the landlords' motives, an approach which had been conspicuously lacking in the High Court case. He sent me a draft of what would be some of his final points to Mr Baker:

At this point in time you may be wondering why the landlords have:
1. *Effectively tried to deny a new lease without compensation in 1975.*
2. *Taken four years to issue a draft lease.*
3. *Issued unsustainable writs for forfeiture and breach of covenant.*
4. *Introduced quite unnecessary AFIS.*
5. *Employed two men effectively to supervise grass cutting.*
6. *Indulged in massive court hearings over matters which must be trivial to the landlords, given the* status quo.

7. *Promised certain rent levels and trebled them as soon as they have a signed lease; rents which are peanuts to British & Commonwealth, but which would be crippling for the tenant.*
8. *In the context of this arbitration, employed big guns legally and demanded a formal hearing.*
9. *Disputed judgements handed down by a court of law.*
10. *Made totally misleading statements in evidence.*
11. *Obstructed every attempt of mine to introduce evidence, including:*
   (a) a huge song and dance about trading accounts
   (b) denial of all but the barest of information concerning airfield costs, and
   (c) delivery of airfield movement logs seconds before the counter-submission date and covering a useless two months' winter period only.
12. *Denied to the tenant the right of tuition for 28 years and then opened up a rival club offering just that facility.*

The landlord's motives in all this must be a matter of speculation. . . .

In short, the landlords have a clear intention to develop the airfield and the introduction of regulations is but a step in this direction; the Tiger Club does not fit into this picture and the landlords' case, I am sorry to say, does seem to me to be laced with hypocrisy and vindictiveness.

To cut a very long story short, on 1st July Mr Baker awarded a rent of £4,700 for 1979 and £10,000 for 1983, together with reasonable awards in connection with members' block landing fees for their own aircraft which were less controversial.

The landlords did not appeal and later in the year, after they had requested another formal hearing on the subject of costs, Mr Baker decided that they should pay five-sixths of his costs and two-thirds of our own. Our sealed offers had been much closer to his decision than theirs. I later learnt that the landlords' own costs had come to a staggering figure of £49,500. Since they did not appeal, I assumed that they did not have a bottomless pocket for legal fees, or maybe their shareholders were complaining.

Thanks to Graham's efforts, another catastrophe for the Club – and for me personally – had been averted and another episode in the Redhill Saga was over.

By now the Tiger Rag was getting back to normal and other interesting Club news was appearing apart from the situation on the aerodrome:

It may be the imagination, but the weather this spring has seemed particularly rotten for flying. In April the airfield was deemed unusable for several days which, I think, is without precedent, and just about every Sunday we seem to have been plagued with low ceilings and general gloom. Three aerobatic competitions have already fallen victim to the weather, and at the traditional spring event at Little Snoring for the McAully icy squalls of more than usual Norfolk ferocity made any type of flying an extremely risky business; congratulations are due to the pilots of the Club Fournier and Stampe for extricating the aircraft from the airfield without mishap and thanks also to the local farmer who allowed the aircraft to use a newly-sown field for an into wind take-off.

The proposed new Stampe Trophy at Downlands, having been cancelled once because of the weather, was rescheduled three weeks later only to be cancelled again; in the interim the owner of the strip had received a visit from the friendly local planning officer and decided that an aerobatic competition might be unnecessarily provocative.

Despite these set-backs enthusiasm for aerobatics at the Standard level has never been higher and there has been a record number of members entering on the faithful Stampes.

Utilisation of the Club aircraft has no doubt also suffered as a result of the weather and is now only painfully edging past last year's all time low; whether we shall ever get back to the pre-radio levels of a couple of years ago, which were modest enough, remains doubtful. There is still no news of the search for an alternative site but preliminary negotiations have been started on one possibility. All the aircraft with the exception of the Turbulents have now been fitted with some sort of permanent radio installation. The last to be fitted and to be flown is Tiger 'OAA, which at the same time is being converted to dual control with standard centre-section tank. Although purists will regret the passing of the Super Tiger it is essential that we have a back-up for 'CDC, and the performance of 'OAA will still be very much better than that of a standard Tiger. . . .

The recent Awards Ceremony of the Royal Aero Club was attended by Her Majesty The Queen accompanied by Prince Philip. It was a prestigious gathering presided over by Bev Snook and organised with military precision by Fred Marsh. All branches of sporting aviation were represented, with a strong contingent from the Club. Our congratulations to Benjy for the award of a Bronze Medal, and also to Pete Kynsey and David Timmis, who collected the premier trophies for aerobatics and precision flying respectively.

The Queen is the Patron of the Royal Aero Club and, as Bev pointed out in his speech of welcome, her attendance at this annual function personally to make the awards was an outstanding honour to the whole of the sporting aviation movement and a great encouragement to us all. Both she and Prince Philip chatted to a great many people at the reception including Club representatives, and they both had some highly interesting comments to make.

Peter Jarvis has decided to stand down from his position on the Committee as Senior Check Pilot. He has explained that his weekends will now be fully committed to Ray Hannah's display team, flying the Spitfire, Mustang and other 'warbirds'! The Committee and Directors of the Club have enviously agreed that they should not stand in the way of this decision and have invited Brian Smith to step back into his old job. Brian will continue to be assisted by Jim Alderton, who has been fairly busy recently introducing new members to the Tiger and the rather complicated flying situation at Redhill.

Assisting Jim Alderton was another local member, Derek Wright. Derek had a small farm down the road from the airfield where he offered parking space for the Club syndicate glider in its trailer. He could always be relied on to turn up at short notice during the week to carry out familiarisation flying with a new member as well as the normal check flights. He also had a part share in a Bolkow Junior based in the hangar and had agreed to stand in for Neil on the Aerodrome Sub-Committee. Even more invaluable, he had a trailer converted from a caravan chassis which was used on many occasions both by the Club and various members to transport dismantled or broken aircraft.

The *Rag* was also featuring a message from Neil on the subject of the Air Show which had been fixed for the 1st September:

Tub-thumping does not come naturally to me and, whilst I hesitate to adopt this stance on the first occasion that I address you as your new Chairman, the importance to the Tiger Club of the forthcoming Air Show at Redhill calls for something along these lines.

There are a number of reasons for staging an event such as this. Firstly, it is something that, without being arrogant, we believe we do as well as anyone else. So it is something in which we can justly take pride.

There is also the pleasure of working together to make a success of such a high point in our calendar. Of course many of the jobs to be done are far from glamorous, but it is only by creating a cohesive team (I hope that is not a contradiction of terms in the context of the Tiger Club!) that we can expect the day to be a success. And this leads to one of the most important reasons for organising an air show. The beleaguered Club finances would so welcome an injection of funds that would enable us to look to the future with greater confidence – a future that might even involve owning our own field.

Planning for the 1st September is now well advanced with Jeanne Frazer again assuming the responsibilities of Display Organiser and Brian Smith the organisation of the flying programme. Without giving away any secrets, I think I can say that he is putting together an interesting display.

But, and here comes the tub-thumping, we need your help, both in the build-up to the 1st September and on the day, when there will be a myriad of jobs . .

Another forthcoming attraction was the re-emergence of the seaplane section. David Shepherd had located a pair of floats for a Super Cub and had been all the way to Switzerland to fetch them; he now generously offered them to the Club. They were first fitted to 'VPT in the hangar and then, in order to obtain the Certificate of Airworthiness (the word 'seaworthiness' is not used in this context) they had been tested on Norman's lake, Castle Water near Rye. The Committee agreed to the operation on floats subject to a minimum utilisation being achieved, because there was only one Super Cub, which was required for other flying including glider-towing. Tom Freer wrote in the *Rag*:

Our seaplaning programme is therefore based on the philosophy of a short but intensive season. The operating base will be Scotney Court, near Lydd; and the purpose will be to enable as many pilots as possible to have the opportunity to fly a seaplane, and, if they wish, obtain a seaplane licence.

To organise this type of intensive programme we need to know in advance who is likely to want to fly the seaplane . . . how many hours they intend to do . . . in fact we must be in a position to say what total hours we expect to achieve. . . .

Eventually 72 hours were achieved and the Super Cub on floats was flown by 37 members. However one major problem emerged. The CAA required the Scotney Court gravel pit lake to be licensed if instruction for a seaplane rating was to be undertaken, something which had not been necessary in the past. People with existing ratings, including many which had been issued in the USA, were not affected. To obtain the necessary 'aerodrome licence' would be a major undertaking and it was postponed until the following year.

Although the *Tiger Rag* was now adopting a slightly more serious tone than in the past, the occasional light-hearted article was sent in by members for publication. One arrived from Maxi Gainza; Maxi was an *emigré* from Argentina who had settled in London with his family to study for various esoteric University degrees: one, I remember him telling me, was medieval English literature. Later he became a regular contributor to *Pilot* magazine. This article was entitled *Confessions:*

This happened a very long time ago so don't be alarmed: I have since reformed!

It was a grotty January afternoon at Redhill when even Smithy stayed on the ground. Not that I was any keener than our boy ace to fly under a thousand-foot overcast of strato-cus; but unlike him I had a visitor to impress – my brother-in-law from Argentina who, as usual, was full of horror stories about flying in the pampas, in which he, a low-houred private pilot like myself, acquitted himself far too well for my ego. I had no choice but to strap him into old 'TKC and take off into the drizzle blowing in from the west.

But not just for a few bumps around the circuit. I had a far better idea. Well, if glider pilots could do it – or was it pigeons? – so could I. In fact, I knew I could take a Stampe through cloud, thanks to a memorable escapade with Brendan the day his seat belts came undone halfway through a slow roll. But that's another story and, needless to say, Wonder Boy is still with us, thank God and very much reformed, too!

In any event, once airborne I set course on a steady climb due east, and putting on a clipped English accent for period effect I informed my Argentine compatriot up front that we were going on top, no need to flap, old chap, piece of cake, really. . . .

And so it was. A few tense minutes later, eyes glued to the compass and the turn-and-bank indicator, the enveloping milkiness grew brighter; there was a flash of blue above me and suddenly we were punching through rose-tinted cloud-tops and slowly rising over a vast, empty sea of bundled mohair into clear sky. Twisting my head round I saw the twin trail of inward-curling spirals whipped up by our wings as we climbed out of those vapoury depths.

I poled the Stampe around 180 degrees and slow-rolled it straight into the westering sun, then half-rolled again and let it drop inverted, stomach butterflies a-flutter, until we were skimming the cloud-tops and occasionally ripping through them in heart-stopping flashes of golden light. We turned back due east, mindful of holding our position relative to the ground, and tail-chased our shadow over tumbling valleys and twisting ravines and billowing slopes, all the while yahooing into our masks and thinking "this is the life."

Sunset was soon upon us, though, and it was with great reluctance and hardly any sense of urgency that I turned my mind to the task of getting us back home. Redhill, I reckoned, couldn't be more than five minutes away, so I would be down before the sun sank in the horizon. What I didn't know was that by then it would be well past sunset on the ground; that indeed it was already getting dark under that pastel-coloured blanket of cloud.

I let down on a northerly heading, and again, after some tense minutes watching the altimeter wind down to 800 feet, Marcelo called out that he could see . . . a wide river beneath us! Yes, so could I, all through streaming rain, plus no end of shipping and floodlit docks and red-eyed chimney stacks and aerials, and far off on our port beam, the odd million lights turning on in the deepening gloom, beckoning Londoners home to tea.

In a flash I had reversed course and reached out for the nav. chart, but it was already too dark to map-read. Now you may say that any self-respecting Tiger Club member can find Redhill from anywhere within a 50-mile radius – especially aboard 'TKC. But I was still a newcomer to these shores, and as for

Marcelo, all he could he offer was moral support – which, bless his soul, he did, prattling away inanely about how magic and *déjà vu* it all was; the wind in the wires, rainy London sliding beneath us, sweet Thames running softly, and how about picking a field before night closed in on us?

They all seemed uncomfortably small and square, except for one longish strip of grass at the edge of a wood and cut at both ends by more trees. I circled low over the field once – not that I could make out much detail in that failing light – and slipped-spiralled in to land.

It was only a 'precautionary' landing, but in my book it rated as a full emergency. Hence my priorities: first and foremost, *survive*. Second (having skimmed the trees and secured the field), *walk out of it*. Third (an overgrown ditch suddenly materialising in the middle of the field in line with my approach and the plane now sinking fast), *remember Michael!*

I gunned the throttle to counteract the sink and ruddered away from danger, and landed no worse than I would have done at Redhill behind the spinney (alas now gone) which screened the touchdown area for 26 from uncharitable eyes outside the Club hangar. We stopped with room to spare, all in one piece, to be greeted by the relentless applause of cold rain on the plane's fabric and on our leather-clad beans. It hardly seemed to matter.

There was a footpath leading through the wood towards some lights I had seen during the approach. By the time we reached the first door of a row of council houses and rang the bell we were thoroughly drenched and looking perhaps a trifle alarming in our bulky clothes and glistening World War II flying helmets. But not for Mrs Norrie.

"Oh, you must be the pilots!", a small woman in her late forties with permed dark hair and twinkling eyes cried out flinging the door open. "Come in, you poor boys – my, you are wet!", and she showed us into a tiny sitting room even before we could utter words to the effect that We Came In Peace. She briskly introduced us to her mother, an old, smiling lady propped up on a sofa at the back of the room, and then said:

"We heard you circling overhead, and I knew you were looking for a place to land. Then we stopped hearing you and I thought, there, they've found it! You picked the right field – the only good one in this area."

How could she know, I wondered, stepping out of my sodden flying suit and letting her bundle away our gear.

"A young RAF pilot force-landed his Hurricane on that field back in 1940 during the Battle of Britain," she went on, laying the suits out by the electric fire. "It all happened right above our heads, you know. . . . He rang our doorbell, just like you. Why, he even looked like you!" she added to the tall young charmer by my side. "He asked if he could use the telephone – as I'm sure you will. Here, give them a call while I get you some tea."

She disappeared into the kitchen leaving me to the delicate task of ringing the Club to inform them that the Stampe was slowly filling up with rainwater in a field near Tonbridge.

"Is the plane alright?"

"Yes, Michael – and so are we, by the way."

"Are there any cows on the field?"

"Not that I could see . . ." (Cows have a weakness for doped fabric, so I am told.)

"Well, make sure there aren't any and that you tie the plane down for the night. See you in the morning."

Only now could I enjoy my tea and being mothered by Mrs Norrie. She called a friend to drive us into town and back to the Stampe with makeshift tie-downs, got in touch with the farmer who owned the field, booked us a room at the local, told us to leave our kit with her, and invited us back for breakfast. As we were leaving, she brushed aside our words of thanks:

"You brought me such memories," she said.

We were up early next morning and in good time for our breakfast following a quick inspection of the Stampe sitting forlorn in the rain. The weather was marginally worse than on the eve, but by mid-morning it still looked very much the same and was reportedly letting up a bit over Redhill.

"Couldn't you just follow the Ashford line back to Redhill?" Mrs Norrie asked, uncannily reading my thoughts. "It's only five miles south of us . . . Here, let me show you on that map of yours."

She cleared a space on the breakfast table to spread the half-mil out and we obediently gathered round her while she 'briefed' us on our return mission to Redhill.

"I'll come to see you off," she announced. "Haven't seen a biplane in ages!"

And so we trudged back to the field, two goonish figures in Biggles gear escorting a dainty lady in a white raincoat, blue headscarf and matching wellies.

The plane's bucket seats were brimming with water – we had thoughtfully removed the cushions the previous night – and it took a while to bale it all out. Still, to my immense surprise and relief, the engine fired up on the first swing.

We took off heading south and immediately turned back to make a low farewell pass in front of Mrs Norrie. She waved excitedly with her umbrella, a tiny figure of a woman in the middle of a rainy Kent field, alone with her memories of a distant summer and of a downed RAF boy.

We found our way back alright – never mind at what height – though not to the hero's welcome I half expected, nor for that matter the carpeting I more than half dreaded. The latter was only a question of time.

Some weeks later Brendan and I were grounded by the powers-that-be after inadvertently cavorting in a Stampe through the Gatwick Zone above 7.99 octas, in the process of which Brendan's flash ski gloves fell out of the cockpit and were seen plunging a long way into the clouds. Unbowed, we bought ourselves an early-model hanglider which we promptly wrote off, landing B. in hospital with a broken arm. But that, too, is another story.

In the spring some of the anticipated fall-out from the AFIS mandatory radio regime occurred and was reported in the *Rag's* 'Aerodrome News':

Talking of radio and accidents, there have been two unfortunate mishaps to Club members' aircraft on the aerodrome recently, mercifully without serious injury to the pilots or occupants. In the first case a Tiger was turned onto its back by an out-of-wind 30-knot gust at the point of touchdown. It is a familiar story, and in such circumstances, if a go-around is not made a landing dead into wind is essential; after all the grass is there. And yet the radio does not seem to have been of much help as a warning of such conditions.

The second was more serious and resulted in the loss of Tom Storey's beautiful Mew Gull; it also made headlines in the national Press. Some 450 m from the threshold of runway 19, two drainage ditches had been dug across the runway and had been left open for several days. Why these ditches were not filled in immediately or the runway moved we have not been told, and the fact that most pilots had become aware of the problem or could see the ditches on finals is not much consolation to the unfortunate pilot of the Mew Gull who, flying a tricky aircraft especially from the point of view of forward visibility, obviously had no inkling of impending catastrophe. In this case also, the mandatory radio carried by the Mew Gull was of no help, since inexplicably no warning was apparently given or received. Having been informed *ad nauseam* that AFIS is there to give 'information useful for the safe and efficient conduct of flight' and such information will include 'runway surface conditions when appropriate' and how essential it is for all aircraft to be equipped with radio to receive such information etc. . . .

The Mew Gull had only just been repaired after its previous mishap on the tarmac. The pilot in this case was Desmond Penrose who had bought the Arrow Active from Benjy. He had been carrying out a trial flight with a view to acquiring another classic aircraft. Understandably Tom was furious: the aircraft was uninsured. Des later gallantly agreed to buy the wreckage and have the aircraft rebuilt himself. But would this mistake have been made in a pre-AFIS era? Somehow I doubted it.

Another event which occurred at this time and which did not appear in 'Aerodrome News' was that there were national Press reports that Mr Bristow was putting in a bid for Westland Helicopters, which had run into financial trouble and was likely to go into receivership. It was rumoured that a long time ago Alan Bristow had been employed by Westlands and had left the company after a row to start his own helicopter business at Redhill. Whether his initiative now had anything to do with Bristow's parent company British & Commonwealth was not revealed, but it caused a certain amount of excitement because some people thought that it might mean Bristow Helicopters departing to Westland's large grass airfield at Yeovil.

The whole affair was even causing anguish to Mrs Thatcher and would later cause a serious political crisis with Mr Heseltine. Mr Bristow eventually withdrew his bid because the Ministry of Defence would not guarantee future orders. At the time I wondered whether somebody might just have overplayed their hand in the jungle that exists between big business and politics.

The Club news column in the August edition of the *Rag* covered most of the summer's events – flying, social and accidental:

Continuing the tradition of always commenting on the weather, in July there was a long sunny calm spell – ideal for all sorts of flying and making no small contribution to utilisation. Yet the Club's aircraft are still not being flown as much as they should be, which is still a reflection of the generally high cost and other things about which enough has already been said.

The Garden Party at Middle Wallop on that glorious first weekend in June showed what could be done. 75 hours were flown in Club aircraft during the two days, including 37 glider launches and plenty of Turbulating. Our warmest thanks are due to the CO of the Army Air Corps and his staff for their hospitality and help, and also to his colleagues at Netheravon who again hosted the Sunday morning breakfast patrol. For the statistically minded the attendance was well up on 1984 with a total of 282 members, their children and guests and 57 members' aircraft and four gliders joining in the fun. We were also particularly pleased that five aircraft and 16 visitors arrived from Osnabrück AC, our twin Club in Germany, which for the first time combined its biennial visit with the Garden Party. (I suspect that the 'atmospherics' at Redhill had something to do with this.) Last but not least a small financial surplus was achieved for the Legal Fund and in this context we will forgive the CO for his query on arriving at the marquee as to whether 'all these aircraft were on radio'!

MIDDLE WALLOP GARDEN PARTY COMPETITION RESULTS

Short Take-Off Contest
1. Bill Browning
2. Matthew Hill
3. Geoff Salt

Spot Landing
1. Mike Dentith
2. David Body
3. Roger Marson

Flour Bombing
1. Harvey Tring
2. Martin Gambrell
3. Clive Rose

Aerobatics Free-Style Competition
1. David Body
2. David Keene
3. Gavin Dix

Tiger Stalk Treasure Hunt
1. David Keene and Gavin Dix
2=. Neil and Phyllis Thomason
2=. Roger Preston and Sue Gaveston

Balloon Bursting Contest
Abandoned due to failure of balloons to gain sufficient altitude

Since the Garden Party, our President – Norman Jones – has celebrated his 80th birthday, and a small lunch party was given in his honour at Rye. Bev Snook, representing the founder members of the Club, announced that Norman was being given an Honorary Life Membership of the Royal Aero Club – a great honour – and in his speech in reply our President demonstrated again that he has lost none of his enthusiasm for sporting flying and for everything the Tiger Club stands for.

The Dawn-to-Dusk competition has been in full swing and so far 23 logs are in the process of being submitted with some exciting flights, one of which achieved some national publicity for a well-known charity. David Body and Phil Bolderson, forsaking the vagaries of the English weather, set off for France in Stampe 'WEF to compete in the Coupe d'Anjou at Angers, a traditional aero competition for Stampes only. Considering their lack of practice they both performed creditably and came back full of praise for the delights of open-cockpit touring in France.

The Turbulent display team has been having a busy summer under the leadership of Bob Downing; its display has been particularly popular at summer fêtes and small shows. Our congratulations to Marcus Norman and Jane Barker who got married in the depths of Wiltshire where they have completely renovated a beautiful little cottage. Members were out in force for the celebration party and were treated to a fine display by the Taylor/O'Brien Fournier duo in the dusk of a perfect summer evening. The Fourniers are ideal for this sort of occasion as the noise level is just right for normal conversation.

Unfortunately the summer increase in activity has produced a crop of minor accidents, all of which can be attributed to pilot error. . . .

Briefly, for the edification of everyone, the Fournier was left with its canopy open broadside to a strong wind: result – badly cracked canopy. The Super Cub was tipped on to its nose taxying downwind on a difficult and gusty gliding site: result – bent prop and engine shock load. A Turbulent propeller was broken taking off on rough ground and in a strong crosswind – we know that the machine concerned is particularly light on the tail. And last, the Beta suffered a heavy landing resulting in a broken prop and other damage.

The Committee has spent some time agonising over these accidents and has delivered verdicts in accordance with Club rules. Please be warned!

As we go to press, the Club is beginning to buzz with activity in anticipation of the show at Redhill on the 1st September We hope everyone can make it and if you've not received a circular for tickets one is enclosed with this copy of the *Rag*, The weather can't be as bad as in 1983!

Thanks to Neil's patient diplomacy, arrangements with Mr Dalrymple for the Air Show had been proceeding relatively smoothly. We had even been granted a 'concession' to carry out one banner-towing pick-up on the airfield the day before the show to advertise the event. One other improvement from the financial point of view was that we managed to obtain a certain amount of sponsorship for individual display acts. Most of this came about through contacts that members already had, and in return the sponsors received a certain amount of publicity not only in the local Press and programme but also from the show commentators. Thus we had the Carless Standing on the Wing, The Marlborough Pitts Specials, the Unipart Fournier Duo, the Emcel Stampe Duo and the Pritchard Formula 1 Air Race for the second time.

Other Club members also rallied round in every way possible, persuading their businesses to take advertising in the programme and providing all the printing at cost. We also received maximum co-operation from all the other airfield tenants and the Redhill Flying Club was offered a slot in the flying programme. In fact everyone was pointed in the same direction and even the weather was kind to us.

Afterwards there were two reports for the *Rag*, one from Benjy in his best style and another, slightly more pedestrian, from me. Martin Evans, the Editor, printed them both:

The Tiger Club Air Show on 1st September was everything we could have wished for ourselves. Just to awake to a sunny morning was in itself a blessing, and the fears of a repeat of last year's washout fled. That the sunshine followed us to Redhill as well was a cheery bonus.

We got to the alrfleld OK but getting in was like breaching Fort Knox, such was the detour the arrows made us follow. I have a sneaking feeling someone moved a sign or two. But the sight that greeted us as we breasted a slight rise to get our first glimpse of the field was such that, for a moment, I thought the detour had led us to one of Gatwick's long-term car parks. Line upon line of cars stretched as far as the eye could see across the north of the airfield. My hat off straight away to Raymond Chudley; his organisation of the car parking was nothing short of brilliant.

The moment we stepped out of the car a feeling of near-carnival took over. With a mounting sense of anticipation we meandered around the busy stands and eventually wound up at the big Tiger Club marquee. If we were surprised at the numbers who had, like many of us, already arrived by midday – our guess was about three thousand cars – it was as nothing as was the sight of so many Club members in one place at the same time. Everyone was there. The Boss, Norman Jones, away just this once from his home in Rye, was already surrounded by members who wanted to meet him. I overheard Jeanne Frazer, as she paused from directing the whole shebang with her walkie-talkie, say: "You know, I've never met him." A phrase I heard many times.

Then out of the marquee into the vast and crowded Club enclosure. The keen westerly wind which set the banners flying stayed with us all afternoon and was later to give the opening formation quite a buffeting. The rest of the weather hadn't quite made up its mind what to do. The sun played hide and seek with the high cloud and every time it hid then it seemed a good idea to grab a cup of coffee from the first-class buffet within the marquee – we were in and out like yoyos.

The now almost traditional opening of the flying was a sight to behold. A 15-plane formation was led by five Tigers with Brian Smith marshalling from the front and all superbly positioned. Behind them bounced six Turbulents led by Bob Grimstead and tight behind them were four more biplanes led by Neil Jensen in his Bücker. And above them all flew the Super Cub, weaving about as photographs were taken.

Came the break, and the Turbs dropped down to do their slot with what for me was a new twist, a hairy-looking cross-over at ground level – as one flew under the hoop another tore by from the opposite direction.

I had meant to ask for a copy of the detailed programme, but mindful of my new position – or lack of it – I didn't bother. After all, why not just enjoy the change! It was surely the first time in many years that I had nothing actually to do with the day. And so Trudi and I did just that. It was great. So if I don't mention pilots and helpers by name you'll understand.

I was joined at times in the enclosure by others of the 'oldies' and together we watched that afternoon's flying critically, and why not, for we had all done the same things in earlier years. In every case the question of comparison came up and in every case the answer was the same. The present teams have lost none of the touch we used to claim as ours.

From the remarkably tight Marlborough two-plane Pitts formation, which was absolutely – almost mechanically – precise in everything it did, to a direct two-plane comparison, that of the Stampes of Pete Jarvis and Brian Smith. It was, at least in my eyes, no contest. Not that I didn't realise that there were probably four of the country's best pilots up there, but it was the slower Stampes that best portrayed the wonderful grace of flying with their gentler and quieter showing. As ever the smoke-streaming inverted ribbon-cut was spectacular, and if the stiff wind didn't exactly help Brian, the apparent slow approach highlighted the dramatic effect. 'Tied together' stayed that way, no doubt to the relief of Jim Alderton, who had filled in at short notice, and the Standing on the Wing was as popular as ever. Unquestionably a highlight of the show was the totally unexpected – at least for me – sight of seven parachute-dropping biplanes. Not even in the days of plenty – Tigers I mean – can I recall such a sight. It was truly a magnificent one-off.

Of aerobatics, the standards were as high as ever. It was great to see the Cosmic Wind *Ballerina* back in action and, if I momentarily hark back, forgive me, but I couldn't help recalling Peter Phillips' immaculate 16-point rolls from earlier years and I missed 'em. And didn't Lomcovaks once look more exciting, or were they just more out of control in those days?

The Spitfire and Hurricane, the Vampire and Meteor were duly seen and ah-ed and oh-ed over. After the intimacy of our Club flying, the space these bigger veterans needed made their appearances almost cautious, if it wasn't for the nostalgia dare I say almost dreary . . . yet I know of the limitations imposed, and it's only my point of view anyway.

The Formula 1 Race was great fun, as much for Brendan O'Brien's breathless mid-Atlantic commentary as for the spirited flying. Spirited it was, for the course was excellently placed, so that Brendan's flawless machine-gun flow could the better be appreciated as the eight tiny craft tore around. Forgot in the excitement to note who won – probably Steve Thompson. Another nice touch was the repartee between John Blake and Brendan, although some of the 'in' comments must have left the thousands of spectators a bit in the dark, but judging by the laughter most of them sensed the message.

The finale truly belonged to *Sally B* the B-17. With a loving touch Keith Sissons contrived to show her, not just as a big bomber, but as a character in her own right. And so with a woman's instinctive flair she showed herself to best advantage, ever turning before her admirers and never out of our sight. It was display flying at its very best.

The day was long and good and full of happenings. I would guess over 10,000 were there, and all would want to come again. From the magnificent array and parade of vintage cars, the colour and bustle of the many stands to the music of the band, it was an occasion to be proud of. To everyone who helped, and especially those who unselfishly gave of their time in the unsung places, and who probably didn't even see the Show, I offer on behalf of all of us in the Club our heartfelt thanks.

"Ladies and Gentlemen," announced the rather breathless commentator at 10 o'clock to the several hundred people who were already on the field. "Welcome to the 1985 Tiger Club Air Show – the flying programme will begin at 2 am!" A forgivable slip of the tongue in the circumstances because by that time we already knew that the public, *our* public, was jolly well going to turn up in force to see the show, *our* Air Show.

As Roy Davis pointed out to me, it was the 53rd Tiger Club show he had been to since joining the Club in 1961 and it was by far the best. But of course it was only the third time that we had organised an air show at our home base since our arrival at Redhill in 1959. In a sense the 1983 event – ruined by the weather – had been a dress rehearsal, but the foundations of the organisation then had been very soundly laid by Jeanne Frazer and this year there were more people to assist her. One major improvement was having everybody on the south side of the display runway instead of being split up into two camps, so to speak, as in 1983.

The weather, that missing figure in air show balance sheets, was on our side – just! After a torrential August we were desperately worried about the condition of the ground. Geoff Tait had planned to have, if you please, a tank amongst his military ground exhibits. Mercifully, the week before had seen a few good drying days and the grass, which always recovers quickly at Redhill, was firm and dry. On the day itself, there was a strong wind – yes – but right down the runway.

Attendance figures have not been officially calculated. By two o'clock, most cars that were going to arrive had done so and only a few had to be halted briefly at the entrance to allow the Formula 1 heat to start. Club members on the paying gate and the ladies – I am told that ladies are much better at collecting money off the punters than the men – deserve our unstinting praise; they can never have worked so hard. Ray Chudley was surprised to have to hurriedly organise a second car park on the western side of the arena. Certainly quite a lot more cars could have been accommodated but it would have been essential to have a second entrance to do so.

Also to the point, this public had money to spend; the trade stands and catering stalls reported a brisk business all day. Mike Hood with his joy-riding Rapide told us that he had never had it so good, and what a perfect compliment it is to an air show on a grass airfield to have such a beautiful and graceful machine solely doing the joy-riding.

We are all experts now at putting up posters in the most suitable places. A well-timed advertising campaign in the local Press and radio, together with the essential pre-publicity for advanced sales, achieved its purpose; even the Club's aerial banner towed round the local area played its part. There was a splendid turn-out of visiting aircraft for the Carless Petroleum arrival competition. All and much else contributed to the success of the event. Plans are afoot for a repeat performance next year. A reasonably healthy profit has been achieved from the 1985 Air Show and it proved a sorely needed tonic to the Club in these difficult times.

After the Air Show, the predicted development of the airfield started to take place in earnest, and the site was cleared for a new control tower and terminal building on the area where the signal square used to be and where there was once a pleasant clump of trees. The 'terminal' was to include passenger lounges, airport offices, Customs areas and so on. As for the hard runway, an appeal had been made against the initial refusal and the Public Inquiry opened in December.

There was a preliminary report in the *Rag*:

The Planning Inquiry into the hard runway has now duly got under way in the Council Chamber at Oxted and so far has occupied four days. It will be resumed in January, so this is only an interim report. The public attended in quite large numbers, which understandably dwindled during the course of the week.

So far it has been the Aerodrome and the District Council who have been putting their respective cases under lengthy cross-examination. At the next session, it will be the turn of the objectors. There has been a notable lack of aviation expertise from the parties although an Air Commodore is acting officially as the Assessor. We just hope that he has flown a Tiger Moth!

Experts of all other types have been much in evidence and nearly a whole day was spent on the esoterics of noise measurement. The consultants for the East Surrey Hospital, who are naturally concerned that £15 million has very recently been spent on a modern hospital only half a mile from the end of the proposed runway – and without double glazing – have been very interested in the Club's views and have promised us a slot in their time and, I hasten to add, at their expense to make these known. They thought that they only had a small grass aerodrome with a few Tiger Moths and helicopters on their doorstep!

Amidst the welter of verbiage, the following hard facts which are relevant to the Club's situation have emerged, and these facts are related to that much-loved word in planning inquiries – 'scenarios.'

Approximately 6,000 'business' movements per annum will be introduced into the existing traffic levels. (At this point someone complained that the country lanes leading to the aerodrome would become cluttered up with Rolls-Royces!) Aircraft using the runway will be restricted to a maximum of 6,750 kg all-up weight. A legal agreement is in place with the British Airport Authority at Gatwick for a maximum of six IFR movements per hour. Helicopter movements will be unaffected. The north-south grass runway will not be used for *ab initio* training. There will be only a 'modest' restriction in recreational flying.

The arguments that have been put to support the case for the hard runway rest largely on the facts that (a) quite recently Fairoaks and Shoreham have been granted one and that (b) a grass runway is inherently dangerous and inefficient. Photographs have been produced of mud-splattered aircraft (taken apparently at Fairoaks and not at Redhill) and also of the new terminal building now almost complete. The CAA has, of course, stepped in with a letter – which has been quoted *ad nauseam* – that a hard runway will lead to an improvement in safety and that statistics were available of aircraft overrunning grass runways because brakes were ineffective on grass when it was wet! And even when it was dry, undercarriages could be severely strained. In other words the aerodrome is running the 'safety' horse for all it is worth and, for public consumption, as we discovered to our cost in the High Court case, it is an extremely difficult one to beat.

The alternative 'scenario' if permission for the new runway is refused (incidentally 900 metres long and 23 metres wide with plenty of room for future expansion) is that the airfield will 'wither and die' and that the Tiger Club is hardly functioning anyway.

If permission is granted, it is not very difficult to guess what the future holds in store. As a starter we have already been told that if a favourable decision is given early, the 1986 Air Show will not be possible because work will be put in hand immediately. However the Inquiry is still in progress; quite a few tricks have been won and no doubt there will be a lot more to win when the opposite case is put, but whether these will be sufficient to win the game is still very doubtful. In the meantime, we are still looking round for an alternative site and, in the light of the fact that we will certainly have our own planning problems to face, the Inquiry over Redhill has been an invaluable education.

I smiled when I heard Fairoaks mentioned. Permission for the hard runway there had been granted in 1978 and the Fairoaks Aero Club (motto: 'The Art and Sport of Flying') had been driven off the airfield before the development had taken place. One of the early tactics then adopted was an edict from the owner that the Club's Tigers should be fitted with brakes and tailwheel – a highly expensive and unnecessary modification – but imagine trying to contest that regulation in the High Court! In the circumstances I was mildly surprised that it had not already been suggested by our landlords!

As for the Air Show, Neil had already written with our formal request to hold our Air Show in 1986.

Mr Dalrymple replied:

"In your letter of the 25th November you mention that in your opinion the possibility that a hard runway may be under construction in 1986 should not preclude the holding of an air show. . . .

In the event that planning permission is granted it is this Company's intention to have the works put in hand as soon as possible. Therefore at this stage we can only grant the Tiger Club conditional permission for the holding of an Air Display at Redhill Aerodrome on 20th July 1986. Whilst we appreciate the Club's desire and enthusiasm regarding a 1986 Air Display we can only put the facts to you as they are at this moment in time, and should the Club wish to organise the Display at its own expense, bearing in mind that such permission could be cancelled, then that must be the Club's decision.

However, should there be no decision from the Public Inquiry by 15th April 1986 it is agreed that the Tiger Club Air Display will go ahead on 20th July 1986 notwithstanding a Public Inquiry decision between 15th April and 20th July. . . .

You will appreciate that the fee for holding an air show at Redhill Aerodrome has remained at £800 since its conception in 1983. Bearing in mind your request to keep the increase to a minimum we suggest a fee of £2,000 for the 1986 Show. Any works required to put the aerodrome back into an operational state will be invoiced to The Tiger Club Limited."

It was a particularly insensitive letter and we had no hesitation in showing it to the objectors at the Inquiry. As it turned out the decision was first delayed, and then finally in August the hard runway appeal was turned down. Eventually, as a compromise, the show went ahead in June but we only had three months to prepare for it . . .

As for an alternative airfield, a good deal of time had already been spent poring over Ordnance Survey maps and visiting possible sites, not only in Surrey and Sussex but also in Kent and Hampshire. They were not difficult to find since airfields of all types were listed in a CAA publication.

Furthermore their history was already fully documented in meticulous detail in various publications produced by aviation societies. The airfield that we were determined to find was one that we could call our own, since we did not wish to 'muscle in' on one already in use and, even if we did, the options were extremely limited. In fact I was amazed to discover how many disused airfield sites there were, and they fell roughly into three groups: those that were established during World War I, those during World War II and those, like Redhill, between the wars.

Most World War I sites had disappeared due to urban sprawl. Although there were a few World War II grass airfields still recognisable such as Coolham and Chailey, those like Tangmere with hard runways and buildings were too big to be practical, and to find somewhere remotely suitable was going to be very difficult. Early on in the exercise I listed a few of the essential requirements:

OUTLINE REQUIREMENT FOR LANDING GROUND AND SITE FOR RECREATIONAL FLYING CLUB

LANDING STRIPS

One approx. E-W, 750 m by 75 m.
One approx. N-S, 500 m by 75 m.

The two strips should be grass, level, well-drained and approx. at right angles to one another. Agricultural operations (arable) could take place up to the edges of each strip subject to access at any one point of a minimum 75 m wide. (Livestock farming adjacent to strips could include sheep but preferably not cattle). At the threshold of each strip at each end, obstacle clearance, i.e. hedge, fence, should not be more than 2 m high. The direct approaches to each strip should be free of high obstacles, e.g. trees, pylons, telegraph wires, buildings etc., say for a distance of approx 300 m.

SITE FOR BUILDINGS ETC.

As close as possible to the strips, and with access to one of them at any point via level well-drained grass track of a minimum width of 75 m – an area of approx. 100 m by 100 m. This would be for:

1. Hangars for small aircraft
2. Clubhouse
3. Workshop
4. Aircraft parking
5. Car parking
6. Fuelling facilities

ACCESS

Reasonable access via a semi-made-up or made-up single-track road to a public highway would be required.

SERVICES

Water, electricity, telephone and sewerage would be required.

SITUATION
Anywhere in SE England, preferably south of the Thames but as far as possible from residential or commercial development, actual or potential.

ACREAGE
Approx. acreages are as follows:
1. Landing Strips and access – say – 20 acres
2. Site for Buildings etc. – say – 2 acres
3. Road – not known

PLANNING
Purchase subject to planning permission through a possible mechanism of a conditional option with a time limit of, say, 3 years with the purchaser responsible for negotiations!

As far as the 'situation' was concerned it was necessary to take account of the fact that a large majority of the Club members were resident, if not in London, then in Surrey, Sussex and Kent, and that Rollasons were based at Shoreham. It was also vital that the site should be reasonably clear of controlled airspace and not officially in an environmentally sensitive area such as, for example, an 'area of outstanding natural beauty.' Last but not least, even if we located somewhere we would need the owner's agreement to sell. As somebody pointed out it would be like finding a needle in a haystack.

However during 1985 one possible site did emerge, a disused grass airfield near Eastbourne in Sussex. It had been established between the wars in 1933 and had been used by a flying club operating Gipsy Moths. It was still in the ownership of the same family and although, inevitably, there were problems, the Trustees were interested and it would be worth further investigation.

Meanwhile at Redhill the aerodrome director was causing a few more problems. The north-south runway was closed for several weeks with no alternative (as required by our lease) being offered, there was a final refusal to allow banner-towing, and the spot landing competition to replace the Hamilton Trophy, which was to take place again at the Downlands strip, had to be cancelled; we had been refused permission to take off with the Super Cub and a Stampe because of 'waterlogging.' Many members had travelled a considerable distance to take part and Harvey Tring had laid on a barbecue at the strip. They were particularly angry because a Piper Aztec had been given permission to take off from the perimeter track, a common occurence for all aircraft in the pre-AFIS days.

But there was little point in complaining. It was best to look ahead. 1985 had not been a bad year. The membership had held up and there had been a small recovery in aircraft utilisation. Martin Evans produced an optimistic editorial in the winter issue of the *Rag*:

As the pages of the logbooks are closed in 1985, it's the Editor's privilege to reflect on the season past. After just one year of producing the *Rag*, my overall impression is of a year of consolidation and cautious revival after the nadir of 1984.

The year saw 'VPT on floats for a very successful six weeks, reintroducing the tradition that came to a watery end in 1982 – though not without some bureaucratic hiccups from the CAA; the running of our second air show after a two-year interval and a healthy profit to boot; continued enthusiasm and support for competition aerobatics right through from Standard to World level, even if the weather grounded three of the UK events; more team Turbulating than ever before; a second good turnout of entrants for our Dawn-to-Dusk competition; Club members and planes racing in both Formula I and the Digital Schneider Race, though not handicap air racing generally; and a UK Precision team led by a Club member in the World Championships.

The weather was gloriously kind to us for the fourth time at Middle Wallop, but not for most of the rest of the year. Nor was the accident record exemplary either. But the real storm clouds gathering on the horizon are still those that hang over our future at Redhill. Our New Year Resolution must be to search for a new and permanent home for the most unique flying club of them all.

Happy New Year to you all.

Martin also produced a stimulating article on the 1985 Dawn-to-Dusk:

The awards for the 1985 Dawn-to-Dusk Competition were presented by HRH The Prince Andrew on 6th December at the Royal Aeronautical Society.

Winner for the third time was Charlie Shea-Simonds, though flying this time not as a Tiger Club member but as leader of a team representing the Army Parachute Association, which completed a jump at every major BPA site in the country. Charlie not only jumped himself six times but flew the jump plane – an Islander. As usual, the logbook of its entry was a work of art.

In second place were two young ladies who couldn't be members of the Club, since they have less than 100 hours PI each. In the spirit of the event's sponsors, Seagram Distillers, they toured the country photographing breweries and picking up (but not imbibing) samples left for them to collect at several airfields.

Third place went to a superbly photographed tour of a number of aircraft museums.

Of the 15 entries finally submitted, three came from Tiger Club members. Brendan O'Brien took his RF.4 onto the Continent to take advantage of the old FAI rules and re-establish 200 world point-to-point records! These were officially witnessed by John Taylor, sworn in as a Royal Aero Club observer for the attempt in the other Unipart RF.4.

Dennis Creswell crossed the North Sea to commemorate the allied air operations in Norway during the war, whilst your Editor went in search of country houses originally illustrated in 'bird's eye view' in 1708.

As a personal reflection on the competition, the old adage of 'taking part, not winning' is more true of this event than any other. My satisfaction in the last two years has been in the many pleasant evenings spent dreaming up ideas and planning them during the 'close' season and the culmination of a well-presented logbook which is a permanent keepsake.

The increased interest in the competition in the last two years has thrown up lots of new ideas, yet amazingly no two the same. The human imagination is very fertile and it would be good to see an even larger Tiger Club entry in 1986 in our own event.

Let me make a few suggestions. We have an ideal collection of aeroplanes. The competition was first run in 1964 and restricted to Turbulents following an idea by Norman Jones to promote the marque. In those days the rules restricted flying to the UK, but Don Lovell, the first-ever winner, tells me he flew a distance equivalent to Rome to Redhill! A 1986 entry involving Turbs would be a nice return to the original ethos. Perhaps a ribbon could even be involved.

An RF.4 has won the event thrice previously and an entry sympathetic to its gliding possibilities must be worthy of investigation. Surveying windmills in an RF.4 had crossed my mind.

Looking through the list of past winners shows two victories credited to a Stampe. Who knows but that Charlie couldn't have added a Tiger and his hat-trick earlier if early morning stratus and a cornfield hadn't prematurely intervened. With the pressures the Club now faces, a non-radio, non-licensed aerodrome tour would be in the old Club spirit. A farmer flyer landed at and surveyed 48 farm strips this year. Perhaps reconnoitring potential new homes for the Club would be a winner.

Most of the entries in the last two years have involved very few landings, the two winners being the exception. The 1984 winning entry -- landing in every English county – is now in the Guinness Book of Records, whilst Charlie's 1985 multiple returns to terra firma was an active entry. Long in the pocket this year was the 1984 winner but – using a helicopter to play a round of golf on 18 different courses. An activity-based entry would suit the Super Cub and its short field capabilities.

Finally, from the Club fleet, is the range master par excellence, the D.150 Jodel. The type has won just once before. Last year I flew 'VEF solo and non-stop for 7½ hours and still had eight gallons on board. Range-orientated entrants should choose this mount.

It's difficult to know exactly what the judges are looking for. Although a detailed scoring framework is part of the rules, the final results are never published in detail and the papal machinations are secret. What is evident though is that they are looking for an original idea, excellent photographic and logbook presentations, and an active entry not confined to a tour round the country. My own ideas have already included hill figures, lost medieval villages, seaside piers and zoos. My personal favourite, however, is a floatplane entry but that, I fear, will have to wait for another year.

Finally in the same issue, the quote of the month was pinched from *Pilot* Magazine and was obviously American in origin:

ATC AGONY

Best place a generous helping of tongue in your cheek before reading this allegedly genuine 'agony' letter quoted in the CAA staff newspaper *Airway*:

"I have two brothers. One is an air traffic controller and the other brother was just sent to death on the electric chair for murder. My mother died from insanity when I was three years old. My two sisters are prostitutes, and my father sells narcotics to college students. Recently I met a girl who was just released from a reformatory where she served time for smothering her illegitimate child to death, and I want to marry this girl. My problem is, if I marry this girl, should I tell her about the brother who is an air traffic controller?"

TOP: Charlie Shea-Simonds, who took over the editorship of the *Tiger Rag* and later became Chairman of the Royal Aero Club and founder of the Tiger Moth *Diamond Nine*. Seen here in his own Tiger Moth – probably at Netheravon.

BOTTOM: The Club's President Norman Jones, on his feet at the lunch celebrating his 80th birthday. Photo: Lewis Benjamin.

TOP: The 1984 *Hamilton Trophy* getting ready for the 'off' at the Downlands Airstrip.
BOTTOM: Downlands again: the gathering for the barbecue after the flying.
Photos: Jim Alderton.

CHAPTER 10
1986

As in the previous year, at the end of 1985 there had been no ballot for places on the Committee because there were insufficient nominations – again so much for Club democracy! However there were changes; Denis Hartas and Bob Grimstead had retired, Neil Thomason had rejoined and there was one new face, Judy Kay, who was co-opted to be responsible for PR and fund-raising. In her professsional life Judy worked for a large charity, so she was ideally qualified, and her undoubted talents would soon be very profitably exercised at both the Tiger Ball and the forthcoming Air Show. Also Brendan had let it be known that he would not be available to mastermind the 1987 Ball because he was going to spend six months flying in the Antarctic and Judy would be an ideal replacement.

The first item on the agenda for the year was the re-opening in early January of the Public Inquiry into Mr Dalrymple's hard runway, or 'all-weather strip' as it was politely described. Our own contribution was carefully monitored by the consultants to the East Surrey Hospital. This large Conservative 'flagship' establishment had been opened in 1984 by no less a person than the Prime Minister herself, and their consultants were saying that the hospital would have to spend £2 million on double-glazing if the hard runway went ahead. I idly wondered what Mrs Thatcher would say to that!

It was now time to put the Club's case, which was really quite simple: although we were looking for an alternative airfield, we had not yet secured one. A hard runway would squeeze our activities at Redhill, both in terms of new restrictions and cost, even more than at present. The Fairoaks decision had been put in strongly to support the Redhill case and:

'Now that the runway is built at Fairoaks, the grass areas are no longer used except in an emergency and it is the declared policy of the management there that recreational users are not welcome. We fear that a similar situation will arise at Redhill. In a county where there are two 'general aviation' airfields established, surely it is sensible to give priority to one of them for recreational flying.'

Our case was dismissed by the QC acting for the aerodrome as one of 'special pleading' but the barrister for the objectors, David Mole, closed his final address with the comment that a hard runway, if accepted, would 'release a beast from its cage.'

The next item on the agenda was the Tiger Ball and we had invited Sqn. Ldr. Richard Thomas and his wife Heather to be our Guests of Honour. Richard was the current leader of the Red Arrows and maybe we were hoping to get their display for the Air Show. In his honour we had engaged the RAF Dance Orchestra, but maybe that was because some people were pressing for the decibel level to be lowered from previous years. The event was again a great success with an attendance of well over 300. Judy, no doubt getting into her stride as a new member of the Committee, produced the report for the *Rag*:

Now that the dust – not to mention several miles of spray string – has settled on the 1986 Tiger Ball, I am grateful for the opportunity via the *Rag* of passing on my very sincere thanks to everyone who helped to make the event the success which, I gather from members' kind comments, it was.

Brendan O'Brien, despite his oft-expressed ambition to be allowed to give up the organisational side and throw bread rolls with (or at) the rest of us, was a paragon of efficiency and help throughout the planning stages (honestly!), and as – to quote himself – 'Rent-a-Mouth' on the night, gave an unparalleled performance as Master of Ceremonies, which leaves us wondering how he has managed to evade the attentions of the TV and radio stations for so long.

Turning from centre stage to back stage on the night, Harvey Tring should be congratulated for his tireless work in organising the impressive light show which resulted in Tigers and aeroplanes flying relentlessly round the walls of the ballroom. Harvey gave up countless hours of his time to liaise with the suppliers, ferry the equipment and hand-paint the display, after which he and Roger Preston devoted most of the Saturday morning and afternoon to setting everything up. The morning after – and was it ever! – HT was back in action dismantling the kit in order to return it, and to my mind he is top of the list of the unsung heroes of the event.

Also working hard behind the scenes were Mavis Harriott and Tessa Lovell, who once again tackled the complex job of taking bookings and organising the table plan.

On the night Janet Tring, together with Poppy Body, also did noble work in selling raffle tickets in pursuit of much needed funds, whilst Hannah and Louise Body acted as flower girls, presenting orchids to each lady guest, closely and ably supervised by big brother Marcus, who had already proved a most willing helper in assisting to prepare the ballroom.

Several members were most generous in collecting and donating gifts for the tombola which, as a result, boasted over 30 excellent prizes.

There are many other credits which are due: to our Chairman, Neil Jensen, and Squadron Leader Richard Thomas, whose enjoyment of dinner could not have been enhanced by the knowledge that they were both having to sing for their supper; Heather Thomas, who presented the awards so enthusiastically; the good-natured staff of the Gatwick Hilton Hotel, who had to serve the meal whilst dodging (or failing to dodge) assorted missiles; the

RAF Dance Orchestra; the Ian Lay Road Show; all our generous donors of gifts; Phil Read, who loaned his beautiful scaled replica SE.5 microlight which complemented perfectly the excellent models lent and installed by our good friends at the Croydon Model Aircraft Society; and last, but by no means least, everyone who bought tickets and entered into the spirit (not half!) of the evening. As one Club member put it, the Tiger Ball is like the Olde Tyme Music Hall from the City Variety: 'Ladies and Gentlemen, mainly yourselves.'

In 1986 the Garden Party had been brought forward from the normal mid-summer weekend to a weekend in May so as not to clash with the June date for the Air Show. Middle Wallop was not available, so it was moved to Netheravon, another large grass airfield on Salisbury Plain. Charlie Shea-Simonds had managed to persuade Jim Steele, the Commandant of the Joint Services Parachute Centre, to have us and, although the weather was indifferent and numbers were slightly down on the previous year, it was another excellent weekend with plenty of unrestricted flying.

Although, from reading various issues of the *Rag*, one might think that the Ball, the Garden Party and the Air Show were the only highlights of the year – and without a doubt they were highlights – there was also a whole host of other activities on offer and a calendar was usually circulated with the *Rag*.
1986 was no exception:

FORTHCOMING EVENTS 1986

The following is a list of events in which Tiger Club aircraft will be participating or where the use of the Club aircraft is actively encouraged:

AEROBATICS

26-27 April	McLean Trophy	Bodmin
17-18 May	Falling Leaf	Fenland
24-25 May	R. Legg	Seething
7-8 June	Golding Barrett	Sleap
27-29 June	McAully	Little Snoring
19-20 July	Coupe d'Anjou	Angers
1-17 August	World's	South Cerney
23-24 August	Fenland	Fenland
6-7 September	Thursford Museum	Little Snoring
27-28 September	Tiger	Dunkeswell
3-5 October	Nationals	TBA

Contact David Body for details. Only competition for Standard and Beginners' level included. Contact BAeA for detals of other events.

DISPLAYS

8 June	Church Fenton
21 June	Halton
29 June	White Waltham
7 September	Leigh

Contact Neil Thomason for details.

FORMULA 1 AIR RACING

8-11 May	Dinard
31 May–1 June	Hurn
7 June	Saintes
15 June	Cherbourg
22 June	Redhill
4-6 July	Cranfield
27 July	Humberside
3 August	Duxford
10 August	Cranfield
21 August	Mulhouse

Contact Robin Voice for details.

GLIDER TOWING

26 July–3rd August Sutton Bank
Contact Geoff Salt for details.

CLUB GARDEN PARTY

24-25 May	Netheravon

Circulars going out shortly.
Contact David Body for details.

DAWN-TO-DUSK

Flights between 1 May and 31 July.
Contact David Timmis for details.
Entry forms available at the Club.

WEEKEND AWAY

26-27 April	Badminton

PRECISION FLYING

26 April	Haverford West
24 May	Oxford
21 June	Sywell (Nationals)
12 July	Sibson
11-17 August	Louz (European)
27 Sept	Eaglescott

Contact David Hamilton or
David Timmis for details.

FOREIGN TOURING

30 May–1 June	Weekend in Osnabrück
27 July	Lunch in France
30 Aug–7 Sept	Week in France

SEAPLANE

Operational 22 August to 19 October, usually only weekends, at Scotney Court.
Contact Tom Freer for details.

HANDICAP AIR RACING

24-25 May	World Trade Centre Air Race, London–Rotterdam
20-22 June	Digital Schneider Trophy, I.O.W.
5-6 July	Leicester Air Race, Leicester East
19-20 July	Grosvenor Challenge Trophy, Shobdon
26-27 July	City Livery Trophy, Humberside Airport
9-10 August	National Air Race, Cranfield
17 August	Kent Messenger Air Race, Rochester
September	King's Cup Air Race, date and venue to be arranged.

For the Air Show in June everything miraculously got organised in time. Brian Smith was once again in charge of the flying and Jeanne Frazer the ground with the assistance of some very dedicated lieutenants.

As Neil put it:

"Months of planning are necessary and an unbelievable amount of work has to be undertaken by members who at the same time have to hold down full-time jobs . . ."

A problem arose with the parachutists who, as before, were being 'supplied' by Charlie Shea-Simonds; in order no doubt to streamline the flying programme and to have all the biplanes in readiness for the Balbo, Brian was anxious that the drop should be made from Mike Hood's joy-riding Rapide. Charlie however was adamant: he was out to create a world record biplane parachute jump and if necessary he could line up 11 machines and their pilots himself. He had also spent a good deal of time checking out members for parachute dropping and issuing them with the certificates which were now required by the CAA.

He wrote to Neil:

"There is in my view more talent available within the Club than one or two would have us believe; the problem is that there is little nurturing of this talent. . . ."

Neil eventually poured the necessary oil on troubled waters and Charlie got his way. As Charlie was later to demonstrate with his Diamond Nine Tiger formation, he would be very good at nurturing the necessary talent. As it turned out neither the Balbo nor the record biplane parachute drop could take place on account of the impossible weather. . . .

Another excitement we were all looking forward to was a first participation in a Club show from Ray Hanna's Old Flying Machine Company based at Duxford. Pete Jarvis, who had forsaken his post as the Club's Senior Check Pilot to join Ray's Group, had already whetted appetites with an article in the *Rag* entitled *'Meribel Mustang.'* Pete also flew for British Airtours at Gatwick and he persuaded them to provide the necessary sponsorship. Pete's partner in the Stampe duo, Carl Schofield, had also signed up with Ray, so the arrival of the warbirds would be very much a Club affair, and we were promised the Spitfire, the Mustang and the Kittyhawk.

Airtours also took a stand on the ground to show their mock-up 757 cockpit, and also provided their hot-air balloon which was inflated and flown – with Mr Dalrymple's agreement – at the end of the Show. Most people agreed that the flying was some of the finest ever seen at a Tiger Club Show but the weather saw to it that there was no financial bonanza.

As the *Rag* reported:

It would be very useful if somebody could conduct a survey at an air show to discover exactly why the public comes and what it expects to see when it gets there. There are so many theories flying around on this question that objective answers would be very valuable. One individual rang up before the show to ask, if you please, whether the event was open to the public!

Versions of the sort of thing one overhears in the crowd: "What's a biplane, Dad?"

"I don't know, son, but I think it's a plane with wings on both sides."

Anyway the 1986 Tiger Club Air Show cannot be criticised for not providing just about everything that anybody could want to suit all ages, all interests and all tastes. The ground exhibitions, the motor vehicle cavalcades, the military displays, the bands, the sideshows, the trade stands, the gymnasts and so on, tirelessly directed by Geoff Tait, provided a splendid curtain-raiser to the flying display itself, particularly since the weather effectively blotted out any pre-display aerial activity (only three visiting aircraft arrived all day and then only late). British Airtours was busy selling holidays in the sun and maybe it did all right!

A line of thunderstorms which crossed the area on the Saturday night had left a Sunday morning grey, damp and dismal, with the clouds seemingly amongst the trees and visibility scarcely across the aerodrome. Fortunately the forecasters said it would clear up and that the sun would be through by lunchtime. They got it wrong, of course, but the forecast itself was a small bonus in our favour and it didn't actually start raining until the late afternoon and then not for long. Nothing, however, will compensate for a fine sunny start to an air show day, and although there was a steady trickle of cars through the gates during the morning, at noon we were rather depressed.

But during the next two hours the situation improved considerably, so that by the time the flying display started there seemed to be almost as many cars on the field as in 1985; but this may have been an optical illusion or there were far more exhibitors' cars etc. because gate receipts were down by the equivalent of around 800 cars. Anticipating a bigger turnout than last year, at no small cost and trouble a second entrance on the west side of the field had been opened, and at least this got rid of potential queues for both arrivals and departures.

The flying programme, using a rather generous interpretation of the official minima for air displays, more or less took place as planned in atrocious conditions. The Balbo formation was sensibly cancelled; such a large formation would have lost sight of the field in no time at all. The military jets in the shape of two RAF Hawks had to stay on the ground at Biggin but the Navy Seahawk apparently made it as far as Guildford before having to turn back to Yeovilton.

Luckily most of the non-resident participants arrived the day before, including the Swordfish and Ray Hanna's trio of warbirds. Ray's opening slot in the Spitfire when the weather was at its worst was masterly and how he kept the airfield in view only he can say.

The CAA was present in the person of Barry Tempest, an experienced display pilot himself, and he knew that most of the aircraft could display within the airfield boundaries and at a low altitude. In fact Barry got so enthusiastic that halfway through the day he demanded that his Associate membership of the Club should be immediately upgraded to 'flying' status; maybe he thought that he would be needed!

The Swordfish, after delighting the crowd with its low and slow flypasts with the crew waving furiously, left for home without landing, only to return, having failed to get more than a few miles down its route. This threw the air traffic control and consequently the programme because somebody, and I'm sure that it was not the Swordfish, declared an emergency. The flour bombing got left out, as a result the F1 racers were delayed but eventually got under way in conditions of slightly improved visibility so that at least one pylon was visible from the last one, and put up a splendid race, with Brian Smith just pipping Steve Thompson for the honours.

The mass biplane parachute drop fell a victim to the low cloud base although they did, as the saying is, 'go for it.' Derek Piggott put up a brave display of glider aerobatics after a tow by Geoff Salt which could scarcely have achieved 500 ft. Even the act of towing a glider is of interest to the crowd.

All the other Club acts performed exceptionally in the conditions, many with modified routines, and space does not permit a description of them all. Only advanced and sophisticated aerobatic displays were not possible. The Fournier duo performed well, although somebody swore that they nearly touched! After a number of rumours to the contrary, Keith Sissons turned up in the Sally B after some motorway navigation to receive an unexpected escort from the Mustang and Kittyhawk.

Finally Brendan O'Brien, foresaking his commentator's box, put up a brilliant and impromptu display of crazy flying in his Stampe, although I hope someone will inform him in due course that the Club in the dim and distant past has totalled at least four Tiger Moths in a similar exercise and 'CDC's log books will tell a thing or two about it!

As for the financial aspects, we just about got out of it with the books balanced. Even if it had been a perfect day, hugely increased airfield and insurance charges would have crippled a respectable profit and taken most of the gilt off the gingerbread. If such charges are in prospect in another year, a question mark will inevitably be raised over the future of the event.

It was particularly galling that the aerodrome saw fit to charge the Club – after the event – landing fees for all the display aircraft which arrived the day before, not only for essential practice but also because their pilots and operators deemed it sensible and courteous to do so; this, as it turned out, was a wise decision. It must be some sort of record for a Spitfire to be charged a landing fee returning to an ex-wartime airfield for a flying display, but in this day and age profit overrules sentiment. It was also extremely irritating that the aerodrome also saw fit not to relax its embargo on banner-towing at the airfield, which again put us to unnecessary trouble and expense, besides ruling out an interesting act with which either to open or close the show.

However on the credit side in this direction members will, of course, be pleased to know that we have received a letter from the aerodrome directors congratulating us on the professional manner in which the display was carried out and the efficient way the aerodrome was returned to normal operations.

These niceties apart, it was the weather which finally dashed our hopes of raising some much-needed revenue, but the fact that we escaped relatively unscathed was entirely due to the energy, commitment, skill and goodwill of countless members and friends freely given and gratefully received. Finally if anyone did miss out and would like a copy of the souvenir programme we have plenty left!

In the same issue there were some interesting items in the 'Club News' column:

We are delighted to report that early this year the Club's engineers, John Sarratt, Jim Ellis and 'Dev' Deverell received the AOPA *Engineer of the Year* award, a very well-deserved and long-overdue recognition of many years' devoted and expert work in the maintenance and repair of the Club's aircraft.

We were also very pleased to hear that in June Charlie Shea-Simonds was elected Chairman of the Royal Aero Club in succession to Bev Snook, who has filled this post with distinction for several years. The Club is very proud that such an important position in the national sporting aviation scene continues to be filled by a member of the Club – and a very active one at that
. . .

Congratulations also to Tony Calvey who has won a flying scholarship for disabled pilots at the Oxford Air Training School. Tony, who is a racing motor-cyclist specialising in sidecar racing, lost a leg some time ago in an accident, but this has not prevented him from jumping into the front seat of Stampes for aerobatic rides whenever the opportunity has arisen and no doubt he will soon be flying one himself.

The summer months are always a regular time for visits from overseas members and this year we are very pleased to welcome a number of new members. To renew acquaintance with or checkout on the Tiger and the Stampe is still the main attraction, and we are grateful for the forbearance and understanding shown towards some of the frustrations of flying open-cockpit biplanes with the current radio regime and in sight of new control buildings etc.

Talking of radio procedures, the CAA has just issued a notice stating that it is 'to mount an exercise to monitor on a random basis radio communications to identify specific non-conformity.' Whether the instruction 'take off at your discretion' falls into this category we do not know but this particular radio communication always seems to cause no end of amusement amongst our overseas members.

We have also had a visit from a Japanese aviation journalist, who has since sent us a copy of his magazine with an article in it about the Club, including a picture of G-ACDC. Harvey Tring arranged a translation, from which it was obvious that our Japanese friend was somewhat amazed that we were still flying 50-year-old biplanes, that such a thing as a grass airfield existed at all and that a Gipsy Major engine should leave so much oil about the place!

Recent aircraft visitors to the hangar have included a Fokker D.VII replica microlight assembled from an American kit by Phil Read, an enterprise which roused much interest; it was very disappointing that the machine was not permitted to make a test flight because microlights are banned at the aerodrome. The Navy's Swordfish spent a couple of nights in the hangar during the Air Show and its huge size, even with the wings folded, was most impressive. Finally Pete Kynsey's and John Harper's new Lazer aerobatic mount arrived in preparation for the World Championships. With its constant-speed wooden prop, it is significantly quieter than the Pitts Specials, which is a definite plus point. We wish Pete and John every success at South Cerney.

We've just received a review copy of Annette Carson's latest book, *Flight Fantastic*, which is a history of aerobatics from the earliest times to the present day. The Club's contribution to aerobatics, particularly in the late 50s and early 60s, is very well covered and the book will be reviewed comprehensively in the next issue of the *Rag*. In fact I should imagine that just about every aerobatic pilot in the Club will want to review what is a magnificent and timely contribution to the sport.

Annette was an associate member of the Club and also the BAeA's official delegate to the FAI commission on aerobatics, where she was particularly interested in improving the standards and training of aerobatic competition judges. She was handicapped with poor eyesight and she could neither drive nor fly herself. I admired her spirit and enterprise in undertaking such a major task as the history of aerobatics. I was able to give her a good deal of information from the Club's archives and in fact she became so interested that she was soon volunteering to write a history of the Tiger Club. Perhaps Benjy got to hear of the idea . . .!

Two accidents were also mentioned in the Club News, one a heavy landing by Tiger 'OAA at the Downlands strip. Downlands was now a regular stopover and Mac Maiklem, its owner, had accepted Honorary Membership of the Club. Members found it highly convenient and affordable to clock up a 20-minute sortie there and back. Perhaps it was getting too popular . . .

The other accident was a collision between two Turbulents landing tied together at Wycombe Air Park after the final leg of a Dawn-to-Dusk flight. Quite who came up with this idea has not been recorded and luckily the damage was fairly minor. The pilots were Neil Thomason and David Keene, both members of the Turbulent formation team. The accident aroused the interest of Barry Tempest wearing his 'poacher turned gamekeeper' hat in the CAA. He wrote:

"I understand this (accident) occurred while the aircraft were partici-pating in the Dawn-to-Dusk Competition, and their particular entry consisted of making an extended cross-country with intermediate stops while remaining tied together. While not wishing to pour cold water on the undoubted fruitful imagination of your Club members, may I suggest respectfully that the level of concentration implicit if this type of flying is to be conducted safely is surely imcompatible with the extended duration involved in any Dawn-to-Dusk operation."

I wrote back:

"On a point of information, I can assure you that it was not the intention of the pilots concerned to carry out this flight tied together for the whole day. I believe it was to be for one or perhaps two legs during which photographs would be taken.

The Club's Committee discussed this accident at great length and minuted:

'Formation pilots to be fully briefed on the inherent risks on formation landings and, if in tied formation, the risks of weak links not breaking at 'after landings' speeds.

I am not sure whether the Judges of the Dawn-to-Dusk competition will have any comment to make on this accident, but I would like to assure you that the lessons of it, as far as the Club is concerned, have been well learnt, and as far as the individual pilots are concerned both of them have suffered considerable financial embarrassment as a result.

I sincerely hope that the above will assist you in closing your file on this particular occurrence. . . ."

When the results of the competition were announced, Neil and David were placed last.

It was extremely fortunate that G-APNZ was not one of the two Turbulents involved because we had already committed the aircraft for an important engagement at Benson; John Severne, who was now the Captain of the Queen's Flight, had written earlier in the year:

"1986 is a very important year for the Queen's Flight because we will be celebrating the 50th Anniversary of the formation of the King's Flight in July 1936. On 26th July we will be having a Families Day at Benson

when, in addition to our own families, invitations will be sent to representatives from industry who support us and also members of the Royal Households and their staffs who fly with us. We hope to gather together some aircraft to represent Royal flying over the past 50 years; in particular we should have a Rapide in King's Flight colours which is currently being restored by the East Anglian Aircraft Society. When the King's Flight first formed, our one and only aircraft was a Rapide owned by King Edward VIII.

We wonder whether it would be possible for 'NZ to be with us on the day? It is a significant aircraft to us, not just because of the King's Cup, but because, when the Duke of Edinburgh flew it, it was the first and only time that a member of the Royal Family has ever flown a single-seater aircraft. The Turbulent parked alongside the 146 would make an interesting comparison! If the aircraft is not already committed on 26th July, we would welcome its arrival the day before because the airfield may well be closed on the Saturday morning. We would of course be delighted to accommodate the pilot. . . ."

David, who lived close to Benson, volunteered to be the pilot. Perhaps the occasion took his mind off the embarrassing incident which had occurred only a fortnight before.

The rumours which had been circulating that the hard runway appeal had been turned down were confirmed in August. At the time I was both surprised and uneasy. If British & Commonwealth PLC with their money and connections in Government could not succeed on such a comparatively simple matter, what hope would we have if ever we reached the planning permission stage for a new airfield?

Whatever the appearance, the reality is that these decisions are made by Government ministers. Having digested the Inspector's 54-page report, I came to the conclusion that a certain Air Commodore who had assisted him at the Inquiry had made a significant contribution.

The aerodrome owners and their consultants had been running the 'safety' horse as hard as possible and had also obtained the usual guarded evidence from the CAA that a hard runway *could* make the airfield safer.

But, said the report, it *would* make it safer for a different class of aircraft and there was no reason why grass runways should not be made operationally efficient.

Also there was no evidence of positive demand. Why, there were only nine letters supporting the scheme! It was a pity that this same Air Commodore had not assisted Mr Justice Mustill in another place. Although most people were relieved at the decision, personally I confessed to a slight twinge of regret. As a keen exponent of Formula 1 racers with their flexible spring steel undercarriages I had to admit that, compared to grass, there is nothing sweeter than taking off and landing a Beta on a hard surface.

During 1986, members were becoming impatient at the apparent lack of progress in acquiring a new airfield site. In fact Robin Voice resigned from the Committee over the issue – at least that was what he told Benjy. Although a good deal of work had been done the previous year on the site we were now focussing on – Wilmington – nothing had been agreed and it was difficult to keep everyone in the picture. Also we could not stop the almost continuous investigation into other alternatives. As for Wilmington, we had been in touch with the agents and visited the site, and Neil and I had seen the District Planning Officer, who was not unsympathetic.

The land itself was not actually on the market. It was held by Trustees acting for the family of Mrs Gwynne Longland, who lived at Wootton Manor some two miles away. It had been her uncle, Sir Roland Gwynne, a former Mayor of Eastbourne, who had originally made the land available for a civil airfield. Her sister was Elizabeth David, the well-known cookery writer.

The land agent, Mr Tim Raikes, had immediately told us that the land was not for sale because there was a problem with the sitting farm tenants, Philip Burgess and his father. However there might be a possibility of a long lease with a first option to purchase if the land came on the market.

The site was, frankly, a shambles. The field itself had been put down to corn. There was one hangar in a very dilapidated condition; where a Clubhouse had once stood there was a pile of rubble and masonry which, together with rusting machinery, intruding undergrowth and a general air of neglect, made for a very depressing picture.

However, in my mind's eye I could see that it would be ideal, and the Burgesses had already told me that under the mess there was water, electricity and even the original underground fuel tank. The field itself was small, with an east-west run of 520 metres and a north-south of 380 metres, but there was an adjoining field to the north (not in the same ownership) which, if a fence was removed, would extend this by a further 400 metres. I had also received a great deal of information on the airfield's past from two local airfield historians, Peter Vaughan and Alan Hibbs.

They had sent me a very brief summary:

"The aerodrome was situated in a large field owned by Colonel Sir Roland Gwynne of Wootton Manor and bounded by the A27 on the south side and by the byway opposite Milton Street on the east side.

The enterprise was started by a Mr Allenby who began flying facilities there for himself and friends in the early 1930s and established a Clubhouse for social activities. The facilities (but not the land) were bought in 1935/36 by Mr Harry Love (who built a house called Arlington Meadow in Milton Street opposite) and Mr Geoff Stubbley. They established a proper flying club known as the Eastbourne Flying Club and operated as a limited company. Mr Eric Edgerton was the Secretary. Flying instruction was given by the two owners and by Flight Lieut. Hazel. The engineer was a Mr Woodhouse.

The Club owned about six aircraft, Gipsy Moths and Tiger Moths, and flourished under the new leadership. A new brick Clubhouse was built in 1938. An aircraft which towed a banner for advertising purposes was allowed to operate from the airfield. The flying activities were encouraged by the Civil Air Guard Scheme, which gave financial aid.

All private flying was stopped immediately on the outbreak of war in 1939 and the Club continued for a while as a social club. Because of the proximity of the Long Man of Wilmington, which would have given hostile aircraft an easy landmark to aid attack, the field was not developed for military flying. Instead it was taken over by the War Office and was used as a base for the Royal Engineers.

The flying club was not restarted after the war. The Clubhouse became a farmhouse, the land was farmed and the hangars used as barns. The Clubhouse was demolished about 1970, the land is still farmed and the old hangars, very dilapidated, are still there. Until quite recently the postbox situated at the junction of Milton Street and the A27 bore a small enamel location plate 'The Aerodrome.'"

There was also some sketchy evidence that the field had been used by the Royal Flying Corps during the first World War. In addition, a number of cuttings from *Flight* and local newspapers, a copy of the original aerodrome licence and several photographs had been unearthed.

A number of these cuttings (heavily abbreviated) had intrigued me:

Flight, August 1936

'When we had all settled down to the idea that our English summer had played itself out . . . it returned unexpectedly . . . for the Eastbourne Flying Club's first big show last Saturday. Consequently a score or more privately-owned machines turned up, quite apart from the considerable number of demonstration, trade and Club machines . . .

Wilmington Aerodrome . . . is still its old self – large enough for light aeroplanes but a little troublesome to pilots of bigger types. However everyone got in and and out without heart failure, and . . . the joy-riding Dragon flew with monotonous regularity during the later afternoon.

The show started with an arrival competition on the usual sealed-time lines. . . . Thereafter, demonstrations followed thick and fast . . . the Monospar . . . the C.30 Autogyro . . . the Heston Phoenix . . . Mr Kronfeld's Drone . . . the cantilever Pou . . . the Cirrus Swallow. . . .

Lord Patrick Crichton Stuart's much-raced Hendon Hobo won the Concours d'Elegance, with the Duchess of Bedford's Moth Major second.

211

One of the London Club's Tigers put up a safe and excellent aerobatic exhibition to to fill a gap in the programme.

Altogether a worthy piece of work by the organisers. . . . Those pilots returning to London in the smooth air of the evening obtained an almost unparallelled view of Sussex and Surrey and we, loftily perched in the nose of the London Club's new Dragonfly, saw the whole of London clearly spread out. . . .'

Flight, August 1937

'Nevertheless, interest in the new (Civil Air Guard) scheme was not the reason for the tremendous amount of support given to this event, at which there were probably 10,000 spectators and nearly 100 visiting machines. For months before, Capt E.I. Short, the secretary of the Eastbourne Flying Club, had been in touch with all those who might assist at the meeting, and he managed to obtain not only a squadron of Gauntlets from Biggin Hill but also three or four visitors from the continent, including one of Germany's better-known women aerobatic pilots.

Because of the amount of support given and the number, therefore, of visiting machines (some of which had, in all politeness, to be given a show), the programme was more than long drawn out. . . .

Before No. 79 Squadron took the air. . . Mr Alex Henshaw had duly shot the place up with his King's Cup-winning Mew Gull, while one or two late arrivals flapped around the aerodrome in evident terror. . . .

After the squadron drill Mr –– demonstrated the Tipsy two-seater, Mr –– flew gently round in the Miles Monarch and Mr –– banged the Scheldemusch into the ground a few times. . . . In the meantime Mr –– had shown us exactly what the good old Avro 504 could do – and it must be admitted that the old type of machine is still the best of all for low-altitude aerobatic exhibitions. . . . To modern eyes his loops from ground level were a little soul-shattering. . . . Another arch-expert in crazy flying, the veteran Pashley, decided that conditions were really too breezy and bumpy for a similar display with a Gipsy Moth. . . . Mr R.L. Porteous gave a satisfactory indication that the Chilton is a very real aeroplane. . . .'

Eastbourne Chronicle, May 1938

'The new President of the Eastbourne Flying Club, Lt. Col. R.V. Gwynne, DSO, DL, cut the first turf on the site of the new Clubhouse at Wilmington flying ground on Saturday evening. A large number of members and visitors were present, including aviators from Shoreham, Hendon and other aerodromes. . . .

The Mayor (Alderman J. Wheeler) spoke of the new Clubhouse as a forward step, saying that he was glad to be associated with a hearty vote of thanks to Col. Gwynne for cutting the first turf. He had always been in favour of flying facilities, and would do all in his power to help the Club.

He, too, hoped the Corporation, and the Government, would take a greater interest in civil aviation. . . .

The new Clubhouse will be a handsome addition to the large flying ground. . . . Accommodation on the ground floor will include a tea lounge, bar lounge, billiard room, club room and reading room, as well as living quarters for the manager. On the first floor will be made further provision for the resident manager, and four bedrooms, with bathroom, are to be included for visiting flyers.'

The Clubhouse was duly built and, as Benjy has already mentioned in a previous volume of this story, flying club managers, as well as their members and friends, enjoyed far superior facilities pre-war than they do today. Perhaps we could recreate a little of that ambience.

At the beginning of 1986, at Mr Raikes' suggestion, Neil and I arranged to meet Mrs Longland at Wootton Manor. It was a beautiful house with much priceless furniture and many heirlooms and Mrs Priscilla Longland was a charming person. She seemed very happy at the prospect of the airfield which had been started by her uncle being restored, and she knew that the younger generation of her family would be delighted. She had only one proviso – that we would not fly over Wootton Manor. After our meeting, I felt that Mrs Longland had been reassured that the Tiger Club was the right and proper organisation to attempt the task.

As 1986 went by, I grew more and more certain that as far as Wilmington was concerned we had to go for it. It was an exciting and worthwhile project. After all, Rollasons with the help of Norman Jones had built, restored and repaired countless light aircraft, and the Tiger Club had promoted and undertaken a huge amount of sporting flying; could we not now repair and restore a real Club airfield?

Our lease at Redhill was due to expire at the end of 1987 and, although technically we had a legal right to renew it, we could not go on fighting British & Commonwealth PLC for ever. We could have a proper Clubhouse at Wilmington and, although it would not suit everybody, we could be in total control and it would be ideal for most of the Club's aircraft, especially the biplanes and the Turbulents.

Although there were still difficulties with the Trustees, who were worried about the existing tenants, I had already met Philip Burgess and he was enthusiastic, as indeed were most of his friends amongst the local farming community. Eventually we were able to exchange letters with Tim Raikes containing heads of agreement which would enable us not only to proceed with the planning exercise but also, most importantly, to negotiate with the Burgesses about putting down a grass strip after the harvest in August to enable essential trial flights to take place. And by the end of the year, once again with some help from Graham Plumbe, we had a draft lease on the table.

'Club News,' as reported in the November issue of the *Rag*, was mixed. There had been a second unexplained engine failure on take-off inside two years at Redhill. This time it was the Super Cub. Fortunately there were no injuries and the damage was not too serious, but it did mean that the seaplane programme for the year had to be abandoned, which was a pity because Tom Freer and David Shepherd had moved heaven and earth to get the water at Scotney Court actually licensed by the CAA.

The World Aerobatic Championships had been staged in Britain – only for the second time – at South Cerney. Pete Kynsey had come eighth in an event marred by bad weather and bureaucratic problems created by the Ministry of Defence over the hours available for practice.

Club touring abroad had picked up considerably and the big Jodel Mousquetaire 'TKX had been booked in November by Martin Evans to collect supplies of Beaujolais Nouveau. However the *Rag* also reported:

The Club's directors, after a recent review of the Club's finances, have decided with great reluctance to offer 'TKX for sale in the first instance to a member or members who might be interested in keeping the aircraft at Redhill on a possible lease-back agreement. Although 'the big Jodel' is a very fine aircraft and has been with the Club for a long time, unfortunately its utilisation over the last few years has not been sufficient to justify its retention, and it has suffered particularly from high insurance and fuel costs.

As previously mentioned this was the aircraft which had to be sold in order to settle the final solicitors' bills in the High Court case. Shortly after the announcement, 'TKX was bought by Marcus and Jane Norman and leased back to the Club, which was a happy solution for all concerned. Also at this time we decided to close the Legal Fund appeal for cash in connection with the case, as the *Rag* later explained:

The final bills for the Club's disastrous punch-up in the High Court three years ago with our landlords at Redhill have now been settled in full. For those who may be interested, the legal costs of attempting to defend the principles of 'airmanship, freedom and common sense' were as follows:

The other side's costs, including taxation fees	£18,685
Counsel's fees	£13,020
Fees of 'independent expert'	£1,780
Solicitor's fees	£13,254
Total	£46,739

None of this, of course, accounts for the very considerable voluntary efforts in preparing surveys, affidavits etc., and representations to people whom we thought might be able to assist in preventing the matter reaching court at all.

The Legal Fund raised £37,000 of this total, of which £31,000 came from members past and present and £6,000 from fund-raising efforts and other sympathisers. The balance of nearly £10,000 has been raised from the Club's own resources, together with the heavy financial outlay of equipping and re-equipping the Club's aircraft with radios – a process which is still not complete and amounting to some £15,000.

It has now been decided that the Legal Fund will not be called upon to provide further funds for this 'little, local difficulty,' but the Fund, of course, remains in existence and open, and undoubtedly will be required again. The Committee would like to take this opportunity of thanking everybody for what has been a truly outstanding fund-raising effort which has demonstrated to the aviation world at large – including a certain very large public company – the Club's commitment to its aims and its will to survive and prosper.

As for the lessons of the affair, the cynics must be allowed their say. The lawyers: when they tell you that you have a good case, then is the time to settle. The politicians: there are no votes in sporting flying. Tenant's flying rights: a myth. Small enterprises and red tape: a hollow laugh. The CAA: definitely not interested in the views of pilots. The High Court: an extremely expensive lottery.

What was not reported in the 'Club News' was that in October Benjy and Trudi had left Britain to live in Spain. Initially Benjy had sent his apologies for absence to the Committee for six months only, but he was to stay in Spain for the next eight years. However his irrepressible enthusiasm for the Club was undiminished and I was soon receiving a stream of letters with his ideas and suggestions, his comments and news.

During the winter, Norvela and I met up with him and Trudi whilst on a golfing holiday not far from Torremolinos on the Costa del Sol where they had an apartment. He told us that the first volume of Tiger Club history was well on the way and would we like to have a look at the proofs of some of the early chapters . . .?

The reception and prizegiving for the Dawn-to-Dusk competition was hosted in November, not this year by Prince Philip but by Prince Andrew, accompanied by his wife the Duchess of York, who had just flown solo and was expected to get her PPL shortly. The winner flew a microlight – the first time that an aircraft of this class had carried off the main trophy. Unfortunately the three-year sponsorship deal with Seagrams had now come to an end; I wrote to David Timmis that I was getting worried that the Club was missing out on the publicity and that it was now a good time to review the future of the competition.

I received a reply from the other David – David Hamilton (the two Davids on the Committee worked very closely together). The letter was written on British Precision Pilots Association (BPPA) notepaper:

"I believe that the Dawn-to-Dusk Competition has a long future but it needs careful promotion and management as an ongoing programme. Sponsorship is desperately needed and without it the Tiger Club may well find that it could become a drain on its limited resources.

As you know I was personally able to negotiate the last three-year sponsorship deal partly by using the name of the Tiger Club, partly by using that of the BPPA, with the added benefit of the Royal Aero Club of which BPPA is a member.

In the past the British Aerobatic Association, which grew out of the Tiger Club as the BPPA, has likewise undertaken the organisation of Tiger Club Competitions on behalf of the Tiger Club.

Similarly I should like to take this opportunity of suggesting that the organisation of the Dawn-to-Dusk be undertaken, in the future, under the umbrella of the BPPA.

Nothing would change. The Competition would remain the same as the current Tiger Club event. Most of the personnel involved would be Tiger Club members and that would include David Timmis and myself irrespective of any forthcoming election. The advantages are considerable. The Association would undertake to finance the competition using its resources to obtain sponsorship wherever possible, whilst the Tiger Club would gain continued publicity for an event which it would not have to contribute to on a financial basis. . . ."

I replied:

"I will put your suggestions to the other Directors of The Tiger Club Ltd and also, in due course, to the Committee, but I doubt that the Club will wish to give up the event unless possibly in return for a substantial financial consideration.

I agree that the Tiger Club has 'hived off' in the past a number of sporting aviation initiatives which are now being run successfully by separate associations, but these are in a rather different category. Also, as you well know, the Club's continuing problems at Redhill have made the taking of initiatives and their development very difficult. But this situation hopefully will not go on for ever."

The Club's financial position was none too healthy and the main Dawn-to-Dusk Trophy was valued in the books at £2,000. I did not hear any more from David Hamilton about the BPPA taking over the competition but he is still on the Tiger Club Committee and is still successfully running the Dawn-to-Dusk.

The last little drama to be played out in 1986 was the Committee elections, and the *Rag* gave the details of another 'first' in the history of the Club:

Six nominations were received for three places on the Committee including two standing for re-election. So the Club had its first postal ballot and the election duly took place on 16th December. The response to the ballot was approximately 35% of the membership and the successful candidates were:

Peter Kynsey   154 votes
David Hamilton (re-elected)   111 votes
David Timmis (re-elected)   90 votes

Commiserations are definitely in order for the unsuccessful candidates:

David Keene   78 votes
Nick Onn   67 votes
Howard Rose   63 votes

On balance the year had been another one of recovery after the 1984 crisis. Utilisation had again significantly improved, we had operated 13 aircraft, membership was steady and a reasonable operating profit had been achieved.

As far as the regulatory regime at Redhill was concerned Mr Dalrymple had been comparatively relaxed and there were only a few minor irritations. One of these was that landing fees for single-seat aircraft (i.e those not electing for a block fee) was jacked up to £6.00, the same as for all the other aircraft; another was that if people happened to be a few minutes late and landed after the official airfield closing time they were liable to be charged £14.00.

Some members were annoyed because they now had to pay greatly increased indemnity insurance premiums for the privilege of keeping their aircraft at Redhill, and we were finally and officially informed that, when the airfield was wet, the southern perimeter track could only be used by aircraft on 'essential' business – recreational aircraft need not apply!

We could live with these pinpricks. More disturbing was the last item to appear under 'any other business' in the minutes of the year's final Committee meeting:

'CAA letter on proposal to set up a 'system' of 'approved' display, racing and competition pilots discussed.'

The Club already had its own long-established system of approvals and authorisation cards for all these activities and it was resolved that the Club would oppose such proposals 'unless clear and overwhelming evidence could be produced to prove the need for such a 'system.'

CHAPTER 11
1987

Apart from a predictable ban on ski-flying by the Turbulents during a brief snowfall in January, the immediate problem for 1987 was who was coming to the Ball as the Guest of Honour. We had got quite used to high-profile people, and to continue with another 'Royal' guest Neil invited Prince Michael of Kent, who unfortunately was not available. Next, on my wife's suggestion, we tried Christopher Tugendhat, the new Chairman of the CAA. Mr Tugendhat was a former MP, a banker and an ex-European Commissioner – hence the personal connection with Norvela. Precisely why he was now Chairman of the CAA I never did find out but no doubt it was felt that it might be an opportunity to explain a few things about the Club. We still held the somewhat naïve belief that a Chairman of the CAA might actually be in a position to do something for sporting flying. Again, Christopher Tugendhat politely refused our invitation.

Then Judy Kay got in touch with Club member Christopher (Superman) Reeve, who provisionally accepted and was consequently billed in the publicity for the event as 'Our Host for the Evening.' In fact what Judy intended was that Chris Reeve would be the ideal replacement for Brendan as the 'star' of the show, but here there had been a mis-understanding since he was definitely not expecting to step into Brendan's shoes and, as it turned out, his 'Superman' filming schedule in the USA prevented him from attending anyway.

Finally Neil secured the services of Richard Noble who, with his wife Sally, filled the bill perfectly on another memorable and successful occasion:

Our Guest of Honour, Richard Noble of world land speed fame and now the builder of the new British light aircraft the ARV Super II, is definitely in the Geoffrey de Havilland tradition – 'you don't actually have to be mad to build aircraft, but it helps.' After opening remarks from the Chairman, he entertained us to some amusing stories about Thrust II, and some good advice on how to get money from one's bank manager. He later presented the Club's annual awards, the recipients being introduced in turn by Neil and Judy.

The RAF Dance Orchestra was magnificent, the food excellent and the company 'sympathetique.' A superb evening and night to relieve the winter gloom. . . .

Continuing the 'Royal' connection to the Club, the Duchess of York had accepted Honorary Membership at the end of the previous year, and now that she had gained her PPL the Chairman sent a letter of congratulations:

"The members of the Tiger Club have asked me to send you their heartiest congratulations upon gaining your Private Pilot's Licence.

The media have portrayed very clearly the enjoyment and satisfaction tha you have derived from flying and we sincerely hope that this will continue and grow with your own experience in the air.

As your husband has no doubt learnt as President of the Royal Aero Club, recreational flying does not enjoy quite such obvious public support as it did in, say, the 1930s. We welcome the opportunity that your involvement brings for promoting this demanding yet immensely satisfying sport."

Neil's reference in his final paragraph to 'public support' might have read 'establishment support.' There was no doubt that the help that such an attractive young woman as the Duchess of York might bring to the whole sporting flying movement could be invaluable.

Also in connection with royal enthusiasm for flying, John Severne had now established a Queen's Flight museum at Benson and was looking for a model of a Turbulent to go on permanent display. He knew that a small model of G-APNZ existed and he again emphasised the significance of the aircraft in the history of 'Royal' flying. He had been in touch with HRH but was told that all his models had been passed over to the Royal Aero Club, who had in turn sent them to the RAF museum. However 'PNZ was not among them.

At my suggestion, John then contacted Ralph Hart, who I knew had done a water colour of 'PNZ. Ralph, besides being a skilled aircraft home-builder, was also an expert model-maker, and he immediately promised one of 'PNZ. However it later transpired that one of the Dawn-to-Dusk judges remembered seeing the 'PNZ model in Prince Philip's office at Buckingham Palace. He had kept it back! And John was later able to collect it to go into the Queen's Flight museum.

Returning to the Redhill Saga, in March aerobatic practice over the aerodrome was finally banned. Neil had already requested via the Aerodrome Users Committee that the extremely limited slots we were allowed should be extended in view of the increased demand. The British Aerobatic calendar for 1987 listed no fewer than 12 national competitions, of which seven were for the beginners' Standard class. Mr Dalrymple justified his decision in what for him was a reasoned letter:

"We carefully considered all the options available such as early morning or midday slots, but feel that these would impinge unfairly upon the rights of other tenants and users of the Aerodrome. Further, it is our opinion that to allow aerobatics to take place contemporaneously with circuit flying, given the restricted airspace available to us, would be unsafe.

However, a more serious implication to the principle of allowing aerobatics overhead the Aerodrome has arisen following the development and occupation of the new Terminal Building. . . .

It is our determination that to continue to allow aerobatics to take place within such restricted airspace in close proximity to the Aerodrome Buildings would be extremely dangerous and against all the practices of good airmanship. . . ."

By now the new terminal and control tower had been in occupation for some time and the old RAF control tower had been pulled down. Mr Dalrymple and his secretary had moved from the offices in a converted farm cottage out of sight in the south-west corner of the airfield to palatial new quarters in the terminal building. Quite why it was considered that the new building would be more vulnerable than all the other buildings and hangars on the airfield was not explained.

Although it was eventually agreed that some limited practice slots over the airfield would be allowed during the month leading up to the Air Show, there seemed to be no point in launching an official objection. Thus a recognised practice facility which had been in existence for 20 years without complaint either from other users or local residents was finally brought to an end, and Club aerobatic enthusiasts were denied the convenience and safety of their own airfield where they could be both seen and criticised. From now on aerobatic practice would take place away from the airfield out of sight and potentially more complaints would be caused.

However for seaplane enthusiasts, as Tom Freer explained in the *Rag*, there was much in prospect:

The Club's Seaplane Section is planning a busy season for 'VPT. For this it is much indebted to David Shepherd, who is providing the floats. The programme will be in two parts. Floats on during the weekend of 25th-26th April. Start of the seaplaning, 2nd May. Floats off, 14th June. 'VPT is then available for glider-towing. Floats on again, 8th August. Floats finally off, 27th September.

During May and the first half of June the principal purpose will be to enable members to obtain 'ratings.' However, this does not preclude others who do not wish to obtain ratings from taking part. There is nothing exclusive about our plans. All members who are interested are very welcome to come and try it. The main base is Scotney Court, near Lydd.

During the last week of August and the first week of September the Club is planning an extensive seaplane tour, probably to the Highlands of Scotland (precise route and ultimate destination are not yet fixed). The flying will be shared among those taking part, and the more members there are to share it, the easier such a tour becomes: in 1979 and 1980 we were about six or seven pilots, and five or six cars for logistic support. . . .

But it was not to be. Early in May, after the aircraft had flown a mere three hours, it was capsized taking off from Scotney Court while being flown solo by David Shepherd. From the meticulous and lengthy reports produced both by David and Tom – who was an eyewitness – it was apparent that a strong gust and the light weight of the Cub were contributory factors. Also perhaps David had been surprised by the rapidity at which the aircraft became airborne and had held the stick back fractionally too long. In view of all that had been done to get Scotney Court licensed by the CAA the accident was particularly depressing. It seemed that it was not only seaplaning that was cursed but the Super Cub, which had now suffered its second disaster in less than a year. Although 'VPT was eventually restored to health after its ducking, inevitably at the time it was the end of the Club's seaplane flying.

The original United Kingdom Seaplane Club had been founded in 1961 at Lee-on-Solent, with support and encouragement from some highly placed people including Sir Francis Chichester. The Club had taken over the operation in 1965, since when some 800 hours had been flown on the Tiger and 75 on the Cub, which in the opinion of most people was a much more practical machine. The costs both in terms of maintenance and damage had been high – too high. But flying with floats had been an activity greatly prized by many members. It had only taken place by virtue of the dedicated voluntary help of a few people. It was very much in the spirit of the Club and perhaps – who knows? – it will one day be revived.

1987 was the last year of our agreement with the landlords to hold an Air Show at Redhill since it was also the year that our ill-fated lease was due to expire. Of the three shows that had already taken place two had been ruined by the weather. This year, as the 'Club News' reported, there was something special to look forward to – some foreign participation:

The big news is that it is 'all systems go' for the Air Show on 26th July. The necessary financial guarantees have been obtained and all we need now is reasonable weather.

Some preliminary information is elsewhere in this issue. On the flying side, we have been approached this year by a Group of Italian enthusiasts known as Le Tigri, which operates a bunch of four Tiger Moths and two Jungmanns. They intend to come to the show en masse and are offering formation, aerobatics, dog-fighting etc.

Some very senior members of the Club may recall that nearly 30 years ago (can it be as long as that?) Rollasons exported quite a number of 'brand-new' Tigers to Italian customers at a price of approximately £900 each including delivery. Club members were asked to undertake the ferry flights, a job, needless to say, for which there was quite a queue. Having heard very little of the history of these machines in the intervening decades, it is fascinating to speculate that some of them may again be seen at Redhill on 26th July.

I had myself been lucky enough to secure one of these ferry flights in February 1960 – to Rome – when I had very few solo hours in my log book, and it had been a memorable experience . . .

As far as the finances were concerned there had been some major worries. Jeanne had already told us that she was unable to continue as the organiser unless a major sponsor could be found, and British Airtours and other companies had already turned down our invitation. The bank had informed me that since our lease was shortly to expire they could not increase our overdraft to finance the event. We needed £5,000 up front to enable the show to go ahead. There were indications that some members might be willing to help, so an underwriting prospectus was produced in which, in return for a stake of £1,000, the subsciber would be guaranteed a share of the profits in addition to the return of the original stake and conversely, more important, would underwrite a share of the losses – if any – in proportion.

Four members of the Committee immediately came to the rescue and the fifth volunteer, who was not a member of the Club, turned out to be the person who at the time was auditing the Club's annual accounts. As he said, he fancied a flutter, but please do not tell his boss at Stoy Hayward!

As for the organisation Janet Tring (in professional life Janet Ayres and also highly experienced in the 'trade') offered to take over from Jeanne, and the rest of the small sub-committee continued as in the previous year – Neil, Don and Geoff Tait on the ground side and Brian the flying, providing he could vet the performance of Le Tigri before the show.

During the early part of the summer we went public on the Wilmington project, not only with the Club but also with the local District and Parish Councils. Part of the field had by now been put down to grass and on the 1st June Neil and I landed the Stampe G-AWEF there, the first time an aircraft had done this for 48 years.

Earlier, with the help of Michael Parker, a planning consultant from Lewes, a formal application for planning consent had been put in to the Wealden District Council. Before this we had had various meetings on the site, not only with the planning officers and local councillors but also with officials from the regional tourist and rural industry organisations. No doubt mindful of the potential economic benefits to the area, they all appeared reasonably enthusiastic. Initially, even the owners of Drusilla's Zoo park, which was the main tourist attraction in the district, were in favour.

Also the redoubtable Mrs Moyra Logan of the Airfields Environment Federation had visited the site and had expressed no outright opposition providing, as she put it, 'the consent was personal to the Tiger Club.' She had already written in one of her newsletters:

'There will doubtless be occasions when the move of aviation facilities from an urban location to a more rural environment would be desirable.' However sending in the official application with its accompanying documentation was like exploding a bomb. An immediate campaign of opposition was whipped up by a small group of vociferous and blinkered individuals and, although local Press coverage was even-handed, it tended to fan the flames.

In July two public meetings were held. The first, in Wilmington village, was civilized and we were able to answer reasonable questions. The second, two weeks later, took place at Drusilla's Zoo. A hostile claque had been organised. One woman even screamed: "Does it mean that we are going to be invaded by the French?"

Rational discussion was impossible. All we could do was to wait for the local Council's probable refusal and then consider an appeal and a Public Inquiry at which hopefully, there would be a calmer atmosphere.

In fact the only local residents who would be directly affected were those living in a few houses in a small lane leading off the main road which ran past the airfield. The irony of the situation was that these houses had been built during the 1930s when the airfield was active. One of them was for Harry Love, the CFI, put up by a local builder, one of his pupils. His widow, Mary Love, who also learnt to fly at Wilmington, still lived there. She was able to tell us how her husband had been one of the early members of the Guild of Air Pilots, how there had been a social as well as a flying club with 150 members, how her husband used to say that if you could fly out of Wilmington you could fly anywhere and much else besides . . .

If Wilmington was occupying a great deal of my time there were also plenty of other topics to be discussed in the Club, as the *Rag* reported in June:

Late April and early May, apart from a typical cold and windy Bank Holiday weekend, have been excellent for flying, and utilisation of Club aircraft definitely took a turn for the better with the Stampes again leading the fleet as the Club's most popular aircraft. On the last Saturday in April, Jim Alderton managed to get together an impressive 16-ship Balbo of Club and members' aircraft for a flight round the local area, led by Brian Smith and Ian White in Ian's magnificent Gipsy Moth: a splendid piece of organisation which will be a great help in stimulating interest in the forthcoming Air Show.

On the subject of the CAA, there is still no news on the outcome of the 'hire and reward' debate but we believe that serious efforts are continuing to give legal recognition to the existing situation and to permit 'cost compensation' to continue. What is more immediate and alarming is that the CAA has now published its regulatory proposals on the matter of organised displays and competitions etc. As stated, the new regulations will require any organiser of any aeronautical event and any pilot who takes part to be specifically licensed by the CAA. The Club has made its views on these draconian measures clear to the department concerned and we can but hope that sensible amendments will be forthcoming.

Bob Grimstead writes to say that he has achieved a new height record for a Turbulent in his own highly-modified G-ARRZ, now 25 years old. He reached the staggering altitude of 21,500 feet (with oxygen). If memory serves me correctly the previous record was set about 20 years ago at around 15,000 feet (without oxygen). Height record attempts seem to be a less popular form of sporting aviation these days than in the past. Apart from the need for oxygen, a careful study needs to be made of controlled airspace and transponder requirements. Congratulations to Bob on a great achievement.

The aerobatic competition season has started well with events at Bodmin, Snoring and Fenland. 'TKC unfortunately blew a magneto at Bodmin, but at Snoring and Fenland performed well, with Club members making up the majority of the field and getting into the money without quite carrying off the trophies. In the 'grand prix' division, Tim Barnby and John Harper have made the British team in their own examples of the 'heavy metal.' Pete Kynsey is taking a year off from competition, and Pitts Specials, it has to be said, are definitely not popular south of the Thames!

FARA also has a good season under way with most events as usual in France. The foreign touring element of FI racing is certainly one of the plus factors. The Club's Beta *Blue Chip*, although no longer competitive, is available to newcomers to gain the necessary experience.

The display scene is being enlivened this year by Brendan O'Brien, now returned fresh from the Antarctic where he has obviously been dreaming up new ideas. . . . Much publicised has been his version of the 'truck-top landing,' an act which is popular in the States but not yet in Europe. He has acquired his own specially modified and sponsored Super Cub, together with a lorry which is being driven by Mac Maiklem. The act is confined to hard runway venues so will not be seen at Redhill.

Another less publicised 'first' has been the inverted 'baton pass.' The Committee gave a cautious approval to Brendan and Pete Kynsey to practise this act using a Club Stampe and a 'Standing on the Wing' Tiger. So far the results have been encouraging and some photographs are promised. According to Brendan, it is a 'first' even for the States!

The whole business of 'hire and reward,' the basic Commercial Pilot's Licence (BCPL) and 'Display Licensing' was discussed regularly in the Committee and the minutes from 1987 are full of references. The Club was well represented at the many CAA meetings with interested organisations including the Historic Aircraft Association (HAA) which had recently been formed at Old Warden.

As far as displays were concerned, times were changing fast; the CAA was now referring to the 'display industry.' The HAA and the BAeA were in favour of a system of licensing and, despite our initial opposition, eventually we went along with them but with strong reservations for the racing fraternity who were already obliged to hold competition licences issued by the Royal Aero Club. As for 'hire and reward' (or what we called at the time 'cost compensation') for the non-professional participant, the whole subject was a veritable minefield. The CAA, after a great deal of discussion and debate, had now finally introduced a whole raft of new rules and regulations on what is now called 'valuable consideration.' The general opinion is that they were not only too complicated but also incomprehensible.

The comment on the Pitts Special referred of course to noise complaints. These so exasperated Mr Dalrymple that he banned the Pitts in the hangar which was operated by Tim Barnby and Roger Graham from using the aerodrome. To be fair the single-seat Pitts with the big Lycoming engine and the fixed-pitch prop was simply too noisy and the Club did not feel that it could make any official protest. As for the Beta this produced a letter from Steve Thompson:

"I feel the description of Blue Chip *(Club News, June) as no longer competitive fails to do her justice. While it is true that a Beta has not won a race for some time, Michael Jones showed for some years that* Blue Chip, *if prepared and flown well, is capable of beating most standard Cassutts, the CP.80s and the slower modified Cassutts. There are several machines now racing which fall into this group and more will be flying by the end of the season, so good racing is available for the Beta.*

Blue Chip *remains the only Formula One racer available anywhere at an hourly rate, and represents a unique opportunity for Tiger Club pilots to take part in the only real air racing available."*

During the early years of F1 racing when metal props were still in use and not considered to be an unacceptable risk I often used to transport *Blue Chip* to race meetings dismantled on a special trailer and, to save weight, devoid of unnecessary instruments. The machine had also been modified with a shorter spring steel undercarriage which made it tricky to land inside a reasonable distance. Now that the racer was being made available to selected members and by *force majeure* had been fitted with a radio and battery, she was becoming quite suitable as a fast tourer with a bit of space for baggage! Also the original longer landing gear had been restored.

But in F1 racing, for a Beta to remain really competitive, there was no compromise between speed and convenience.

During July excitement mounted at the prospect of the forthcoming Air Show, particularly the arrival of *Le Tigri*. The four Italian Tigers and one Jungmann were based at a grass field at Treviso in Northern Italy aptly called Campo di Volo Jonathon. They were sponsored by a firm of furniture manufacturers in the town called Frezza, whose chairman, Francesco Frezza, was also a pilot and a vintage aircraft enthusiast. The firm also had agents in London. The trip was publicised as a 'raid,' a word which is used in French and Italian to mean a 'round flight' rather than carrying a military connotation. The 'raid' was also to commemorate the anniversary of Blériot's cross-Channel flight on 25th July and had been considerably expanded by the addition of five Super Cubs from the Italian mountain flight school, taking time off from glacier landings.

Mr Frezza's publicity also carried a political message: European unity and the single market. Even Mr Dalrymple became enthusiastic and agreed not only to a 10% reduction in the Air Show fee and free landings for participating aircraft but also for arrangements for the Italians to clear Customs inbound from France in the new terminal building. Brian put together a mouth-watering provisional flying programme with the 'race' item reverting to the traditional Club pre-arranged handicap event instead of Formula 1.

Provisional Flying Programme

Cosmic Wind	Pete Kynsey
Balbo	Tiger Club
Turbulents	Tiger Club
Swordfish	RN Historic Flight
Unipart Duo	John Taylor
Flour Bombing	Tiger Club
Glider	Tiger Club/D. Piggott
Pitts Special	Richard Pickin
Balloon bursting	Tiger Club
BBMF	BBMF Coningsby
Italian Equipe	Le Tigri/Historic Trentine
B-17	Sally B *Memorial Flight*
Stampe Duo	Tiger Club
Inverted Ribbon Cut	Tiger Club
Crazy Flying	Brendan O'Brien
Firefly	RN Historic Flight
Parachuting	Tiger Club
FW.190 Replica	Rod Dean
Tied Trio	Tiger Club
Race	Tiger Club
Balloon	British Airtours

For the programme on the ground there was also something new – the Brooklands Connection, as a Press release explained:

'1987 has seen the forging of a strong link between the famous BROOKLANDS RACECOURSE (celebrating its 80th anniversary this year) and the TIGER CLUB of Redhill Aerodrome, which will culminate with a special 'Salute to Brooklands' exhibit at the forthcoming TIGER CLUB AIR SHOW....

Two weeks ago four of the Club's vintage aircraft landed at Brooklands, on a strip specially prepared for the occasion, to take part in the launch of the Brooklands Museum Trust. Last Sunday, the Tiger Club paid a second visit in the form of a flypast during the Brooklands Society Reunion.

Visitors to the Air Show in July will be able to see exhibits by both the Brooklands Society and Brooklands Museum. In addition, 30 to 40 cars and motor-cycles of the types used at the famous circuit will be on view, bearing such magical names as BENTLEY, FRAZER-NASH, LAGONDA, RILEY, MG, ALFA ROMEO, MERCEDES and MARENDAZ SPECIAL. Motor-cycle enthusiasts will recognise the names of ZENITH, DOUGLAS, BROUGH SUPERIOR and COTTON BLACKBURN. A selection of pedal cycles used for racing at Brooklands completes the display.'

As it turned out, the weather for once was completely on our side and as reported in the *Rag* the show was an outstanding success:

Blessed with near-perfect weather, this was the most successful Show we have ever held at Redhill in terms of crowd attendance. As in previous years, our thanks must go out to all those members who gave so unsparingly of their time and effort in the thousand and one things that needed doing. It is always invidious to mention names but Geoff Tait's organisation of the ground exhibition and setting up of the event, ably assisted by Charles Ravenhill, was as in previous years faultless. Janet Ayres in taking over from Jeanne Frazer as display co-ordinator and promoter had a very high standard to follow and succeeded admirably. Brian Smith put together a flying programme in the best Club tradition which went without a hitch and which the crowd loved. David Body's posters will again become collectors' items and as in previous years Brendan O'Brien's commentary received most of the fan-mail.

The main highlight was, of course, the visit to the Show of the Italian *Le Tigri*, unassumingly and skilfully led by Giancarlo Zanardo. It was splendid to see five biplanes, including four venerable Tigers (three of them were ex-Rollason's) arriving perfectly on schedule in the best Tiger Club tradition and all the way from Italy. An excellent and spirited display was put up on the day itself with the supporting and unusual duo formation of Super Cubs from the Trentine Patrol (the Italian mountain flying school). We were delighted that both *Le Tigri* and the Trentina agreed to take part in the Balbo, thereby

227

enabling some sort of record to be achieved for the mass formation. We were also very grateful that Snr Francesco Frezza suggested having a party the evening before on the airfield so that British and Italian pilots and their friends could get together, and a splendid occasion it proved to be; the wine mysteriously appeared from a van which had come all the way from Italy – and from where else? All in all there is absolutely no doubt that the international flavour provided by our Italian friends made the 1987 Show especially memorable.

The five underwriters received a very worthwhile return on their investment.

However the aerodrome director was not pleased. A few days after the show I received a long letter from Mr Dalrymple containing a string of peevish complaints. He complained about the crowd control; he complained that the pilots were only in contact with the AFIS for '10% of the time'; he complained (with some justification) about the exuberance of one pilot who flew 'unexpectedly straight at the control tower' at the conclusion of the 'biplane four' act; he complained that the military vehicles which Geoff Tait had organised for the ground exhibition included a Sherman tank; he complained that the Club marquee which had been put up at our expense had been used to to entertain the Italian pilots the evening before the show without his permission.

Finally he abruptly informed us that now that our licence agreement to hold an annual air display at the aerodrome had come to an end he would 'not entertain any future application . . .' I had the distinct impression that he might have complained because it had been a fine day!

The Club's annual Garden Party had been arranged for the weekend after the Air Show at Gransden. Neither Middle Wallop nor Netheravon were available, and a plan to visit Bodmin in Cornwall had fallen through for lack of support; it was too far to go. Gransden was a small private field near St. Neots owned by Mark Jefferies, who was an aerobatic enthusiast. It had three grass strips and was restricted to experienced pilots. There were quite a few light aircraft and microlights based there already and we were very grateful to Mark for making the field available to us at short notice, including a magnificent old barn for the barbecue.

Norvela and I drove there on the Saturday afternoon to be present at the evening's festivities but returned to London the same night. On the Sunday I was acting duty engineer at Redhill and during the day received the dreadful news that the Stampe 'TKC had crashed during a flight from Gransden killing both its occupants – Marcus Norman and Cathy O'Brien.

After the euphoria of the Air Show it was the second tragedy to strike, because one of the Italian pilots, the owner of the Jungmann, had been killed carrying out an aerobatic display at La Ferte Alais on *Le Tigri*'s return journey through France.

Both Marcus and Cathy were committed members of the Club; Marcus was very keen on aerobatics and Cathy, also a pilot, was helping to run a company specialising in vintage aircraft restoration. By profession Marcus was an architect who some months before had drawn up plans for a suggested Clubhouse at Wilmington. I was particularly upset that I was unable to attend his funeral service near his home in Wiltshire at which many moving tributes were paid, including a Stampe flight. After an absence of several years Norvela and I had decided to enter *Mowgli* for the Fastnet race and a full crew had been organised. Perhaps it was just as well; I felt like a break and an ocean race like the Fastnet would take my mind off what was the worst accident in the Club's history.

The other Stampe, 'WEF, was out of action after the Air Show with a cracked crankcase, and it was decided in the meantime to impose a ban on aerobatics in all Club aircraft until, as the *Rag* put it, 'certain procedures had been thoroughly investigated and reviewed by the Committee'; we were also waiting for the AIB report. On my return I learnt the awful truth. Eyewitness reports were confirmed; there had been a structural failure. The aircraft had been carrying out aerobatic manoeuvres and some people said that Marcus was practising air restarts. The failure had occurred to the aircraft's tie-rods, which were long stccl bolts linking the lower mainplanes. A similar system is used on the Tiger.

In 1971 there had been a fatal accident to a Stampe in France caused by a failure of the tie-rods and a temporary ban on aerobatics had been imposed. At the time Rollasons were overhauling and converting a considerable number of imported Stampes, and had been approved by the CAA to manufacture through sub-contractors its own design of tie-rod because they were virtually impossible to obtain in France. The AIB report criticised the Rollason tie-rod and in particular drew attention to the fact that the threads on the ends were of the machine-cut variety, not rolled, a modification that Rollasons had made to the original design no doubt because of difficulties in manufacture. It also queried whether this modification had been approved. At all events Rollasons carried the can.

Fortunately the Club's insurance policy also covered Rollasons and the reasonable claims of the relatives were eventually met though not without a considerable delay and the involvement of lawyers.

As far as the review of Club procedures was concerned, the Committee at its September meeting minuted the following:

◆ *Permitted manoeuvres in Stampe to be revised and the following to be excluded: Flick Rolls, Vertical Rolls (all types), Outside Loops, Push-outs. Pilots' notes being revised.*

◆ *New G meters to be fitted to G-AWEF including one non-resettable.*

◆ *Weight Placard to be fitted prominently in cockpit.*

◆ *Air restarts to be banned.*

- *Aerobatic check pilots to review checking procedure in view of lack of practice facility over the airfield (P. Kynsey to advise).*
- *Continue with competitions in G-AWEF at Standard level only.*
- *Aerobatics on G-AOAA and G-AYHY being reviewed with amendments to Pilots' Notes.*

Pete Kynsey, who was representing aerobatics on the Committee, later circulated a letter spelling out exactly what should be accomplished during an aerobatic check, and all members with an aerobatic authorisation were asked to sign that they had read the revised edition of the Stampe Pilots' Notes. Pete also required some people to be personally checked by him. Structural failure in aerobatic aircraft, although rare, is not unknown and the Stampe as a type had a much better record than most but 'TKC, which was one of the Club's most popular aircraft, had given us a terrible lesson.

Although he need not have done so, Brian Smith had already offered his resignation as Senior Check Pilot. He wrote:

"I feel it would be appropriate for me to step down in order to clear the way for any fresh approach that may be decided upon. Pete Kynsey seems the obvious replacement. He has far fewer family and work commitments and his recent semi-retirement from aerobatics might provide the sort of time the job requires. Additionally he recently represented the Club at the Wilmington public meeting in a 'senior pilot' capacity. Bearing in mind the importance of this project it would seem logical to keep some form of continuity running."

Pete accepted the recommendation, which was endorsed by the Committee a month later. Today some 14 years later he is still the Club's chief pilot.

Meanwhile we were waiting for the District Council's decision on our planning application for Wilmington and inevitably the Stampe accident resulted in adverse publicity. Although I was expecting a refusal, I was extremely interested in the reasons which would be given.

Basically, these were two in number. First, the impact of an airfield would be unacceptable in this 'sensitive' rural location and on the 'peaceful character and amenities of this attractive locality.' The site was 'adjacent' to the Sussex Downs' Area of Outstanding Natural Beauty. Second, there would be traffic problems on the trunk road which ran alongside the airfield because of the layout and visibility of the junction leading to the airfield turn-off.

In my view the first reason was meaningless; it contained a number of purely subjective value judgements. Who in fact decides that a rural location is 'sensitive' and that the character of a locality is 'attractive' and 'peaceful'? Was not an airfield and a flying club also an 'amenity'? As for the Sussex Downs, the whole point was that the site lay *outside* the designated Area of Outstanding Natural Beauty; it was borderd by a trunk road on one side and an active railway line on the other. There was already a former military grass airfield right in the middle of the AONB which, although in some ways more suitable, had already been ruled out *a priori*. It seemed that the District Council was moving the goal-posts. As for the traffic problems, there was plenty of room for more than one wholly practical solution, although it might be necessary to remove one tree.

At this stage it was far from certain that we would be proceeding with an appeal against Wealden District Council's refusal and the Public Inquiry which would follow. The lease and the option to puchase the land had still not been completed and there was a worrying delay. Unseemly pressure by a handful of locals was being placed on Mrs Priscilla Gwynne-Longland not to sign and she, quite naturally, had been upset by the local publicity.

There was even a scheme being floated to buy the land from the Trustees to prevent an appeal going ahead. I invited her and her family on two separate occasions to visit Redhill and meet the Club, which they duly did. They were all reassured and remained enthusiastic. However Mrs Longland, understandably, felt it would help her locally if she resigned as one of the Trustees.

I was adamant that we could not proceed with an appeal until we had the necessary legal documents agreed and signed. It was not until January the following year that this was finally achieved and another year had gone by in the search for a new home for the Club.

Continuing with the Redhill Saga, although our lease expired at the end of the year we had the right under the Landlord and Tenant Act to renew it. The landlords could overcome this if they could prove that they required our hangar for their own use. If this happened and we had to leave we were entitled – also under the Landlord and Tenant Act – to statutory compensation in proportion to the rateable value and to the number of years we had been in occupation – 29 years to be precise. Therefore it was necessary to apply to renew the lease.

The situation was discussed regularly by the Committee during the year, particularly as the landlords were offering a two-year extension providing we gave up our rights under the Landlord and Tenant Act. Only two members of the Committee were in favour of continuing at Redhill at all costs and it was eventually minuted that legal costs would not be incurred in trying to renew our lease in the County Court.

However Mr Dalrymple had other ideas aside from sensible negotiation and at the end of June I received the following letter:

"We refer to your invoice No. F26989 dated the 31st May 1987 addressed to your member Mr A. Barber. That invoice, together with a cheque in

your favour in settlement, was inadvertently delivered to us and opened by us in error. We subsequently forwarded the invoice and cheque to you and we assume that you have now safely received both.

We have, however, further reflected on the contents of that invoice and have the following observations to make.

The invoice raises charges for the hire to Mr Barber of two of the Club's aircraft, a Tiger Moth and a Jodel D.150. According to current CAA records only one of the Club's aircraft is presently registered in the Public Transport category and has an appropriate Certificate of Airworthiness."

I replied:

"We are in receipt of your letter of 26th June.

There is no secret about the matter to which you refer. It was dealt with in an exchange of correspondence between your solicitors and our surveyors at the end of January 1985.

Certificates of Airworthiness for all the Club aircraft are issued and renewed by the Airworthinness Division of the CAA and before that the Air Registration Board.

The Tiger Club is strictly a private Club, non-instructional and in no sense a public transport operation; we have always been advised that Public Transport certification is not required.

As far as Hire and Reward is concerned the CAA are currently conducting an urgent study of the whole question and the many anomalies which appear to exist. The fact that we obviously have to charge our members the cost of their flying in Club aircraft is not a relevant issue."

I might have added that the Club did no joy-riding and no advertising and that quite a few members of the CAA, including some in very senior positions, regularly 'hired' the Club's aircraft. Mr Dalrymple, however, despite the extraordinary pretext of an envelope 'opened in error,' was not to be put off. With the aid of yet another firm of solicitors he launched the legal battering ram of a forfeiture action in the High Court. I noticed with dismay that the solicitor who was writing the letters was Mr Hewitt, the same person who acted for Redhill Aerodome in the mandatory radio case. Mr Hewitt had now changed firms and he was definitely not a lawyer of the negotiating type.

The *Rag* now took up the story under the heading 'Hire and Reward':

Although this subject features elsewhere in the *Rag* and in previous issues, on this occasion one particular aspect deserves a special mention, since it has been forceably brought to the attention of the Club by legal action from our landlords at Redhill.

Briefly, we've had to face a claim for forfeiture of our lease and associated massive costs because the majority of the Club's aircraft did not have

Certificates of Airworthiness in the Transport Category (Passenger). Unfortunately, the fine print of the rules can be used to carry an interpretation that if anybody pays a brass farthing for the right to fly any aircraft, then that aircraft should have a C of A in the Transport Category (Passenger). Most of the Club's aircraft have up to now been on Private Category C of As or Permits, a situation which has been well known and accepted both by the CAA and our landlords for years.

After exhaustive discussions, sympathy and much shuffling of the problem from one department to another, the CAA has finally advised that it would probably be best if the aircraft were 'recategorised.' Perhaps the fact that the complaint has come from the subsidiary of a very large public company has had something to do with it and certainly the Club is in no position to test the legality of the situation in court. Consequently, for most of December, the Tiger, Stampe and Jodels – not to mention the single-seaters – have had to be grounded on this account.

Fortunately, this particular manoeuvre on the part of our landlords to use this matter to remove us summarily from our hangar has, for the time being, been defeated and it is certainly strange that this action should have been taken just at the time when the Club was trying to renew its lease on amicable terms, with the intention of trying to locate and move to another site as soon as reasonably practical.

Needless to say, the price of this technicality has, and will be, considerable both in terms of legal and statutory and other costs, but, by the time this *Rag* appears most of the aircraft will be in the air again. However, if anybody has any bright ideas on how one obtains a Transport Category (Passenger) C of A on a single-seat aircraft, please let us know!

The final advice came from the CAA's legal department. As someone joked at the time: "The CAA is now run by lawyers, not by men and women of common sense."

As for single-seaters, even the CAA's lawyers agreed that Transport Category (Passenger) for them was laughable and exemptions were duly issued for the Turbulents, RF.4 and the Beta.

It reminded me of the time, many years before, when Rollasons had managed to obtain what was then known as a General Purpose C of A for the Turbulent, hopefully to be used by clubs for post-*ab initio* flying. When the document arrived it stated as one of the conditions:

'This aircraft may carry a passenger providing he or she is a member of a flying club'!

The Club's two-seat aircraft today are still certified in the Public Transport Category and an important slice of the Club's income is received from joy-riding in the Tiger or from what are now known as 'trial flights.'

In addition to these episodes in both the Redhill and Wilmington stories, the end of the year *Rag* had other interesting reports: first, there was the traditional Osnabrück visit:

The weather was perfect on the weekend of 25th/27th September for the 1987 visit to Redhill by the Osnabrück Aero Club. Six aircraft – a mixture of Robins, Pipers and Cessnas with 15 visitors – arrived during Friday and Saturday.

Our guests made visits to London or to Squerry's Court, a 17th-century mansion near Westerham. Everyone enjoyed our meeting with a typical English pub evening and meal at the Dog & Duck on Friday and our larger gathering to dine together at the Skylane Hotel on Saturday. It was particuarly pleasing to have the support of several Tiger Club members not usually into the touring scene, especially as this weekend marked the 21st year of these Club visits. May 1966 in Osnabrück was the initial meeting.

Then there was another good turn-out for the Dawn-to-Dusk:

Of the 30 or more entries in the 1987 Dawn-to-Dusk Competition there were 17 flight reports completed. The standard of reports was consistently very high, in fact the highest we have seen. It was the opinion of the judges that many of the reports could have won first prize in previous years.

The sponsors – BAC Windows – and organisers have the plans for the 1988 competition well in hand and look forward to an interesting and larger than ever entry.

There was the usual aircraft news and a major story on the weather:

No apologies this issue for opening with the favourite topic – the weather. Thankfully the hangar escaped major damage during the famous October hurricane and all the aircraft safely tucked up inside were unscathed. Considering that nearly a hundred light aircraft in Southern England – many of them actually inside hangars – were seriously damaged, this was a slice of good fortune. Following the high winds and floods of October, nearly every weekend in November suffered from fog and low cloud. In December the weather picked up a bit, but by then most of the Club's aircraft had been grounded with 'paperwork' problems.

News on the aircraft front is that Super Cub 'VPT is now flying again, apparently none the worse for its unfortunate ducking on floats last May. Tiger 'SKP is very nearly ready to take over from 'CDC as the Club's front-line dual Tiger, 'CDC being overdue for a complete overhaul. The RF.4 is having a C of A and a new engine, and Stampe 'WEF is being fitted with a 720-channel radio – one of the minor consequences of having to have a Transport Category C of A. All in all, despite the lack of flying, there has been plenty of work for Rollason's engineers.

Newcomers to the hangar include Ian White's very smart Gipsy-engined Stampe replacing his beautiful Gipsy Moth which has been sold. As Ian would probably readily admit, the Stampe does have certain advantages . . . !

Members were also asking when we would be getting a replacement Stampe, and there was talk of another seaplane project. For 1988 Jeanne Frazer and Geoff Tait were planning with the Croydon Airport Society for another Show and for the Tiger Ball there would be no argument about who would be Guest of Honour; it would be Club member Bob Pooley, who had recently been elected to the prestigious position of Master of the Guild of Air Pilots.

Finally in the *Rag* there was a review of a new book on the Tiger Moth:

What better person than Stuart McKay to provide us with a new book on the Tiger? Stuart is the chief guru of the DH Moth Club, which for the past decade or so has done so much to promote the cult of the Moth, mainly through the medium of a splendid magazine and also, I might add, with a little assistance from the Tiger Club and its fraternal organisations throughout the world. Comparisons will of course, be made with Alan Bramson's and Neville Birch's *Tiger Moth Story* first published in 1964 and which ran to three editions before being revised and enlarged in 1982. *The Tiger Moth*, however, is a different sort of book in that it is essentially a pictorial history of the aircraft and a splendid one at that.

The publication is of a high standard and worth the money for the photographs alone, many of which are in colour. Several Club machines are featured, both past and present, and connecting the feast of pictures are the familiar Tiger Moth themes – the family tree, trainer of the Empire, maid of all work, air show star, the modifications (good and bad), the sporting aircraft *par excellence* and the vintage show-piece the world over.

The book stimulates one yet again to attempt to analyse the continuing success of the type. It isn't just that more than 8,000 were built nearly 50 years ago, nor that its essential flying characteristics are anything to write home about: given the choice, most sporting pilots would fly a Stampe. I suppose in the ultimate analysis it is due to the facts that the aircraft has the well-deserved reputation for always being re-buildable and that, if you can handle it successfully, you can handle almost any other light aircraft, both old and new. Nearly 50 Tiger Moths turned out in 1987 for the Moth Club's splendid rally at Woburn and as this book so admirably shows, the aircraft, like an old soldier, will never die and, while green grass fields remain, will show remarkably little sign of ever fading away.

Stuart's book set me musing on the dim and distant past when the Club operated Hornet Moths, a Puss Moth, a Fox Moth and even a Jackaroo as well as the ubiquitous Tiger Moth. Many people including myself were members of both Clubs and some were saying that the two organisations should work more closely together. But they were wrong. Stuart was brilliantly promoting the de Havilland 'marque' worldwide as an end in itself. The Tiger Club used the Tiger Moth as the sporting aircraft *par excellence* and it would be unthinkable for the Club ever to be without one but, essentially, it was a means to an end – to other goals in sporting and recreational flying.

1987, to use the hackneyed quote, had been a year of 'triumph and disaster.' Also, although there had been a slight increase in membership, there was a slump in flying hours. As for Redhill, we were now living on borrowed time with an expired lease, which was a liability, not an asset. All the old enjoyable Club flying at the aerodrome was lost and gone forever – aerobatics, formation, spot landing competitions, flying off skis, speed trials with racing aircraft, gliding, night-flying, early morning departure for Dawn-to-Dusk flights, flying off the perimeter track in the winter, and the rest: they had all disappeared. There was a faint glimmer of hope during the year when I read in the financial Press that there had been changes at the top of British & Commonwealth PLC. A new entrepreneur had taken over as Chairman, Mr John Gunn. The Cayzer family, according to the reports, were pulling out their cash and their influence from the conglomerate. Perhaps when Mr Gunn came to examine B & C's considerable aviation portfolio, he would notice that he had a well-known flying club tenant at Redhill and would be sympathetic.

Unfortunately it was a glimmer soon to be extinguished. B & C were still paying huge sums of money into the Conservative Party's war chest and Mrs Thatcher for the third time had been returned to power in 1987. It seemed that money, greed and shareholder power were still ruling OK.

But what were the prospects for a new airfield? Someone gloomily pointed out that the last time any form of planning consent had been given to a new site was Popham in the late seventies and under a Labour government.

But we had acted on our landlords' suggestions, as reported in the Press that 'we should go out and find a nice little field' and 'it was up to us to find somewhere else to fly,' and in Mr Norman Tebbit's much-quoted phrase "Get on your bike" we had done just that. But would anyone in power listen?

The Queen's Flight at RAF Benson!
Photo: Author's collection.

TOP: Wilmington airfield in 1988, with mown strip and Arlington Reservoir in the distance. The two houses in the left foreground were built pre-war for Eastbourne Flying Club members! Photo: Jim Alderton.
BOTTOM: The Chairman and Manager were greeted at Wilmington on their first arrival by a gathering of local well-wishers. Photo: Author's collection.

TOP: Wilmington again with the hangar in the background.
BOTTOM: But what remained of the hangar and apron was a shambles.
Photos: Author's collection.

TOP: Almost the last day at Redhill aerodrome. Mavis Harriott and Tessa Lovell with the author. Photo: via Tessa Lovell.
BOTTOM: The author and Beta *Blue Chip*, in radio communication and preparing to make a final departure from Redhill early in 1990.
Photo: Jim Alderton.

1988

Under the Club constitution the Chairman of the Club only served a maximum of three years; so at the beginning of the year Neil stepped down and the Committee unanimously elected Don Lovell in his place. Neil, however, was not to be let off the hook and after a ballot he was elected Vice-Chairman. With the prevailing uncertainty musical chairs for the top positions for the sake of continuity was a good idea.

As for the Committee elections at the end of 1987, with the departure of Benjy to sunny Spain and Brian's resignation as Senior Check Pilot there were two vacancies, and since there were no other candidates David Keene and Howard Rose, two of the unsuccessful candidates in the previous ballot, sportingly accepted nominations to fill the vacant slots. David volunteered to organise the Garden Party in place of Dave Body, who took over aerobatics, and Howard, who was a Lloyds underwriter specialising in aviation, was immediately given the old 'insurance' slot. This was very welcome since 'Titch' Holmes had retired both from the business and the Committee many years earlier and there had not been a replacement. Now the unwritten and unpublicised convention that our man in Lloyds could for his own reasons blackball a new membership application and veto any flying activity that he considered an unacceptable risk could be restored. Furthermore advice on accident reports was invaluable. For the Club this was always reassuring and Howard was the ideal person to step into Titch's old shoes. He was a long-standing member, flew regularly at Redhill and from my point of view he was also a keen yachtsman!

Pete Kynsey was soon into his stride as our new Senior Check Pilot and produced the editorial in the *Rag*'s first issue of the year:

As I take up my post as Senior Check Pilot, may I start by wishing you all a very successful New Year – and good flying to boot. 1988 is a year in which the Club faces major problems over its base for operations, and as we search for the security of a fixed home the Club needs all the support it can get from its members. So why not start the year in the most practical way – by flying the Club fleet and helping to improve utilisation.

Authorisation cards have been sent out with this copy of the *Rag*. If you haven't received one, it's probably because you haven't flown a Club aircraft in the last 12 months. To get a card, you need to see a Check Pilot. Whether or not you'll need a check flight depends on your experience. The aggravation of doing this can be avoided by just flying a few hours each year at Redhill. It will keep you familiar not only with the aircraft but also with any aerodrome changes and, importantly right now, will help the Club's finances by improving utilisation.

Most Club pilots don't seem to have flown all the various types available. (There are 10.) So next time you visit the Club why not try a different type? The opportunity may not be there in the future!

There have been a few changes at Redhill over the last few months. The circuit direction on the north-south runway has been reverted to east of the airfield as it used to be (avoid the village, please). There are now runway lights on the east-west (26L/08R) alternating with the green plastic markers and PAPIs (like VASIs) to the left of the thresholds. Unlike the plastic markers, these are not easily seen and will do expensive damage to an aeroplane taxying over them.

'WEF has returned for aerobatics with a new set of Pilots' Notes. Please read them when you're next at Redhill and, if you're cleared for aeros, sign to say you're familiar with them. If you are flying around the eastern side of the London Central Zone, be sure to avoid the new City Stolport SRZ. Its position is marked on the notice board. In fact, before you next fly just ask yourself if you're really familiar with the controlled airspace that surrounds us at Redhill. Light aeroplanes straying into zones and TMAs don't help us to protect the little freedoms we still have.

Club news for the early part of the year was that January had been the worst on record for weather, and only 11 hours were flown, but that things had picked up a good deal in February. There had been unexpected hold-ups in re-categorising the Jodels for 'Transport' certification, and the CAA were now bowing to pressure from the militant environment lobby and requiring much larger registration letters to be painted on all light aircraft, which was another costly nuisance. The new sizes seemed particularly hideous and incongruous on very small aircraft like the Turbulent.

On the other hand, on the social front the Dawn-to-Dusk reception and prize-giving at the Royal Aeronautical Society with Peter Vanneck standing in for the Duke and Duchess of York had gone well. For the first time, incidentally, the winning entry had been a flight outside Europe – in Canada, following the trail of the fur traders.

Also, as was now almost being taken for granted, the Ball, under Judy's expert organisation and with Brendan back as master of ceremonies, had been another resounding success, particularly from the financial angle.

One item not recorded in the *Rag* appeared in the Committee minutes: there had been a break-in at the hangar and our tiger's head mascot had been stolen from the Clubroom. This had originally been donated by Tom Foxworth and had been there for more years than I could remember. Nothing else was missing and presumably it was now a collector's item. I hoped that its loss was not going to be a bad omen.

At Redhill our landlords were now becoming impatient. Our own position was quite clear. Whatever the outcome of the Wilmington appeal, it would be unlikely that we would have a decision until well into 1989. It was therefore essential to continue to run the Club at Redhill until the end of 1989 and to allow a few months after that to remove ourselves from the hangar. Graham Plumbe had already had a meeting with Mr Dalrymple and his solicitor, Mr Hewitt, and had explained to them that whatever the outcome of legal proceedings they would have the greatest difficulty in getting us out inside two years and that he would strongly oppose any increase in rent in the meantime.

George Fry and Mr Dalrymple, with prompting from Ken Smith, now arranged to have lunch with my father. Ken, who at that time was not a member of the Committee, always played the role of the 'candid friend' as far as the Club and me personally were concerned. Norman, although still a director and shareholder of The Tiger Club Ltd and President of the Club, was now well into his eighties. At the meeting Mr Fry and Mr Dalrymple said that they would like the Club to leave by the end of 1988, earlier if possible. In return, providing we gave up our rights under the Landlord and Tenant Act, including our right to statutory compensation, we need not pay any rent and landing fees and they would not introduce any new aerodrome regulations which would adversely affect the Club.

They also dangled the carrot of an air display which would have anyway been too late to organise. Considering that our annual outgoings to the aerodrome in terms of rent and landing fees were less than the statutory compensation to which we were entitled it was an insulting offer and Norman was not taken in. However what was more surprising were the final paragraphs of George Fry's subsequent letter to my father:

"Lastly, you mentioned to me that if the Club does not find a new home, you thought there might be no alternative but for it to disband. After all the years I have spent in flying, I know you will believe me when I say that I would be truly sad to see this happen. I suggested therefore that if you did not find another home, if you wished, it might then be possible to come to an arrangement whereby we continue to run the Club. . . .

Obviously, it would all have to be worked out if and when the time came but, assuming it was viable, this could then offer a prospect of a very satisfactory way of keeping the Club going and of safeguarding the interests of its employees. In such circumstances, we would hope that you would continue as President and that Michael and Ken would be prepared to continue to play an active role on the Committee of the Club."

When I later mentioned this suggestion to the Committee it was, needless to say, unanimously opposed!

No doubt at the failure of this initiative, Mr Dalrymple resumed his usual tactics of harassment. The official airfield hours of operation were reduced, losing us valuable flying time at the end of the day unless, of course, we were willing to pay a charge of £40 plus VAT which was the published night-flying rate. Two members who kept their Stampes in the hangar and flew them regularly were denied the option of a block landing fee because it was claimed that our lease had been forfeited. Finally Pete Kynsey was refused permission to fly Neil's Jungmann to Geoff Masterton's strip at Chessington for essential maintenance. This prompted a good deal of correspondence and a letter from Neil to Mr Dalrymple:

"Despite what you say in your letter of 29th April, it is reported to me that your AFISO was very positive in using the lack of insurance cover as a reason for withholding permission for G-BECW to depart from Redhill. I see that you acknowledge that a mistake was made in this respect but your letter carries no hint of an apology.

On the question of Peter Kynsey's request to depart non-radio, I find it incredible that this should be denied him. You cannot possibly claim that it would have been unsafe or inconvenient to other users for a non-radio departure to have been made. Light signals could have been used and he could have followed whatever departure procedure the AFISO chose. Furthermore, it was made clear that there was no question of the aircraft returning to Redhill that day.

My letter of 22nd April suggested that your company's policy would appear to be directed towards discouraging aviation in every possible way. Your letter demonstrates my contention admirably. You hide behind the non-radio ruling within the Aerodrome Rules and Regulations, yet it was you who devised these singularly restrictive rules and regulations and imposed them without discussion upon the users of the aerodrome. There is no other airfield in the same category as Redhill that is as harsh and unbending in its attitude towards its users, and certainly none that would refuse a non-radio departure in similar circumstances.

It is no surprise to me at all that certain aircraft owners have found your regime intolerable and moved away, despite Redhill's inherently attractive qualities including its convenient location. The lack of visiting aircraft also speaks volumes when one recalls how many used to drop in at weekends in the past."

While all this was going on, Mr Fry agreed to listen to our counter-proposals. Basically these were that in return for two years free of all charges at Redhill and the option of holding an air display in 1989 we would give up all our rights and leave by the end of 1989. Mr Fry interpreted this as a cash payment to the Club of £35,000 to be in the form of a post-dated cheque to be presented only when we had vacated the hangar. Although the offer was superficially attractive, I did not wish to accept any responsibility or liability for any members' aircraft that might be left in the hangar at the end of the year after we had left and I was worried that our compensation might be held up on that account. I also proposed that at least our 1989 rent might be offset against the compensation.

Mr Fry rejected these points: 'It was completely unacceptable,' he wrote, 'that there should be any aircraft left in the hangar' and that 'we should offset any rent due in 1989.' He was 'saddened' that his proposals had been treated with 'circumspection' and he concluded by withdrawing the offer. The truth was that by this time there was no trust between tenant and landlord and I doubted whether our respective solicitors could have achieved a settlement. Mr Ian Gavin Brown, a friend of Graham's who was now acting for us, had already told me that Mr Hewitt appeared to 'hold a grudge against the Tiger Club.'

Of course most of this was not made public at the time but the *Rag* was reporting the aircraft situation and the Croydon Air Show:

It has been a long spring, with the usual mixed weather, but the main preoccupation has been getting the Club's aircraft flying again and completing the programme of changing the C of As from 'Private' to 'Transport (Passenger) Category.' Happily, this has now been achieved on all seven types of the Club's passenger-carrying aircraft and the 'problem' of the single-seaters has also been solved with an official CAA Exemption. It still, however, remains a mystery why all of this should have been necessary in the first place, but in the current climate 'ours is not to reason why' and, in the process, spare a thought for the long-suffering Adrian Deverell who has had to cope with all the extra paperwork involved.

Unfortunately, this particular business has coincided with major overhaul work due on the Club's biplanes in 1988. Stampe 'WEF's C of A ran out in April and, under the new regime, a major overhaul is required on its engine. 'CDC has been laid up for a complete recovering since last autumn and the C of A on 'OAA expires at the end of July, again with a new engine required. However Tiger 'SKP is now fully back in commission – better than new after a major rebuild following its accident in 1985. While it is appreciated that some members have been perceived to have been suffering acute withdrawal symptoms from the lack of biplanes, in particular the Stampe, patience will be rewarded!

All of this meant that it was a real cliffhanger mustering sufficient aircraft for the Croydon Air Show on 30th May. The Committee would like to take this opportunity to offer whole-hearted thanks to those members who volunteered the use of their own Tigers, Stampes and other aircraft for the occasion – in particular to Mike Cowburn and Mike Thrower, who provided their own Stampes for others to fly and without which the Show would have been in real difficulties. As it turned out the full programme went ahead in the best tradition of the Club, marred only by lousy air show weather. The last time an air show took place at the old Croydon Airport was in 1980, sponsored by the Sutton Borough Council and the Croydon Airport Society and organised by 'Benjy' Benjamin, the then Vice-Chairman of the Club.

This year, with the same sponsors, the event was masterminded by Jeanne Frazer in somewhat more difficult circumstances in view of further building development at the site and the understandable attentions of the recently created CAA Air Show Department. However, despite the weather and the problems, the Show was a classic and, hopefully, will be written up in a future edition of the *Rag*. As in 1980, we have again been told that a future flying meeting at Croydon will be impossible but who knows?

As most people may be aware, the Club started at Croydon Airport in 1957 only two years before the Airport was finally closed and, as it happens, Benjy is heavily engaged, from his retreat in Spain, in producing a volume of reminiscences recalling the early years of the Club. The book should appear soon in a limited edition and on sale to members. In it he will no doubt recount that the first recorded flight by a Tiger Club aircraft took place from Croydon on 20th January 1957 in Tiger Moth G-AOAA. That this aircraft should have been one of the stars of the 1988 Croydon Air Show must be some sort of record, as indeed was the participation of Clive Elton leading the tied trio and hardly looking a day older since he was one of the original 1957 stalwarts.

Back to the present. In response to a request from our old friends, the Kent Gliding Club at Challock, Geoff Salt has undertaken a programme of checking out members for aero-towing there using the Super Cub. As a result some six new pilots have been qualified and more than 150 tows were achieved in May, which has been a welcome boost to aircraft utilisation.

Members visiting the hangar at Redhill will have noticed that Jodel G-ATLB now sports a series of stickers on its fuselage advertising various firms in the travel industry. Straight away, let me assure people that this has absolutely nothing to do with the aircraft's new status in the Transport (Passenger) Category! The aircraft is being campaigned by Brian Manning in this year's series of handicap air races and Brian has succeeded in obtaining very worthwhile sponsorship from a number of sources in return for a sticker on the aircraft. These days handicap air racing is a very expensive business and has somewhat gone out of fashion in Club aircraft; the Club (as well as Brian) stands to benefit from this exercise and who knows, for old times sake, 'TLB might get a decent handicap again, and some prize money!

The Garden Party was due to be held at Felthorpe in July. David Keene and I had already visited the site to make the arrangements. It was a delightful small airfield in Norfolk with two wide grass strips at right angles to each other 450 metres long. It was decided to restrict participating aircraft to Tigers, Stampes, Cubs and Turbulents.

Out of politeness I happened to ask our hosts, the Felthorpe Flying Group, whether there was any radio. Their reply made the quote of the month: "We've been given a frequency but we haven't got a radio!"

A refreshing letter was also received on the same subject from an enthusiast at Crosland Moor:

"Just a few words to let you know that you have the complete understanding, support and sympathy of myself, the other pilots based at Crosland Moor Airfield and I believe, all real pilots throughout the UK.

We can't think of far worse situations than yours, and we all admire your tenacity, perseverance and good humour in continuing to operate in what must be a very hostile and alien environment for pilots.

Don't be discouraged, keep on flying. There has to be room for non-radio, open-cockpit fun-flying south of the Wash!

You are always assured of a warm welcome here at Crosland Moor – you don't need a radio and you won't be charged a landing fee."

There might have been room for fun-flying south of the Wash, but would there be room south of the Thames? The Garden Party went well despite a smallish attendance due to a poor forecast. I particularly remember enjoying the ferry flight there and back in 'PNZ, the first time I had flown a Turbulent cross-country for years.

By now we had received notice that the Public Inquiry into Wilmington would be held in December at a hotel in Alfriston, the nearest village with any significant population. It was already a tourist attraction in its own right, but was also a hotbed of local protest. However we were receiving a few encouraging letters, one of which included a long piece of doggerel verse which was published in the *Rag*. Some of it made some interesting points:

So much of the past we have lost all the traces,
But the greatest of change is the influx of new faces.
The eminent protesters might not be that old,
But they would surely admit they are no longer so bold.
Figures and words have been banded around,
But the proof of most statements will never be found.
As one of the old and no longer so bold,
I cannot accept all I am told.
'Noise would be more than we should bear,'
In a very short time we no longer would care.
'Demand will bring more and much bigger planes,'
Development would be blocked by road, river and trains.
'Traffic on show days would block the main road,'
Why not stay in on those days and enjoy your abode.
'Tornados and Tiger Moths no doubt would collide,'

If the airfield was open the war-planes would subside.
'Farm animals and monkeys so badly would suffer,'
Low fighter-plane noises are very much rougher.
'Five thousand weekend flights into our sky,'
Is not physically possible however they try.
What will be said in eighty-eight,
At the loss of the chance at Milton Gate?
Many young locals would like to fly,
But without an airfield how can they try?
We tolerate the horses that travel our lanes.
Surely our airspace could be used by the planes.
In our effort to protect our tranquillity and leisure,
We must be denying many others their pleasure.
The peace in the parish would be mildly disturbed,
But people who enjoy life would not be perturbed.
On summer nights, when there's time to spare,
I'll be wondering if we have been quite fair.

The mention of Tornados referred to the fact that the whole area was currently being used for low-flying practice by NATO jets, and the monkeys were those resident at Drusilla's Zoo, whose owners had decided to change their minds and object. But it was the 'new faces' and the 'eminent protesters' who would be the main problem . . .

Reverting to Redhill, the *Rag* reported in October:

At our home base uncertainty continues; despite strenuous efforts and a few false dawns, at the time of writing no further progress has been made on any form of settlement of the situation with regard to the Club's lease at Redhill. As reported in the national Press, British & Commonwealth have now hived off their very substantial aviation interests with the notable exception of Redhill Aerodrome. Recently various surveyors have been seen in abundance measuring this and that, fuelling persistent rumours that the airfield, or parts of it, are to be sold for development. The tarmac (including the grass area) outside the hangars and the perimeter track to the terminal building have been resurfaced to a high standard, the cost of which could hardly be justified for light aircraft use. The lease on Hangars 1 to 3 has apparently now been terminated and the few remaining aircraft housed there may have to leave.

The hiving off of very substantial aviation interests referred to a £359 million management buy-out of 250 subsidiary companies including, of course, Bristow Helicopters. B & C were also involved in legal disputes and other manoeuvres with their money-broking subsidiaries and they were now anxious to develop their property assets which, according to to a

248

newspaper report, included a 500-acre site at Redhill which contained '300,000 square feet of warehouses and offices.'

With our negotiations at deadlock locally, Norvela as a shareholder in both B & C and the Tiger Club decided that an approach to the new Chairman, Mr Gunn, might be worthwhile. A long correspondence ensued. We went to the AGM and put down a question. Mr Gunn promised a 'sensible solution' but nothing came of it. First, we were referred to a young director of B & C Properties, Mark Creedy, who had also been appointed to the Redhill board. He merely confirmed Mr Fry's position; they only had an 'obligation' to pay statutory compensation; if they were going to pay anything more they required full vacant possession on or before 25th December 1989 and all rents and other charges to be paid in the interim. Norvela then said that that may well have been the legal position but, in view of the way the Club had been treated over many years, what about 'moral obligation'? And she said that she would raise the matter again at an Extraordinary General meeting which had been called to gain shareholder approval to take over a company called Atlantic Computers.

This brought an immediate response from B & C's new company secretary, a lady called Maria Callaghan with whom Norvela was on good terms, who said that a question would not be in order and that it was not in the interests of B & C's shareholders to be 'generous' to the Tiger Club.

Further fruitless letters were exchanged with Mr Gunn. All we eventually received was a packet of legal documents from Mr Hewitt. They contained an ultimatum requiring our signature within 14 days giving full and vacant possession of our hangar before the end of 1989 without further negotiation.

And so this approach came to an end. It was my opinion that large public corporations who spend millions of other people's money buying and selling other companies and contributing to political parties are rarely inclined to be 'generous' when there is a beggar at the gate.

Also B & C had troubles of its own. Their share price had fallen from a high of 570p in 1987 to 200p and their investment in Atlantic Computers had been a mistake . . .

In October there was a stupid accident at Redhill which spoilt what had been otherwise an accident-free 1988. It is best described by the *Rag*:

The 'SKP affair (and I can think of no other way of describing it) arose on the final approach to Runway 19, and bears a certain resemblance to the wholly unnecessary loss of the Mew Gull some time ago when the unwitting pilot, with the benefit of a total lack of information from the Airfield Information Service (AFIS), ran into a poorly-marked ditch dug across the runway. On this occasion the pilot of 'SKP, approaching in turn behind several other aircraft and having been given the usual farcical 'discretionary' clearance to land, suddenly found himself in collision with a van on the northern perimeter track. It subsequently turned out that the driver of this van, after being held by a red traffic signal for several minutes, was given a green by the same AFIS straight into the path of the landing Tiger Moth.

Fortunately, neither the pilot of the Tiger nor the driver of the van was hurt in the accident, but the Club has been left with what was virtually a brand-new Tiger very badly damaged and which will take months to repair. Predictably the aerodrome management and the AFIS and/or their insurers have denied all liability for the accident and for the damage to both the Tiger and the van, saying that written circulars have been issued in the past warning pilots 'to keep high over the peri-track' and pointing out that the traffic signals are there for the benefit of the helicopters only!

The Committee, in reviewing the accident under Club rules, decided that it was not bad airmanship since it was normal practice for a pilot to look out of one side of a Tiger in the final stages of the landing (in this case it was the left side) and that, having made certain that the way ahead was clear, he was entitled to rely on the Rule of the Air that vehicles should give way to aircraft on aerodromes in all circumstances. What the Club's insurers will do and what the Club can do to recover its very substantial uninsured losses in this affair without yet another costly legal action remains to be seen. Any attempt at constructive comment on this idiotic sequence of events seems totally superfluous, except possibly to remind everybody that NO RELIANCE SHOULD BE PLACED ON INFORMATION OR ON THE LACK OF INFORMATION RECEIVED FROM AFIS AT ANY TIME.

The official report did not mention that the van, which belonged to Bristows, had for years been in the habit of driving round the same perimeter track to visit a blister hangar where they had a store. In the past there had been no incidents of any description, but that was before the arrival of AFIS and the traffic lights.

Needless to say we put in a claim for uninsured losses, which is an expensive and lengthy business requiring assessors and lawyers. Eventually it was paid and I was told that the aerodrome's insurers had contributed half.

Although there was plenty going on at the Club in 1988, inevitably a great deal of my time was taken up with preparations for the Wilmington Inquiry. With the benefit of hindsight and, naturally, the eventual result, there were several worrying aspects. Michael Parker, our consultant, had told me that we would need an advocate to present our case. The barrister, of course, would require solicitors to advise and act as a post-box.

Immediately the frightening spectre of costs loomed before my eyes. The one consolation was that, if we lost, we would not have to pay the costs of the 'other side.' But why did there have to be 'the other side' and the adversarial system in the first place? It was simply an Inquiry, an official investigation conducted by an Inspector instructed by the Secretary of State for the Environment. Surely this person could listen to the evidence, ask the necessary questions, allow reasonable and civilised debate and discussion to take place and form his or her own conclusions? No, I was told, lawyers are essential. It is a quasi-judicial process. What was not mentioned was that this allows politicians to quote the *sub judice* rule in order to avoid embarrassing questions. There are quite a few lawyers who specialise in Public Inquiries and David Mole accepted our brief. I had heard him at the Redhill Hard Runway Inquiry where, acting for the local residents, he had given an impressive performance.

Another worry was the attitude of the Airfield Environment Federation (AEF); Mrs Moyra Logan, who lived in South Nutfield, had founded the organisation and was now its chief executive. The declared aims of the AEF were 'to promote a fair balance between the development of a healthy aviation industry and the sensible protection of people and the environment from its adverse effects.'

By now the AEF was respected in general aviation circles as far as planning matters were concerned, and Mrs Logan was regularly invited to speak at conferences and seminars. In the interests of good relations several flying clubs, including the Tiger Club, were members. Furthermore, Mrs Logan had been a guest of the Club at Redhill and had been given a flight in a Club aircraft. Earlier, in 1974 when our landlords refused to renew our lease, and which was really the year when the Redhill Saga began, Mrs Logan wrote to the Club:

"I have been meaning to write to you ever since the news broke that the lease of the premises you occupy on Redhill Aerodrome was not to be renewed. One tends to write readily in anger, and to miss opportunities for expressing pleasure or gratitude. So, as a family, we felt that it was time for us to say thank you to the Tiger Club.

We moved here only three years ago, and even as we viewed the house, we enjoyed a performance of one of your members in the middle distance. The Tiger Club has been for us very much part of the South Nutfield package we bought. Therefore, we were sorry to hear of your possible departure. With you would go part of the character of this village. It could be said that we are in a particularly favourable position here in that your perfomances tend to take place at a comfortable distance – in fact our terrace provides quite a good viewing point – but by now we feel mildly affectionate and proprietorial when returning aircraft fly over us to come in to land!"

Later, wearing her AEF hat, she wrote that it was their aim 'not to attempt to make flying impossible' but to seek 'some formula for agreement.' Also she recognised that 'talking of responsible club management is rather preaching to the converted when addressed to me.' As already explained she had visited the Wilmington site. Also I had written to her, enclosing our preliminary submissions and requesting the advice of the AEF generally. However I was then quite surprised to receive a full AEF quotation for 'an environmental and noise survey including reports,' cost £2,600. I did not go ahead with this because, frankly, I considered it would be a waste of money. The AEF did not have a reputation for supporting new airfield development in Planning Inquiries. Later Mrs Logan confirmed this by saying that 'although there were aspects of the site and the proposed use which were appealing we would not be able to give our unreserved approval.'

However I did expect that at least the AEF would remain neutral. I was therefore considerably annoyed to discover in the run-up to the Inquiry that the AEF were supporting and assisting the Cuckmere Valley Society, an organisation which had been formed solely to object to the arrival of the Tiger Club. What was even more distressing was that Mrs Logan had submitted a statement, a copy of which was never supplied to us, that spare capacity for recreational flying existed at many other airfields in south-east England including Redhill! Quite apart from the fact that no evidence was ever produced for this statement, it was particularly offensive. Surely a Club with an international reputation with 600 members, not to mention members of the Royal Family, was entitled to a home of its own after 30 years of existence?

The final bombshell came the following year after the result of the Inquiry was announced. The AEF was to receive funding from the Department of the Environment to the tune of £22,000 per year. In my view it was a quite scandalous abuse of taxpayers' money and I said so at the same time as resigning our membership. On reflection if we had known this before the Inquiry, we would have recognised the real *politik* of the situation and withdrawn our appeal.

Next, before the Inquiry there was a spate of obnoxious propaganda in the form of posters and leaflets. A few examples will give the flavour of some of the appeals made to local residents:

'*The Tigers use uncontrolled airspace.*'
'*Do not believe that you will only suffer a short-term devaluation of your property.*'
'*Do not believe that you will get used to the noise.*'
'*Do not believe that you are safe and that an accident won't happen here.*'

Although the inspector at the Inquiry was hardly likely to take much notice of this sort of rubbish, it was worrying that so-called responsible people could produce it in the first place.

Finally a story appeared in the local Press that the Secretary of State for the Environment, Mr Nicholas Ridley, was a cousin of Mrs Gwynne Longland and therefore he should distance himself from the affair. A spokesman for the Department said that if that was the case he would not be dealing with the final decision. It was a little light relief.

On the other hand there was some good news. The CAA aerodromes department inspected the field and wrote to say that it would meet the standards of a licensed aerodrome without undue difficulty. Not that we needed an aerodrome licence but it did refute some ill-informed objections that the airfield was too small to be safe. Also the responsible director in the National Air Traffic Services confirmed our submission that Wilmington was and would be clear of all nationally controlled airspace for the foreseeable future, and more importantly added:

"With regard to the possible move of your Club from its existing location to Wilmington, I think that we all recognise that any decrease in traffic in the vicinity of one of Europe's major aerodromes is to be welcomed, and the reduction in airspace congestion in the area will inevitably be to the overall benefit to flight safety."

I hoped that the Inspector would take due note of both these points. But the problem was that for some reason or other neither the CAA nor NATS were officially permitted to exercise any influence on the views of an inspector conducting an airfield Inquiry.

I wrote a report of the actual Inquiry itself at some length in the *Rag*:

The public local Inquiry into our appeal to re-open the old Wilmington airfield took place as planned in a reasonably spacious hotel in Alfriston during December. Originally scheduled to last four days during one week, it overran four more days during the following two weeks, and thankfully the Inspector was determined to complete the proceedings before Christmas. One day was set aside for the Inspector to visit the site and to tour all the places where it was alleged that residents, visitors, animals and birds would be upset by the existence of a small airfield.

At a fairly early stage it was suggested that a flying demonstration by a Tiger Moth would be in order, and on the day of the site visit Brian Smith was able to bring G-AOAA down from Redhill on a decidedly murky morning to demonstrate to the Inspector himself an arrival, take-off, circuit and landing and the absolutely minimal noise levels that would be experienced.

Not to be outdone, the locals dragged out a British Airways captain who lived in Wilmington village and another pilot who kept a Robin DR.400 on a private strip in the neighbourhood on a diversionary flying demonstration which, apart from taking place after the Inspector had left the site, was a tactic which in our view did not find particular favour. The same British Airways pilot later gave evidence at the Inquiry that in his opinion the airfield was too small, that the circuits and joining procedures which we had drawn up to avoid local houses were impractical (needless to say his version of the 'correct' rejoin would take an aircraft right over his house) and that the official CAA field length and 'safety factors' for a Piper Super Cub showed that it would need some 700 metres for take-off and landing!

Fortunately this particular farrago of nonsense could not be applied to any other type of aircraft the Club proposed to base at the airfield since, mercifully, official CAA 'field lengths' do not exist for them. In fact frantic research for any sort of published figures for a Tiger Moth proved entirely negative, and the point anyway completely ignored the fact that the airfield before the war had seen the succesful *ab initio* training of plenty of pilots who subsequently took part in the Battle of Britain and later in civil aviation. The British Airways captain was also somewhat at a loss to explain why he had allowed himself to carry out a flying demonstration, taking off from a strip of some 460 metres in an aircraft with a published field length, including his safety factors, of 1,100 metres!

Aside from these peripheral technicalities, the main proceedings were taken up with the evidence of a galaxy of experts ranged against each other on both sides of the question: planning, noise, traffic, agricultural and zoological, to name but a few. On the side of the objectors self-appointed representatives also had their say: ramblers, ratepayers, downsmen, amenity and rural England experts, conservationists etc. Fortunately we were spared Friends of the Earth, Greenpeace and British Rail (a main line railway runs within half a mile of the site).

Perhaps the whole business can be best summed up by the line from the poem:

'If you can bear to hear the truth you've spoken twisted by knaves to make a frap for fools . . .'

On the question of letters written to the Department of the Environment in connection with the appeal, the final tally on our side was 150, of which exactly 100 came from members, including several from America. Of these, all, without exception, were extremely well-argued, well-written and well-presented and through the *Rag*, on behalf of the Club and knowing full well the time and effort that must have been expended, may I express a heartfelt thank you. The remaining 50 in favour – a surprisingly large number – came from people with apparently no connection with the Club and, apart from local well-wishers, included local councillors, professional people, pilots and aviation enthusiasts, and last but no least virtually all the national representative aviation organisations with an interest in the welfare of sport and recreational flying.

The local objectors, after a strenuous campaign, finally mustered by our count some 200 letters against and a sizeable petition. Hopefully it will be noted that over 50 of these letters came from residents of Seaford five miles away, no doubt inspired by a scurrilous newspaper report that the town would be overflown by 400 Tiger Moths! In fact, when the objecting letters were finally analysed, it emerged that of the 500 or so people living in the immediate vicinity of the airfield and who might fairly claim to have reasonable cause for anxiety, precisely 22 objecting letters were received.

As far as the urgency of the position at Redhill was concerned, our counsel, Mr David Mole, compared our situation with that of a sinking ship and of the immediate necessity of launching a lifeboat before the passengers were forced to jump into the water – a picture with which we cannot disagree! The decision on whether and when that lifeboat can be launched now rests with the Inspector and is subject to being upheld or overruled by the Secretary of State for the Environment. At best we are unlikely to hear anything for several months. Although, with the help of an excellent team, we have put up a very strong case, the whole exercise has been very expensive and with no certainty as to the final result. We are keeping our fingers crossed but it is not an ordeal which I personally would care to repeat!

In truth a whole book could well be devoted to the Wilmington affair, which from start to finish had taken four years. As for the objecting letters, it was the ones, so to speak, which were *not* written which would be significant: the phone calls, the nods, the winks to the highly-placed civil servants of the 'Yes, Minister' variety. I fondly hoped that there would be a few of these in our favour as well!

As for the costs, after the final bills had come in Mavis gave me a summary. Over the whole four-year period the total sum came to a staggering £42,000. Needless to say – and I must not be disrespectful – by far the largest proportion, nearly £20,000, went to lawyers. *Apropos* and talking of our own letters of support, Don had written to members with a circular giving guidance on some of the points they could make to the Department of Environment, mentioning by the way:

"Redhill has served us well in the past but, due to the actions of the aerodrome management, it has witnessed a major decline in the affairs of the Club and, sadly, there is no question of us remaining there much longer."

The comment was quoted by *Pilot* magazine, who immediately received a letter from the ever-watchful Mr Hewitt complaining that it was defamatory ! But all we could do now was to wait . . .

Back to the reality of the 'Club News' in the *Rag*:

The 1988 Dawn-to-Dusk Awards were made in December at a special dinner held in the Stationers' Hall to mark the 25th anniversary of the Competition. The Duke of Edinburgh, as Chairman of the judging panel, presided and the results are given elsewhere in the *Rag*. The entries were slightly down on 1987, which is a pity, as was also the lack of Club aircraft and Club member participation, Rob Johnson and Frank Wheeler being the sole representatives with a well-deserved second place.

One of the objects of the occasion was to invite as many of the previous winners as possible, of whom there was an excellent turnout including our Chairman Don Lovell, who won the event in its first two years in a Turbulent. In the very early years the competition was restricted to Turbulents and we could well do with more entries from Club Turbulents now! Prince Philip spoke warmly of our President, Norman Jones, and wished the competition well for the next 25 years; also he intends to continue as chief judge. Last but not least, to the sponsors – BAC Windows – our gratitude for their continuing generous support.

On the aircraft front at Redhill, Stampe 'WEF is now back in the air after a prolonged C of A and engine change and as always is proving popular. In view of the accident to 'SKP, 'OAA's engine change and C of A has been brought forward and the aircraft is now back in service. The Jodel D.140 is now no longer available. Jane Norman has had the aircraft up for sale for some time, and by mutual agreement it has been decided that the arrangement whereby the Club used it should be finished at the end of 1988. Condor 'YFD is now undergoing a complete airframe overhaul, and repairs to 'SKP will be started just as soon as this is finished. This leaves poor old 'CDC still at the back of the queue but quite a bit of work on the wings has already been done. Finally it has also been decided with great reluctance and due only to financial *force majeure* to put Jodel 'TLB up for sale. . . .

By this time David Timmis had resigned as a Dawn-to-Dusk judge. He had, he wrote, been a Dawn-to-Dusk judge for 'twelve most happy and interesting years.' Also perhaps it would now give him the opportunity of having a go at the competition himself. However he continued on the Committee, swapping jobs with David Hamilton. He was replaced on the judge's panel by Andrew McClymont, a former entrant as well as being an experienced air race handicapper and timekeeper. Harvey Tring also resigned from the Committee and there were no new nominations.

Benjy's long-awaited book – *The Tiger Club: A Tribute, 1957–1966* – had now been published and was on sale. The publication of the book had coincided with his visit to the UK to make a film. As he wrote to the *Rag*:

A filmed documentary of the Tiger Club is currently in production and provisionally entitled *A Tiger's Tale*. The book *The Tiger Club: A Tribute* sparked it all off. . . .

A full day's filming has already taken place at White Waltham (no prizes for guessing why not at Redhill) to get the flying sequences in before the winter. A few days later, another film sequence was shot at the Palace, where HRH the Duke of Edinburgh kindly agreed to be interviewed and where we were also able to film some of the Dawn-to-Dusk judging. A third day has been spent in the hangar at Redhill with the participation of 'Superman' Chris Reeve (many thanks, Chris, and sorry to the Saturday regulars for the general chaos!). We are trying to portray the Club as authentically as possible, and already some members have been earmarked for modest star treatment! It is not easy to forecast when the planned one-hour programme will finally come together but it is hoped that it will be in the spring of next year.

As adviser to the producer (would you believe 'Loop the Loop Films Ltd'?) I am now urgently seeking 16 mm footage of earlier Club activities, air shows and the like, and especially footage of racing in the late fifties and early sixties. The need is like yesterday.

On the whole 1988 had been a slightly better year than 1987 and in the circumstances of the Club's position at Redhill things had not gone too badly. Norvela and I had actually managed to enjoy three weeks' holiday sailing, doing a race to La Rochelle and later a cruise to NW Spain where we left the boat for the winter.

True, there had not been a full display and other display bookings had declined, but flying hours and subscription income were up and financially we were still breaking even. True also that the Club was a quieter place, and since Mr Dalrymple's decision to tear up the one free landing agreement there had been fewer visiting aircraft. On the other hand several people had had the opportunity and the excitement of flying into a possible new airfield home and the decision had been taken that we would keep the Club going at Redhill for at least one more year, come what may.

CHAPTER 13

1989

At the beginning of the year it was almost business as usual at Redhill. Don wrote the Chairman's letter to members and Pete Kynsey explained the new CAA rules to display pilots:

"A year ago, my predecessor wrote of the challenges facing the Club both in the matter of a new airfield and our future at Redhill. Regrettably, neither of these problems is yet resolved. Although the site of the old Wilmington airfield in East Sussex has now been secured, we still await the verdict of a Planning Inquiry before we know whether it will be available. At Redhill, although one forfeiture action has been dealt with and we still remain in possession of our hangar, the situation remains precarious. Nevertheless, despite ever-increasing restrictions, we are able to keep flying and it is noteworthy that some 240 members managed to take to the air in a Club aircraft in 1988.

To cope with rising costs, including new statutory increases in aircraft operating costs referred to last year, flying rates and subscriptions have again had to be increased and, as far as subscriptions are concerned, the main burden has had to be placed on the flying membership. I very much regret this but unfortunately it is unavoidable, particularly since other sources of Club income, e.g. flying displays and fuel sales, have dramatically declined in 1988.

The usual subscription reminder for 1989 is enclosed, together with the list of flying rates and your flying authorisation card (if applicable). At the time of writing, there is some doubt as to whether the Jodel D.140 and the Jodel DR.1050 will still be available in 1989. Otherwise, apart from one bent Tiger to repair, all other types will be on line.

Finally, on behalf of the Committee, I would like to take this opportunity of expressing our thanks to all the Check Pilots, Duty Pilots, volunteers for weekend tea-making, and the Rollason engineering staff, for their continuing invaluable assistance in keeping the Club airborne in difficult times, and to all members who actively supported our Wilmington Appeal."

"The CAA legislation on Display Flying should be effective from 1st April. Anyone wishing to fly in a display attended by more than 500 people will need a "Display Authorisation." To get one there is no charge, complete the enclosed form (Page One only) and return it to the Club. If you intend to display an aeroplane in front of more than 500 people you will also need to ensure that the organiser has permission from the CAA for the display.

From the 1st April "Hire and Reward" will be replaced by "Valuable Consideration." A PPL holder will be able to receive payment for flying at a display provided that the payment covers the running of the aeroplane and not profit for the pilot. This is an attempt to remove the grey area but will more likely just change the shade of grey. I will keep all Club members holding a DA informed of the changes when they finally occur.

When filling in the form please include all displays, flypasts, practices and formation experience. The Authorisation will then allow you to carry out Aerobatics/SOW/General Flying/Formation as appropriate. General flying includes balloon bursting, flour bombing and flypasts."

Phil Bolderson was nominated to fill the vacancy on the Committee and to provide the essential link with the BAeA, whose new Chairman was Diana Britten. Also at the end of 1987 Geoff Salt had been appointed a director of the Tiger Club Ltd to replace Benjy and so was doubling up his position on the Committee. Although not many displays had been booked, there were plenty of forthcoming events and the Garden Party was returning to Netheravon with the added attraction of an organised visit to the RAF Test Pilots' School at Boscombe Down nearby. There was also plenty of other non-controversial Club news:

The mild winter and lower-than-average rainfall has continued through to the spring but the airfield seems to have been declared unflyable on as many weekends as usual . . . Two new aerobatic mounts have arrived in the hangar: Richard Pickin, having sold his Pitts S.1 to Colin Boardman, has acquired the ultimate competition machine, a Walter Extra 230. Although similar in appearance to Pete Kynsey's Lazer – now sold abroad – Richard will assure you that it is a vastly improved aircraft and don't ask him how much it cost! This has been joined by an ex-Marlborough Pitts S.2 bought by Peter Rutterford and Hugh Smith, who will be campaigning it in this year's National Competitions. This will take some of the load off the Club's Stampe 'WEF which will be available for beginners at Standard level only.

As for Club aircraft on offer, Condor 'YFD is now flying again resplendent in a new green and white colour scheme. Jodel Musketeer 'TKX has now returned to the fold under new owners Alistair White and Graham Piper; they are anxious for it to do as much flying as possible, so do not delay getting checked out or rechecked. At the time of writing Jodel Excellence 'TLB, after a few false alarms, is still unsold. The Club is still hoping to operate it on lease if buyers from the membership can be found at the right price. Turbulents 'SAM and 'RZM, the Fournier and Beta have emerged from winter lay-ups.

I have been taken to task for not mentioning in a previous issue of 'Club News' John Vening's magnificent solo flight from England to Australia last summer in his BA.4 ultralight biplane. The aircraft was the BA.4 originally owned by Peter & Sue Phillips and a star of countless air shows a decade ago. John kept very quiet about his plans and his flight from Goodwood to

Bankstown (NSW) in only just over three weeks apparently went without a hitch. In view of present-day political problems of such a trip, John deserves our heartiest congratulations. Hopefully some day he will tell us all about it!

Giancarlo Zanardo has sent the Club a copy of a new book produced by Francesco Frezza recalling the exploits of *Le Tigri* in 1988. Called *Quel Piccolo Grande Rosso* and again splendidly illustrated, this time the hero is Giancarlo's Fokker Triplane *au* Richthofen which he flew round Italy and Austria. Giancarlo and his colleagues are planning another trip to England this summer and *Le Tigri* will be joined by the Fokker and a replica Blériot monoplane to commemorate the Channel crossing. They are most upset that there will not be an air show at Redhill but they will join us for the Garden Party at Netheravon.

The Tiger Ball on 4th February at the Gatwick Hilton was yet again a great success, with numbers attending slightly up on last year. Brendan O'Brien's enforced absence abroad left Judy Kay in sole control and our thanks to her for the excellent organisation, in particular for complying with a Committee request that the spray string should be kept out of the soup! The model aircraft projectiles were, by the way, supposed to be there but somehow or other they got lost *en route* to the hotel!

Our Guests of Honour, Lord and Lady Brabazon, greatly enjoyed themselves. Lord Brabazon, who is the grandson of the first Lord Brabazon – who held Royal Aero Club Pilot's Certificate No. 1 – is currently the Minister of Aviation but, as he reminded us in an excellent speech, he was not on official business on this occasion. Don Lovell, in his first appearance at the Ball as Chairman of the Club, also spoke well and optimistically for the Club's future. Over the years, the Tiger Ball has established itself as *the* social event in the sporting aviation calendar. It is also an essential fund-raising event and this year in this department all previous records were broken.

We received the Wilmington decision via a letter and report to our solicitors from the Department of the Environment dated 29th March. I was away at the time enjoying a few days' cruising with friends in the Spanish *rias* and Neil had phoned Norvela, who on this occasion had not accompanied me. In fact I was glad that she was there to break the news.

When I eventually read the letter, it was an uncompromising refusal; we were allowed nothing – not a Clubhouse, not a hangar, not an air show, not a single aircraft movement. It was a crushing disappointment but, curiously enough, it triggered my own personal decision that the game was now definitely not worth the candle, and I had had enough. If a responsible Government department could treat a well-known flying club and the rights and aspirations of hundreds of people in this manner, what on earth was the use of trying to renew our lease at Redhill even if the funds for a court battle were available? Although we asked our counsel

David Mole if there was any merit in appealing because there were several errors and inconsistencies in the Report, he replied – for a further fee of £150 – that there was no point: the Inspector was entitled to his own subjective opinion. As I later wrote in the *Rag*:

Having now had the opportunity of studying the Inspector's report, the decision letter, legal opinion and subsequent correspondence, the passage of time has done nothing to alleviate the profound anger and disappointment that this decision has aroused.

A few quotes will be in order:

'The points made by the Club about alternative, recreational use of land have been taken into account, but this is a case where we have had to recognise that the flying they pursue for their enjoyment would be seriously disruptive to the peace and tranquillity of this fine area of East Sussex countryside.' (Minister of Planning.)

The fact that there has been no increase in the population of the area for the past 60 years and that it is virtually an economic wilderness seems to imply that planning consent for an airstrip on Clapham Common would have been easier to achieve. As for noise, scientific measurement and calculation against recognised criteria was agreed on all sides as producing 'low community annoyance' (if a community existed).

'The amount of weight the Inspector put on this evidence is entirely a matter for him.' (Legal opinion.)

If this is so, why waste a great deal of time and money on noise evidence? The answer would have been that, in the absence of noise evidence, it would be right to conclude that the flying would be too noisy. The flying demonstration arranged specifically for the Inspector's benefit was reported as only 'clearly audible' from 300 metres overhead and from 100 metres on take-off. From all other points it ranged from 'audible,' 'just audible,' 'only partly audible' and 'not at all intrusive.' And he was listening! The conclusions (if they were the Inspector's) were that the noise would be 'very audible and noticeable' and cause 'demonstrable harm.' And these, apparently, are considered to be 'intelligible conclusions.' The final conclusion – that this absurd noise objection would override any established need – is another way of saying that no new airfield sites are wanted in this country, nor, for that matter, private pilots. Perhaps we could have been told at the beginning.

The truth was, of course, different. As our planning consultants explained in a letter, 'we had probably upset too many influential people.' For good measure, also too many NIMBYs. Planning consultants in East Sussex generally have a hard time. There were 150 square miles of downland already sterilised against any form of development. Elsewhere, golfers could have golf courses and yachtsmen could have marinas but 'influential people,' who are perfectly happy to be flown on business and holiday from major airports by the same pilots who might well wish to fly a Tiger Moth at an old Sussex airfield, preferred the bleating of sheep on the Sussex Downs to the occasional drone of a Gipsy Major.

We received several sympathetic letters but no practical suggestions as to what to do next. Geoffrey Howe wrote to say that he was 'so sorry' but he had 'no bright ideas,' and the following letter was received from Peter Vanneck:

"I was just so sorry to read in the Rag, *which arrived today, that the Wilmington Appeal was turned down. With a government that seems to be prepared to tackle any entrenched section from the doctors to the dockers, they appear a lot of wimps when it comes to the environmental pressure groups and I do not see how one can change their attitude when the environment issues seem to rear their heads daily in different ways. I wish I had some advice to give you but I haven't, only sympathy."*

As for the field itself, I visited it several times in the ensuing years, most recently in the spring of 2001 when this book was written. Nothing much has changed. There was still the noise of traffic on the adjacent road and the trains in the middle distance. By some quirk of planning law a half-finished house stood on the site of the old Club building. The steel framework of an agricultural barn had been erected, but it had no roof and an ugly chain-link fence with concrete posts encircled the old airfield tarmac area. Everywhere there was still rubbish and desolation. There were rusting wrecks of old cars, and empty fertiliser bags flapped in the breeze. This 'fine area of Sussex countryside' was in every sense a wasteland crying out to be put to some constructive purpose . . .

In the meantime at Redhill, we had received a whole file of documents and copies of company minutes purporting to demonstrate that our landlords required our hangar for their own use, to set up their own maintenance and aircraft valeting business. On the face of it the documents were impressive and included details of staffing levels, profit forecasts, likely demand and so on. Nevertheless it would have been perfectly possible to challenge the *bona fides* of the landlords' claims and there was some reliable evidence that another tenant on the aerodrome was very willing to surrender the lease of other hangars. However, as already explained, we were in no position to incur further legal costs and I instructed our solicitors that from now on I would deal with the matter myself. It was just possible that with some behind-the-scenes help from Graham Plumbe, the landlords' action might be thwarted and I was persuaded to make the attempt.

It was, of course, clutching at straws. At a hearing before the Reigate County Court in May, my application to represent The Tiger Club Ltd in person, both as a director and shareholder, was refused by the Registrar and it seemed that once again financially we were at the mercy of the legal profession.

The beginning of the end of the Redhill Saga was now in sight and I told our solicitors that they were now back on the case to negotiate the best surrender terms possible. Events now started to move very fast. Another hearing had been fixed at court for the 26th June. However the good news was that the bank had suddenly agreed to finance the building or a small hangar, workshops, stores and offices at Shoreham to accomodate Rollasons, whose existing premises were now so dilapidated that a move was essential. The building could be ready at the end of the year and it would be some sort of bolt-hole, if not for the Club then at least for its ancillary engineering equipment. Also two aircraft could be housed if necessary.

I was beginning to feel a little more cheerful. Consequently I wrote to George Fry offering to cease flying at the end of the year, providing that we could have three months after that to clear the hangar and organise the removal of all the aircraft; providing also, of course, that we would not be clobbered for any dilapidations or back-increases in rent and that our statutory compensation would remain intact. We could then leave Redhill on an amicable basis. Somewhat to my surprise he agreed with alacrity.

The necessary papers were signed and sealed by the lawyers and the respective parties at the court on the 26th June and the end of the Saga was now definitely in sight. I dropped in at the hangar on my way back from the court and told Mavis, Jim and John that, as far as I was concerned, all was now over at Redhill. I then promptly left to join my crew to catch a plane to Bayona in NW Spain to fetch *Mowgli* and sail her back to England. It was just as well that another sailing holiday had been arranged!

The *Rag* later carried the story under the heading 'Redhill Goodbye.'

Well, the decision has been taken at last – to quit Redhill Aerodrome after 30 years. It was in September 1959 that the Club first moved into what was then a completely deserted airfield and it will be in December 1989 when the Club's flying will finally have to cease. Thirty years seems a long time and it was only 20 years before that in September 1939 when amateur Club pilots flying for fun were called upon to get the country out of a mess.

In 1975, the Club faced a legal battle to renew its lease, going the whole way through the County Court and the Appeal Court, but unlike that occasion the decision in 1989 to surrender on the best terms available was inevitable. The last decade since 1979 has been a catalogue of strife, aggravation and ever-increasing restrictions from all quarters. The real turning point occurred in 1984 when a certain High Court judge removed from pilots flying at Redhill the essential freedom of choice and individual responsibility without which the Club could never be viable in the long term. The haemorrhage of legal costs which occurred then and subsequently could well have proved fatal, and the uncertain prospect of further court battles in

1989 to renew a lease which would be both burdensome and unprofitable dictated the settlement that finally emerged on 26th June and only then at the doors of the court.

As for the future, the immediate priority is to get the nucleus of the Club's aircraft out of Redhill in good order. Now that the politicians have ruled out the viable alternative – Wilmington – and by implication any other practical site in SE England, the final destination is more than likely to be a long way away. Rollasons, who will continue to maintain the Club's aircraft, have managed to raise the finance and the planning permission for a small hangar and workshop at Shoreham, but there will be no room for aircraft that are not being worked on, and with 180 aircraft already based at Shoreham a flying club is ruled out.

One aircraft which would not be leaving Redhill in good order was Tiger G-AOAA which had come to grief earlier in the month:

"I took off at 15.29 in Tiger Moth G-AOAA to carry out circuits. Before take-off and during the circuit I observed the windsock which showed the wind to be N/10 kts. On finals the AFISO gave the wind as 350/12 kts and I looked at the windsock to confirm this. The three-point landing was normal. Just before touchdown I noticed a small amount of drift to the right and corrected this with left aileron. After landing I carried out a normal touch-and-go. Just before I reached full power the left wing rose, despite the application of full left aileron. The plane became airborne but was drifting to the right and the right wing probably touched the ground. The aeroplane yawed right towards the tower and this was followed by the aeroplane sinking on to the ground hitting nose-first, then the left wings. After the plane stopped I unstrapped myself and switched the fuel off. I climbed out and walked away from the plane waving my arms so that people could see I was all right.

I feel that this was caused by a sudden gust of wind from a NW direction."

The pilot was a charming new member and in true Tiger Club spirit she immediately acquired a replacement machine, G-AFVE, which could be used by the Club. But at the time it was another depressing accident, and it was the third bad Tiger crash we had had at Redhill in almost as many years: I felt that John Sarratt and Rollasons could not go on repairing them for ever. The wreck of G-AOAA was eventually bought by a member but the aircraft never did rejoin the Club fleet.

It was a long hot summer and there had been a spate of other minor accidents. There was also a warning in the *Rag* about Stampe G-AWEF:

This aircraft is fitted with two expensive G-meters – one in the back cockpit, which is resettable, and one in the front which is non-resettable. This means that if the aircraft has been overstressed for any reason, the evidence will be plain for all to see.

Recently the front non-resettable G-meter was found to have a reading considerably in excess of the permitted max. positive G. This meant that the aircraft had to be completely dismantled for an overstress check, including replacement of the tie-bars. It is absolutely essential not only that the aircraft should be immediately grounded if an overstress has taken place (two G-meters cannot both be wrong), but also that anyone contemplating flying the Stampe, whether for aerobatics or not, should make it a vital part of the pre-flight check that the front G-meter is within the permitted limits. Finally, on G-AWEF there is an absolute ban on all flick manoeuvres and the Pilots' Notes are compulsory reading. Further relevant information will be found in *Aerobatics* by Neil Williams (Chapter 12).

Following this a letter was received from Peter Phillips saying that G-meters could record very high readings while taxying and this had happened to him in a Vampire at CFS at Little Rissington. He went on to say that nobody had believed him and we certainly were going to take no chances.

Although the Osnabrück Aero Club did not make it as planned to Netheravon, but came later in the year instead, the Garden Party, the last to be organised from the Redhill office, once again went well:

200 members, families and friends turned out for the annual weekend Garden Party, which returned to Netheravon after an interval of two years. Some 50 hours were flown on Club aircraft and plenty more on members' aircraft on what must have been the hottest weekend on Salisbury Plain for years.

The weekend started on Friday afternoon with a conducted tour of neighbouring Boscombe Down at the invitation of the RAF Test Pilots' School. Most people arrived on Saturday; there was plenty of local flying, gliding and competitions, followed in the evening by an excellent steak supper and dancing to a traditional band.

On Sunday there was the breakfast patrol to Old Sarum followed by more competitions. Unlike the previous visit to Netheravon, this year we flew only off the spacious north airfield; there was no service parachuting and we had everything more or less to ourselves.

The Army could not have been more helpful and we are very grateful to Major Julian Bourne of the Army Air Corps for making all the arrangements, as well as to Charlie Shea-Simonds, who sorted out a problem brought about by the fact that the Danger Area had been declared active because of a weekend exercise, a situation nobody had told us about!

Unfortunately the promised arrival of a two-seat Spitfire did not materialise because Pete Kynsey was *hors de combat* with chicken pox, but those who had booked flights were not disappointed a couple of weekends later at Headcorn.

Giancarlo Zanardo and *Le Tigri* also did not turn up. They arrived at Redhill on the Friday and asked John Sarratt to re-rig one of their Tigers; but we never did find out why they decided not to come to Netheravon, although they did tell us that the weather was hotter in England than Italy. It was probably something to do with their commitments with the Blériot Channel crossing.

Despite these minor disappointments, it was a marvellous weekend much enjoyed by everybody. An uninterrupted supply of cold drinks from the mobile caterers, David Keene's excellent organisation and the delights of non-radio flying were the essential features of its success.

At the end of the summer I started to think seriously about the future and initially it seemed probable that the Club would have to disband. In a few months there would be the last rites and I would be left alone handing over a forlorn, deserted and empty hangar to John Dalrymple. After 30 years there were plenty of memories and even a few ghosts. I would feel – and the poet has put it much better than ever I could:-

'When I remember all
The friends so linked together
I've seen around me fall,
Like leaves in wintry weather;
I feel like one
Who treads alone
Some banquet-hall deserted,
Whose lights are fled,
Whose garlands dead,
And all but he departed!'

But once again, for the Club to disband would be unthinkable. Already it was clear that, despite the uncertainty, just about everybody had renewed their subscriptions for 1989, some with substantial donations to the Legal Fund and, although new members were only accepted with the greatest reluctance, income from subscriptions was running at a record level.

Half-formed thoughts crossed my mind that, building on the success of the Garden Parties, the Club could continue enjoying a nomad existence visiting different airfields at weekends and maybe during the summer months for a week or a fortnight. It would require careful organisation but I remembered the summer camps during my University Air Squadron days and how enjoyable they were. Also with a view to finding some inexpensive hangarage some contacts had already been made.

Consequently, on behalf of the directors, in October I circulated the following letter:

"As many of you are already aware, the Club's lease at Redhill, which ran out at the end of 1987, is not being renewed. The current Tiger Rag which accompanies this letter provides further information. Consequently Club flying and other activity at Redhill will have to cease on 24th December this year, and the Club's hangar and premises will only be available after this from Monday to Friday during normal working hours until 25th March 1990, which is the period allowed for the Club finally to vacate.

The Club will however continue in 1990 and thereafter. Its existence has never been wholly dependent on its presence at Redhill Aerodrome, and its aircraft will remain intact and available to members in so far as is practical elsewhere. Although our first priority is to clear out of Redhill in good order, we will shortly be making plans for flying by members on Club aircraft from time to time at other suitable airfields both in this country and in France. (It is envisaged that flying will be organised on a weekend and weekly basis during the summer months according to a pre-arranged programme.)

Regrettably at the time of writing no alternative airfield and premises are in sight and, following the failure of our planning application at Wilmington, the Club does not have the resources to take any further initiative in the matter in the immediate future.

As you will no doubt appreciate, the next few months will be a time of considerable disruption and hardship for the Club and its staff. However we would like to assure you that through the Tiger Rag, the Committee and other channels you will be kept fully informed of all developments including details of aircraft and flying which will be available in 1990.

Finally we would like to thank you in advance for your patience and understanding during a difficult situation."

Following this announcement, a rumour sprang up, which actually reached the national Press, that the Club was moving to France! The truth was somewhat different.

As part of the plan to fly at different airfields, places in France were obviously on the agenda. It was a well-known statistical fact that France had seven times more airfields available to the private pilot than the UK, and many of these were still grass, friendly and uncontrolled. One approach had already been made to the Aero Club de la Somme at Abbeville and a favourable reply had been received in English.

The secretary wrote:

"Of course we are willing to help a friendly Club suffering from housing problems. We are ready to greet you at the time of your choice during the time you wish."

So much for the rumour, and whether inspired or not the non-executive directors of the Club now took a hand in the proceedings . . .

Also at the aerodrome itself some interesting changes were taking place. Mr Dalrymple had left in somewhat of a hurry and without saying goodbye. Mr David Beety had taken over as Chairman of Redhill Aerodome Ltd from George Fry and was to be the new aerodrome manager, and we were now being asked to pay our rent to a firm of property managers and estate agents who would be dealing with what they called 'the commercial section of the aerodrome.' However there were to be no changes to the AFIS and the radio control situation and the hard runway was still on the agenda. On the other hand we were not hearing very much – in fact nothing at all – about the landlords' plans to take over our hangar for the purpose of running their own aircraft maintenance and valeting business. Quite the opposite! A Club member, Alistair (Chalky) White, who knew a thing or two about airfields, having previously worked for the owners of Biggin Hill, was now making enquiries about a possible short-term lease of our hangar, and he assured me that if they came to anything the biplanes and other aircraft belonging to the Club's private-owner members would be most welcome to stay!

Finally there were newspaper reports of a 'boardroom bust-up' at British & Commonwealth and their share price had now slumped to 92p. So much for small grass airfields being owned by large financial conglomerates . . .

The rest of the story is soon told. Neil arranged with Chris Freeman, the friendly owner of Headcorn, that the Club could just be fitted in there. Headcorn was already busy with a parachuting centre and other flying. Also Chris had his own planning problems. There could be no security of tenure and the facilities were modest – a converted mobile home for a Clubhouse, with toilets 100 yards away across some muddy grass. We would be sharing a hangar not only with other aircraft but with a flock of sheep. But, more important, it was inexpensive and we had a friendly aerodrome owner.

With the assistance of Geoff Salt, Jim Alderton volunteered to take over as manager. Tom Storey and I had meetings to settle the buy-out of the Club's existing shareholders and an acceptable agreement was soon reached.

By this time word had got around. Neil and others had been able to recruit some 60-odd members to raise the necessary funds and purchase shares in packets ranging from £20,000 to £500, and I was more than happy to subscribe myself. Also there was one non-member of the Club who joined in – Jamie, Chris Freeman's son.

As a result, by the time the New Year came round Don was able to write to members to explain:

"As you must know by now, we ceased to fly at Redhill Aerodrome on Christmas Eve, and the intention was that during 1990 the aircraft would be positioned at different airfields so as to keep the fleet together

and offer members the opportunity of flying on an interim basis. It is with great pleasure and considerable relief that I can now tell you that an alternative plan has now reached the stage of an outline agreement whereby a group of Club members will purchase control of the Club from the existing shareholders. It is their intention to establish the Club at Headcorn under the day-to-day control of a new Club manager. It is still too early to provide detailed information about a commencement date, facilities available, flying rates and booking procedures etc. However, Headcorn is a friendly airfield and Chris Freeman, the owner, will make us very welcome.

The prospective new owners of the Tiger Club hope to be able to provide sufficient finance to purchase the Club and then see it re-established as the premier sporting flying club in the country and possibly the world. Additional funding is still needed to ensure our future, and anyone willing to help in this way should contact Neil Jensen or Robin Voice initially. More news will follow soon. . . ."

The agreement, vetted, of course, by lawyers and accountants, was finally signed on 28th February and nine serviceable aircraft, including three biplanes, flew out of Redhill on 15th March. With them went the Club's annual trophies, display equipment, its stock-in-trade, its name, its logo and its goodwill. Only one serviceable aircraft was left out of the deal – the Beta *Blue Chip* which I kept and flew to Shoreham. Tessa organised one of her successful Bring-and-Buys to raise a large sum for the Hospitality Fund, and later there was a mammoth jumble sale to get rid of everything else.

The last Dawn-to-Dusk reception of the Redhill era took place at the Lansdowne Club in December; the awards were presented by Prince Michael of Kent and there had been a record 36 entries and 28 completed logs

The last rites at Redhill were described in the *Rag*:

Record bookings for the final weekends at Redhill prompted the comment that the Club should move more often. As it turned out, the weather had the last laugh: torrential rain, gales and a flooded airfield put paid to virtually all flying from mid-December onwards. There were, however, other compensations, especially the magnificent Christmas lunch laid on by Margaret Burgess and Chris White in the Clubroom; so many people turned up that, for the first time ever, two sittings were needed.

On the final Christmas Eve, by courtesy of AFIS, Redhill *aficionados* were treated to spirited displays of aerobatics in the teeth of a howling gale by Peter Rutterford in his Pitts and Richard Pickin in his Walter Extra. But the weather ruled out all thoughts of a final biplane formation.

Although the Club moved lock, stock and barrel to Headcorn, a small bit of its heart and soul remained at Redhill. Early in 1990 Chalky White did his deal on the hangar and the majority of the private owners, with some notable exceptions, stayed there. Of the staff Jim decided to join his twin brother John at Shoreham but Dev, John Sarratt and Mavis remained to work for Chalky in the hangar. I went to Shoreham now to work full-time for Rollasons.

Since the move from Redhill had ended a long chapter in the Club's history, various letters and tokens of appreciation were received, including a Royal Aero Club diploma and the Lennox Boyd Trophy from the Aircraft Owners and Pilots Association – the second time in fact the Club had received this award. The Committee also offered me Honorary Membership, a privilege which I gratefully accepted. In addition they conferred the same distinction to Frank Hounslow. I was particularly pleased for Frank; he was my colleague and co-director at Rollasons, and without his unstinting help behind the scenes my job at the Club would have been much more difficult.

Later in 1990 the final irony, as far as Redhill was concerned, occurred: British & Commonwealth went into administration, but by then the Saga was over.

Today the Club still flourishes at Headcorn, now under the energetic management of Chris Bellhouse and Gerry Knight. Although no dividends have been paid to the shareholders, none are expected. The Club's 50th anniversary will soon be approaching and that must be some sort of record for a flying club.

APPENDIX 1
TIGER CLUB AIRCRAFT OPERATED DURING 1977–1989

Tiger Moths
G-ACDC
G-AFVE
G-AIVW
G-AOAA
G-ASKP

Stampes
G-ATKC
G-AWEF

Jodels
G-AROW (D.140)
G-ATKX (D.140)
G-ATLB (DR.1050M)
G-AVEF (D.150)

Turbulents
G-APNZ
G-ARZM
G-ASAM

Condors
G-AWSS
G-AXGS
G-AYFD

Super Cub
G-AVPT

Fournier RF.4
G-AYHY

Beta
G-AWHV

Wassmer
G-BDSN

APPENDIX 2
MEMBERS JOINING 1977–1989

A

Wilfred Aarts	1977	Robert Biggs	1978
Jim Alderton	1977	Paula Boraston	1978
James Alexander	1977	Stephen Briggs	1978
Mike Akhurst	1978	Vincent Butler	1978
Karem Ali	1978	Jonathan Bailey	1979
Madeleine Ashbery	1978	John Ball	1979
Richard Acton	1979	Robert Bergsma	1979
John Allison	1979	Harvey Boswell	1979
Anthony Appleby	1979	Piers Bowlan	1979
Ray Attwood	1979	John Bradberry	1979
James Austin	1979	Dennis Bryant	1979
Barry Aldridge	1980	Phyllis Bennett	1980
Anthony Abbey	1981	S. Blizzard	1980
John Adams	1982	David Body	1980
Howard Allmon	1982	Peter Bond	1980
Ian Anderson	1982	Godfrey Bowles	1980
Nigel Aitken	1983	Maria Boyd	1980
Erik Alkeneo	1983	John Bridges	1980
Graham Arthur	1983	Leonard Buck	1980
Maureen Arthur	1983	Niall Burke	1980
Jill Atkinson	1983	HRH Prince Bernhard	1981
April Aslett	1984	Nick Bloom	1981
Anthony Allen	1985	Phil Bolderson	1981
Duncan Allen	1985	Bettina Boxall-James	1981
Kenneth Alwyn	1985	Bill Browning	1981
Robert Ames	1985	Clive Burghard	1981
Nicholas Ashby	1985	Robert Burt	1981
Peter Allison	1987	Graham Barlow	1982
David Andrews	1987	David Baker	1983
Ron Armitage	1987	Timothy Beck	1983
Alan Ashton	1987	Graham Bentley	1983
Janet Ayres	1987	Keith Bentley	1983
		Hans Bergenfors	1983
B		Poppy Body	1983
Cyril Ballard	1977	Geoffrey Bouchet	1983
Phyllis Banks	1977	David Brooks	1983
Colin Boardman	1977	Eric Bartholomew	1984
Robert Buckels	1977	Stewart Becker	1984
Robert Burgess	1977	Christopher Blyth	1984
Jacqueline Banfill	1978	Clifford Bonneywell	1984
Inga Brereton	1978	James Bristol	1985
Walter Bernet	1978	Theo Bruckman	1985

Dudley Beck	1986	Susan Clifford	1979
Peter Benn	1986	Chris Cook	1979
Lee Bowman	1986	Richard Corbett	1979
Stanley Brecken	1986	Evelyn Cropper	1979
John Bridges	1986	Alan Curry	1979
Helen Badger	1987	Astrid Carroll	1980
Harold Bailey	1987	Annette Carson	1980
Jon Banfield	1987	Patrick Caruth	1980
Hubert Batkin	1987	Kevin Clegg	1980
Adrian Bayley	1987	Graham Colover	1980
Gerald Bowe	1987	Judith Court	1980
Warwick Brady	1987	Mike Cowburn	1980
Charles Bailey	1988	Jutta Cunningham	1980
Robin Bains	1988	Michael Cain	1981
Mark Barclay	1988	Michael Chapman	1981
Jonathan Bastin	1988	Donald Coe	1981
Trevor Beadle	1988	Charles Cook	1981
John Bedser	1988	James Cook	1981
Berni Bernadino	1988	Jeremy Cooke	1981
Michael Bishop	1988	Chris Currie	1981
Roger Bishop	1988	Rod Cadman	1982
Andrew Black	1988	Alan Cashin	1982
Jonathan Blacksley	1988	Christopher Chandler	1982
Alan Boswell	1988	William Clarke	1982
Noel Baker	1989	Paul Crispin	1982
Christopher Barton	1989	Roy Crosland	1982
Philip Bevis	1989	Alan Caldecourt	1983
David Bigley	1989	Barbara Caldecourt	1983
Jim Bond	1989	Richard Candelin	1983
David Boyd	1989	Timothy Churchman	1983
		Ray Chudley	1983
C		Naomi Collier	1983
Timothy Carbury	1977	Janet Crispin	1983
David Carter	1977	George Crump	1983
Tony Cattle	1977	Simon Clark	1984
Joyce Collin	1977	David Collett	1984
Martin Cundey	1977	Tony Calvey	1985
Clive Canning	1978	James Cole	1985
Graham Clarke	1978	Matthew Cripps	1985
Robin Coffey	1978	Michael Crofts	1985
Patrick Conlon	1978	George Crumbie	1985
Bruce Cooper	1978	Graham Chadd	1986
John Crawford	1978	Alan Church	1986
Terence Cawthorne	1979	Dermot Campbell	1987
Arthur Challoner	1979	Glen Chainey	1987
Terence Clifford	1979	Tony Clarry	1987

John Clements	1987	**E**	
Stanley Cooper	1987	Carey Edwards	1977
Nigel Cottrell	1987	J.D. Elliot	1978
Michael Cuming	1987	David Evans	1978
Martin Cowburn	1988	Tony Edmunds	1979
Cavan Carnele	1989	Jonathan Elwes	1979
Simon Cattlin	1989	Carolyn Evans	1979
Christopher Cook	1989	Edward Etherington	1980
Alan Coppard	1989	Martin Edser	1981
		Stephen Evans	1981
D		Richard Eastman	1982
Raf van Deeren	1977	Martin Evans	1982
Alan Dix	1977	Jean Evans	1983
Fred Daem	1978	John Ewer	1983
Marylyn Doncarlos	1978	Lilane Ewer	1983
Barry Douch	1978	Leonard Evans	1984
George Dall	1979	Penny Evans	1984
Paul Daniell	1979	Derek Ellwood	1986
Jean Delvaux	1979	John Emiljanczyk	1986
Michael Daniel	1980	David Evans	1986
Terry Dann	1980	Jennifer Evans	1986
Margaret Dann	1980	Brian Edwards	1988
Ronald Davidson	1980	Julian Everest	1988
John Davies	1980	Adrian Eves	1989
Barry Deubelbeiss	1980		
George Dimeris	1980	**F**	
Bob Downing	1980	Derek Faulkner	1977
Willem van Dam	1981	Gideon Fiat	1977
Mark Daniel	1982	Jeanne Frazer	1977
Barry Davies	1982	Joy Frazer	1977
Henry Donovan	1983	Feller Felix	1978
Erik van Dordrecht	1983	Peter Foley	1978
John Dowsmith	1983	Jenny Foxworth	1978
Withold Dyozinski	1983	James Fuller	1978
David Day	1984	Peter Fish	1979
Arnold Desmond	1984	Wreford Fisher	1979
Colin Deans	1985	Simon Frazer	1979
Michael Digby	1985	John Froelich	1979
Cecil Digby	1986	Peter Fenton	1980
Andrew Darke	1987	Edwin Ford	1980
Francois Dassen	1987	Peter Finnucane	1981
Francis Donaldson	1987	Julian Forshaw	1981
Michael Downey	1989	Gillian Froelich	1981
		Rupert Farbridge	1982
		John Faulkner	1982
		Anthony Flynn	1982

Joe Frankel	1982	Patrick Gallagher	1987
Alan Fraser	1982	Peter Goldberg	1988
Brian Fields	1984	Nicholas Gribble	1988
Kevin Fresson	1984	John Gulle	1988
Roger Fiennes	1985	Jason Green	1989
Roy Fowler	1985		
Michael Frey	1985	**H**	
Colin Finlay	1986	Roger Hadfield	1977
Roald Faux	1987	Eileen Hallam	1977
John Ford	1987	John Heathcote	1977
Jonathan Foster-Pedley	1987	Ole Hemstad	1977
Colin Ford	1988	Lars Henrysson	1977
		Ian Hewitt	1977
G		Paul Hinkley	1977
Alan Garnett	1977	Rodney Hobbis	1977
John Grohman	1977	Francis Holmes	1977
Karen Gates	1977	Martin Holmes	1977
Roy Godwin	1978	John Hopkins	1977
Richard Goode	1978]	William Houston	1977
Deidre Goodwin	1978	August Hagen	1978
Roger Graham	1978	Martin Harding	1978
John Gifford	1979	Jean Harding	1978
William Gower	1979	Anthony Harmsworth	1978
Hugh Grehan	1979	James Harington	1978
Erica Griffiths	1979	Joseph Hartranft	1978
Bob Grimstead	1979	Suzie Henderson	1978
Kay Grimstead	1979	Michael Hobby	1978
Michael Glanfield	1980	Tizzie Hodson	1978
Roger Goodger	1980	Helge Holmedal	1978
James Graef	1980	Graham Horder	1978
Richard Grant	1980	Geoffrey Hunt	1978
Robert Green	1981	Gerald Hackemer	1979
Philip Greenwood	1981	Roger Haldenby	1979
Peter Gosheron	1981	John Hall	1979
Martin Gambrell	1982	Maclin Hancock	1979
Michael Gibbs	1982	Philip Harris	1979
David Gray	1982	Michael Harwood	1979
Geoff Green	1982	Bob Head	1979
Archie Grice	1982	Roger Hinchcliffe	1979
Paul Gwin	1982	Wendy Hinchcliffe	1979
Richard Gandelin	1983	Charles Hobbs	1979
Suzanne Gaveston	1983	Martin Holloway	1979
Barry Griffiths	1984	H. Holmedal	1979
David Goodenough	1985	Chris Huckstep	1979
Denys Gould	1985	Sven Hugusson	1979
Geoffrey Gear	1986	Keith Hunt	1979

Paul Hunter	1979	Jessica Holmes-Watkins	1988
Peter Hunter	1979	Christopher Harrison	1989
Martin Haines	1980	John Haswell	1989
Jorma Halle	1980	David Heckert	1989
Peter Harrison	1980	Kevin Hood	1989
Arthur Hill	1980		
John Hope	1980	**J**	
Robert Hopkins	1980	Brian Jones	1977
Edith Hopkins	1980	Nils Junehill	1977
Josephine Holroyd	1980	Ann Jackson	1978
George Hopper	1980	Peter Johnson	1978
Ronald Hyder	1980	Alan Johnston	1978
Maurice Hynett	1980	Kenneth Jarrett	1979
Julie Hanks	1981	Michael Jeffcock	1979
Jack Hards	1981	Kevin Jones	1979
Richard Hawke	1981	Russell Jones	1979
Stephen Haye	1981	Daniel Jenvey	1980
Peter Howard	1981	Robert Johnson	1980
Oliver Howe	1981	Steven Jones	1980
Paul Howell	1981	Michael Joseph	1980
Murray Hamer	1982	Malcolm Joslin	1980
Anthony Harold	1982	Peter Jackson	1981
Brian Hartley	1892	Mark Jenkins	1981
Bernard Haussaire	1982	Hugh Jenner	1981
Roy Highfield	1982	Norvela Jones	1981
Trevor Howe	1982	Scott Jones	1981
Chris Harding	1983	John Joyner	1981
Eric Hamill	1983	David Joyce	1982
Paul Hatch	1983	Lucy Jensen	1983
Herbert Hewlett	1983	Brian Johnson	1983
Roger Holland	1983	James Johnston	1983
David Horn	1983	Gordon Jameson	1985
Robert Haddad	1984	Mark Janney	1985
Paul Heath	1984	Rory Jeffes	1985
Matthew Hill	1984	Caroline Jensen	1985
Richard Hubbard	1984	Trevor James	1986
Frank Hawke	1985	Karl Johnson	1986
David Henderson	1985	Richard Jones	1986
Edward Hoit	1985	Hans Jorgensen	1986
Colin Harrison	1986	Guy Jackson	1988
Michael Holden	1986	Esgil Jesperson	1988
Timothy Horne	1986	Matt Johansson	1988
Angela Hill	1987	Meredith Johnson	1988
Jonathan Holland	1987	Christopher Jefferson	1989
Nigel Hughes	1987	Malcolm Jefferson	1989
Georgina Hunter-Jones	1987		

K

David Knight	1977
Pete Kynsey	1977
Gordon Keymer	1978
Patricia Keymer	1978
Alfred Knowles	1978
Edward Kettell	1979
Adrian Knegtel	1979
Brian Knock	1979
David Keene	1980
Robert Kofoed	1980
Asif Khan	1981
Leslie Kentfield	1982
Julian Klein	1982
Barry Kynsey	1982
Brian Keeler	1983
Judy Kay	1984
Joseph Keighley	1985
Michael Kennedy	1986
Margaret Kenney	1987
Adrian Keenan	1988
Jonathan Killerby	1989
Kieran Kielly	1989

L

Jean-Luc Lands	1977
Simon Lea	1977
Brian Lecomber	1977
Malcolm Lecroissette	1977
Michael Luxton	1977
Clive Leach	1978
Jeremy Leasor	1978
David Lewis	1978
Anne Lloyd-Bostock	1978
David Lowe	1978
Donald Lord	1979
Ian Lundberg	1979
Martin Leeuwis	1980
Steven Leport	1980
Peter Lert	1980
Andrew Lineham	1980
Ronald Livingstone	1980
Tony Lloyd	1980
Paul Longley	1980
Betty Lake	1981
Paul van Lonkhuyzen	1981

Robert Lovell	1981
Anthony Lansdowne	1982
David Lipscombe	1982
Norman Lees	1983
David Lewis	1983
Roger Ludgate	1983
Keith Lines	1984
Peter Larsen	1985
Roger Lenton	1986
Robin Livett	1986
Norman Lowes	1986
David Leigh	1987
Bentley Lowther	1987
Aileen Lacey	1988
Thomas Logan	1988

M

Kevin Machell Cox	1977
Betty Martin	1977
Roderick McFarlane	1977
George McKay	1977
Roger Meerts	1977
Lionel Moon	1977
Michael Markey	1978
M.F.P. Marshall	1978
Peter May	1978
John Mayhew	1978
Colin Moon	1978
Christopher Marshall	1979
Ian Marshall	1979
Roger Marson	1979
Jonathan Marten-Hale	1979
Susan Masterton	1979
Raf Mestdag	1979
Keith Miller	1979
Mak Mitchell	1979
Les Morley	1979
Anthony Machin	1980
Terence Murphy	1980
Paul MacCready	1981
William Macintosh	1981
John Mallinson	1981
Ian Mann	1981
Raymond Marley	1981
Victor Matthews	1981
George Mitchell	1981

Hector Monro	1981	James Newman	1985
Eric Muller	1981	Jonathan Napier	1986
Christopher McKay	1982	Rex Nicholls	1986
Tim Molloy	1982	Paul Noble	1987
Haydn Morgan	1982	Richard Noble	1987
Lawrence Mullaly	1982	John Norris	1987
Edmund Murton	1982	Graham Northcott	1988
Peter Madams	1983	Bruce Nicholson	1989
Pauline Mallinson	1983		
Peter Moss	1983	**O**	
Brian Mundy	1983	David Oddy	1979
Brian Manning	1984	Dennis Osbourne	1979
Nicholas Marston	1985	David Oates	1980
Ian Mills	1985	Cathy O'Brien	1980
Michael Morrison	1985	Michael O'Brien	1980
Mac Maiklem	1986	Sean O'Callaghan	1980
Michelle Marais	1986	Josephine O'Donnell	1981
John Markham	1986	Paolo Oliviero	1981
Maurice Martin	1986	Nick Onn	1981
Simon Mayhew	1986	Nick Owen	1981
Lucinda Mead	1986	Mark Outridge	1982
John Miller	1986	Tudor Owen	1982
Patrick Murray	1986	Keith Old	1984
Arne Mengel	1987	Donald Olvey	1986
Helen Morris	1987	Philip O'Dell	1987
John Marley	1988	Eamonn O'Donoghue	1988
John Mickelburgh	1988	Kenneth Ovenden	1988
Anthony Mitchison	1988		
Werner Muenker	1988	**P**	
John McKechnie	1989	Michael Peare	1977
David Miles	1989	Ronald Penney	1977
		Fred Poff	1977
N		Ronald Price	1977
Anthony Northway	1977	Keith Palmer	1978
Philip Newell	1979	Henry Peare	1978
Eric Newitt	1979	Rhys Perraton	1978
Gerald Newitt	1979	Christopher Philpott	1978
Nicholas Newport	1979	Miranda Preston	1978
Neville Nixon	1979	David Page-Thomas	1979
Susan Noble	1979	Hugo Paridaens	1979
Mark Northway	1979	David Parkhouse	1979
Arne Nylen	1979	John Parks	1979
William Nash	1981	Anthony Perris	1979
Christopher Norman	1981	Roy Phillips	1979
Victor Norman	1981	Alan Pierce	1979
Marcus Norman	1982	David Platt	1979

Keith Purchese	1979	Malcolm Routh	1979
Richard Parker	1980	Charles Ranald	1980
Norman Pealing	1980	John Randle	1980
Kenneth Peare	1980	Alick Reid	1980
Jonathan Pedley	1980	Jean Richards	1980
Josephine Pennel	1980	Jeremy Ridge	1980
Desmond Penrose	1980	John Rundle	1980
John Pike	1980	Mark Ramsay	1981
Robin Poole	1980	William Rawlinson	1981
Alan Pritchard	1980	Ferdinand Reinlieb	1981
Trevor Pegram	1981	Tim Robson	1981
Richard Pickin	1981	Tim Ruck	1981
Kathleen Pritchard	1981	S. Rupp	1981
Louise Proctor	1981	Christopher Reeve	1982
Ned Putnam	1981	Amanda Rigden	1982
George Parsons	1982	Frederick Rivett	1983
Len Ferry	1982	Marco Raymakers	1984
Derek Piggott	1982	Michael Riley	1984
Peter Poole	1982	William Rogers	1984
Warren Pyke	1982	Phil Read	1985
Dermot Patterson	1983	Peter Rutterford	1985
Anthony Pearce	1983	Norman Rhodes	1986
David Purnell	1983	Alwyn Roberts	1986
Ronald Parsons	1985	David Roberts	1986
John Paxton	1985	James Roland	1986
John Penfold	1985	Ian Ramsay	1987
Roger Preston	1985	Clive Richardson	1988
Ronald Price	1985	Anthony Richmond	1988
Ian Page	1986	David Roberts	1988
William Perlmutter	1986	Robin Russell	1988
Graham Piper	1986		
Peter Pitt	1986	**S**	
Colin Parsons	1987	Elisabeth Sandys	1977
Lee Proudfoot	1987	Paul Sheldon	1977
Robert Palmer	1988	Bruce Wearing Smith	1977
		Graham Saw	1978
R		Bernd Schillen	1978
Charles Ravenhill	1977	Peter Sears	1978
Christian Roux	1977	Barry Simon	1978
Nick Radford	1978	Geoffrey Smith	1978
Noel Reed	1978	Dorrie Smith	1978
Sheena Reid	1978	Terence Southcott	1978
Andrew Ringrose	1978	Sam Spindlow	1978
Jim Roland	1978	Eric Steenson	1978
David Randyll	1979	Rowan Stephens	1978
Ronald Rounce	1979	Brenda Stroud	1978

Philip Swinstead	1978	Joseph Sullivan	1985
Ian Sandon	1979	Karl Schafers	1986
Martin Saunders	1979	Stephen Smith	1986
Jonny Seccombe	1979	Hans Martin Steinle	1986
D. Shepherd	1979	Alistair Stenhouse	1986
Meryl Sherry	1979	Kenneth Struthers	1986
Eric Skelton	1979	Thomas Siwecki	1987
Pauline Smith	1979	David Smith	1987
Stephen Smith	1979	Ian Stockwell	1987
David Starkey	1979	John Sully	1987
Edward Sutsh	1979	Filipe Johnson C. Silva	1988
Hugh Scanlan	1980	Andrew Stuart	1988
Henry Sharp	1980		
Charlie Shea-Simonds	1980	**T**	
Ian Statham	1980	Roger Tribe	1977
Margaret Sutcliffe	1980	Sue Thompson	1978
Julian Sylvester	1980	Robert Thring	1978
Derek Sephton	1981	Chris Tringham	1978
Denis Smith	1981	Adrian Tellier	1979
Leo Smith	1981	Raymond Thornton	1979
M. Smith	1981	John Timms	1979
Carol Statham	1981	Eberhard Trams	1979
Anthony Stepney	1981	Ronald Traynor	1979
David Stirton	1981	Arthur Tait	1980
Geoffrey Swaffield	1981	Jane Taylor	1980
Anthony Salter	1982	Howard Thompson	1980
Robin Smith	1982	Ian Turner	1981
Andrew Stinchcombe	1982	John Tanswell	1982
Christopher Stringer	1982	Peter Tawse	1982
Philip Sale	1983	Colin Taylor	1983
Milan Slahor	1983	Alan Thomas	1983
Geoffrey Smee	1983	Harvey Tring	1983
Stephen Spence	1983	Brian Tapp	1984
Michael Steer	1983	Jonathan Taylor	1985
Maurice Stevens	1983	John Trumper	1985
Paul Street	1983	Frank Taylor	1987
Gerald Stubbs	1983	Mike Thrower	1987
John Schottenheimer	1984	John Tylenda	1987
Tim Snider	1984	Stuart Tizzard	1988
Lionel Sole	1984	John Tavener	1989
Jeffery Spall	1984		
James Stewart	1984	**U**	
Ronald Sayer	1985	Anthony Unwin	1983
Bernard Sedgewick	1985	Geoffrey Urquart	1984
Hugh Smith	1985	Peter Underhill	1985
Alan Snowden	1985		

V

Guide Verbist	1979
Gerritt Vanderweerd	1980
Caroline Vaughan	1983
John Vening	1985
Hugo Vonwiller	1988
Peter Valentine	1989

W

Clive Wales	1977
David Walker	1977
Roger Warren	1977
Kenneth Wheatley	1977
Thomas Wood	1977
Patricia Wapshott	1978
Brian Webb	1978
Gordon Winterbourne	1978
David Wise	1978
Charles Wotherspoon	1978
Alexandra Waller	1979
Michael Waller	1979
Terry Warren	1979
John Watkins	1979
Daniel Woolf	1979
Ian Woolacott	1979
Jenny Wakem	1980
Howard Walker	1980
Brian Ward	1980
Russell Watkins	1980
Neville Welch	1980
Michael Wennink	1980
Arthur White	1980
Pym White	1980
Adam Whitehead	1980
Clare Whitehouse	1980
Jan Wildbergh	1980
Anthony Wiltshire	1980
Patricia Wiltshire	1980
Paul Wood	1980
Robert Wright	1980
Tim Wellburn	1981
Richard Wheeler	1981
John Ware	1982
Peter Warden	1983
Anthony Wickens	1983
Dewi Williams	1983

Adam Wise	1983
Ernest Worthley	1983
John Webb	1984
Oswald Weisz	1984
Simon Wheeler	1984
Donald Woodland	1984
Mark Woodland	1984
Ronald Wright	1984
John Warham	1986
Timothy Waters	1986
John A. Webb	1986
Susanne Whelpton	1986
Richard Whitaker	1986
Ian White	1986
Malcolm Wigglesworth	1986
Robert Wilson	1987
John Wood	1987
Alex Wajih	1988
Anna Walker	1988
Adrian Webster	1988
Francis Wheeler	1988
Timothy Williams	1988
Paul Welsh	1989
Timothy Williamson	1989
David Woodford	1989

Y

HRH Duke of York	1983
HRH Duchess of York	1986

Z

Orville Zeller	1977
Giancarlo Zanardo	1987

APPENDIX 3

ANNUAL TROPHIES AWARDED BY THE TIGER CLUB
1977–1989

There were four main Trophies awarded annually.

1) The Dawn-to-Dusk (sometimes called the Duke of Edinburgh Trophy); this was open to all comers, not just members of the Club.
2) The Clem Pike, awarded to a Club member who over a period of time had made an outstanding contribution to the well-being of the Club.
3) The de Salis, awarded to a new Club member who had contributed most to the aims of the Club during the first year and a half of his or her membership.
4) The Tony Smith, awarded for aerobatics and to the Club member highest placed in the Tiger Trophy, a competition organised by the British Aerobatic Association in the Standard class.

In addition there were medallions awarded annually for air racing, aerobatics, foreign touring and glider-towing, also a Chairman's medallion. Because these were not awarded consistently every year, the winners have not been listed here.

Finally, all the other original Club trophies, all awarded for aerobatic competitions, had by 1977 been handed over to the British Aerobatic Association.

Dawn-to-Dusk Trophy Winners

1977 Marylyn Wood – Alan Butcher
1978 Pat Holmes
1979 John Blake – Stratton Richey
1980 Charlie Shea-Simonds – Amanda Mitchell
1981 Charlie Shea-Simonds – Julie Hanks
1982 Howard Cox – Christopher Turner
1983 Howard Cox – Christopher Turner
1984 Eddie Coventry – Don Bullen
1985 Charlie Shea-Simonds – Patrick Long
1986 David Southwell – David Cook
1987 Robert Purves – André Dumas
1988 Christopher Harris – James Stevens
1989 Iain Lawrence – Leigh Jones-Fenleigh

Clem Pike Trophy Winners

1977 Roy Davis
1978 Bill Chesson
1979 Michael Jones

1980 David Hamilton
1981 Robin Voice
1982 Mavis Harriott
1983 Frank Hounslow
1984 Tom Storey
1985 Jeanne Frazer
1986 Geoff Tait
1987 Brian Smith
1988 Neil Jensen
1989 Tessa Lovell

De Salis Trophy Winners

1977 Ian Hewitt
1978 Sue Thompson
1979 Helge Holmedal
1980 Charlie Shea-Simonds
1981 Jonny Seccombe
1982 David Body
1983 Marcus Norman
1984 Poppy Body
1985 Matthew Hill
1986 David Evans
1987 Toney Calvey
1988 Patrick Gallagher
1989 Alan Boswell

Tony Smith Trophy Winners

1978 Alan Dix
1979 Peter Kynsey
1980 Roger Graham
1981 Barry Tempest
1982 Keith Miller
1983 Richard Pickin
1984 Marcus Norman
1985 Nick Onn
1986 David Body
1987 Mike Morrison
1988 Jonathon Foster-Pedley
1989 Tony Edmunds

APPENDIX 4
TIGER CLUB (1990) LTD
LIST OF ORIGINAL SHAREHOLDERS

Jim Alderton
John & Anne Ball
Martin Barraclough
Chris Bellhouse
Keith Bentley
James Black
Geoffrey Bouchet
Roger Brookhouse
Suzanne Brookhouse
Andrew Chadwick
Tony Clarry
Roy Crosland
Mike Digby
Tony Docherty
Clive Elton
Martin Emery
John Ford
David Frankel
Jamie Freeman
Tom Freer
Maximo Gainza
Suzanne Gaveston
Chris Gibbs
James Gilbert
Tony Haigh-Thomas
David Hamilton
James Hamilton
Ralph Hart
Angela Hill
David Hood
Peter Jarvis
Neil Jensen
Chris Jesson
Michael Jones

David Keene
Marwan Khalaf
Peter Kynsey
Don Lovell
John Mallinson
Margo McKellar
Philip Meeson
John Mickleburgh
Brendan O'Brien
Keith Old
Nick Parkhouse
Richard Pearson
David Phillips
Richard Pickin
Peter Pilch
Peter Poole
Robert Pooley
Charles Ravenhill
Howard Rose
Pat Sellar
Barry Smith
Brian Smith
Rowarth Spurrell
Tom Storey
Adrian Swire
Neil Thomason
Steve Thompson
Robin Voice
Ken Wales
Anna Walker
Frank Walker
David Wise
Philip Wolf

NAME INDEX

(NB References are to chapter years [e.g. 80 signifies the year 1980], and * indicates more than one reference in that chapter year.)

286